To See the Dawn

THE COMMUNIST INTERNATIONAL
IN LENIN'S TIME

TO SEE THE DAWN

Baku, 1920—First Congress
of the Peoples of the East

Edited by John Riddell

PATHFINDER

New York   London   Montreal   Sydney

Copyright © 1993 by Pathfinder Press
All rights reserved

ISBN 978-0-87348-769-6
Library of Congress Catalog Card Number 93-85321
Manufactured in Canada

First edition, 1993
Fourteenth printing, 2025

FRONT COVER PHOTO: Delegates at Baku congress

BACK COVER PHOTO: (from left) Najiye Hanum, Khaver Shabanova, and Bulach Tatu, members of congress Presiding Committee
Courtesy of City Library, La Chaux-de-Fonds, Switzerland

COVER: Eric Simpson

PATHFINDER
pathfinderpress.com
Email: pathfinder@pathfinderpress.com

Contents

Maps 8

Introduction 11

Call to the Baku congress 41

PROCEEDINGS

Opening rally 51
Zinoviev, 53 / Radek, 59 / Kun, 62 / Quelch, 64 / Rosmer, 65 / Reed, 66 / Steinhardt, 67

Session 1.
Tasks of the Congress of the Peoples 69
of the East
Narimanov, 69 / Report by Zinoviev, 72

Session 2.
World political situation 93
Report by Radek, 94 / Buniatzadeh, 113 / Shakir, 117 / Haydar Khan, 118

Session 3.
Discussion: Turkestan, Mountain republic 121
Narbutabekov, 121 / Korkmasov, 128

Session 4.
Guest speakers / India / Turkey 135
Zinoviev, 135 / Quelch, 138 / Rosmer, 140 / Fazil al-Qadir, 142 / Declaration by Indian Revolutionary Association, 142 / Shablin, 143 / Declaration by Enver Pasha, 144 / Statement by Ibrahim Tali, 149 / Resolution on Turkey, 153 / Zinoviev, 154 / Addendum: Speech by John Reed, 156

Session 5.
National and colonial questions 163
  Report by Pavlovich, 163 / Matushev, 190 /
  Ryskulov, 197

Session 6.
Soviets in the East / agrarian question 205
  Report by Kun, 205 / Theses on Soviet power in the
  East, 215 / Report by Skachko, 219 / Theses on the
  agrarian question, 231

Session 7.
Council for Propaganda and Action / women of the
East / concluding remarks 239
  Resolution on Council for Propaganda and
  Action, 240 / Zinoviev, 241 / Rojabov, 242 / Report by
  Najiye, 243 / Bibinur, 246 / Tajiyev, 249 /
  Yegorov, 250 / Narimanov, 252 / Zinoviev, 253

Manifesto to the peoples of the East 263

Appeal to the workers of Europe,
America, and Japan 279

Composition of the congress 289

APPENDIXES

Appendix 1.
Declaration of Soviet government on
rights of peoples of Russia 295

Appendix 2.
Appeal to all toiling Muslims of Russia
and the East (*Council of People's Commissars*) 299

Appendix 3.
Address to the Second All-Russia Congress of
Communist Organizations of the
Peoples of the East (*V.I. Lenin*) 303

Appendix 4.
Theses on the national and colonial questions
(*Second Congress of the Communist International*) 319

Appendix 5.
A new world (*Baku City Executive Committee, Communist Party of Azerbaijan*)   329

Appendix 6.
Workers of Armenia have cemented an alliance with toiling Azerbaijan
(*Delegation from Armenia*)   333

Appendix 7.
Zionism: an exchange of views at the Baku congress   339

a) Thousands of Jewish toilers need land (*Mountain Jews*), 339

b) Settle and colonize Palestine on communist principles (*Jewish Communist Party/Poale Zion*), 341

c) The slogan must be 'Hands off Palestine' (*Jewish Sections, Communist Party of Russia*), 346

Appendix 8.
Correcting abuses of Soviet power in Asia   351

a) Corrections must be made, and made quickly (*Twenty-one delegates to Baku congress*), 355

b) Communist tasks among Eastern peoples (*Political Bureau, Communist Party of Russia*), 368

c) Appeal to Red Army soldiers fighting in the East (*Council for Propaganda and Action*), 370

Notes   373

Glossary of names and terms   395

Index   407

Photographs are found after page 212

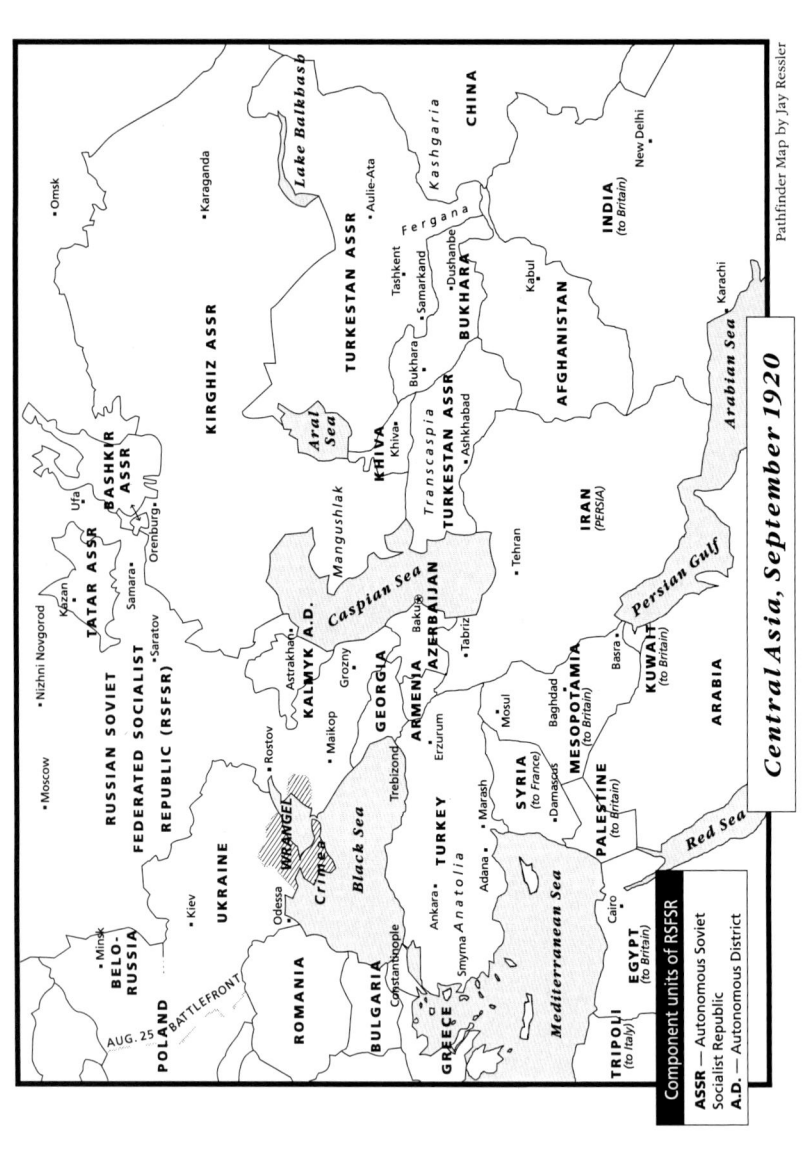

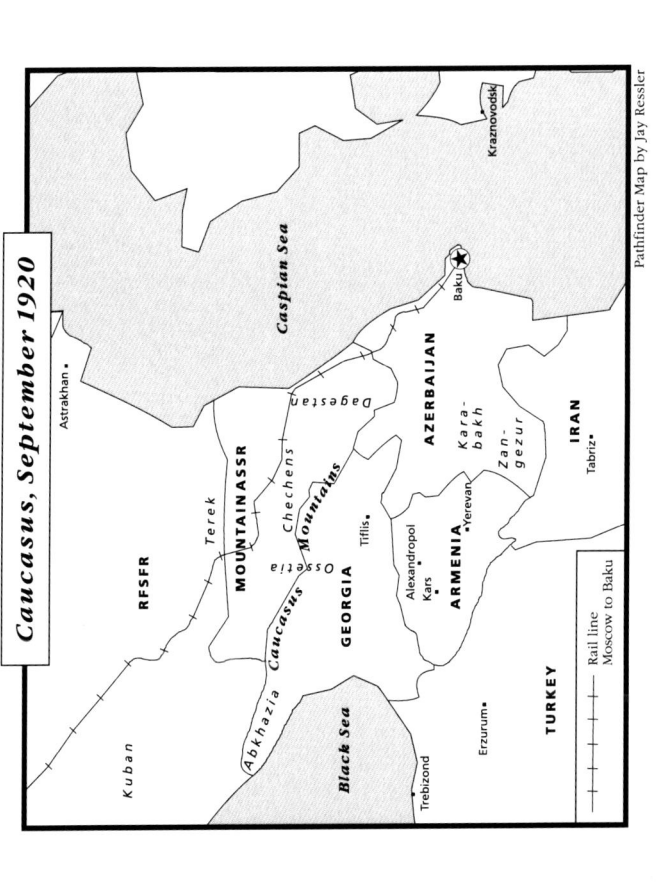

Introduction

The First Congress of the Peoples of the East, held September 1–7, 1920, in Baku, capital of Soviet Azerbaijan, registered a new stage in the emancipation struggle of colonial and oppressed peoples and in the world struggle for socialism. This stage had been opened by the October 1917 revolution in Russia, in which the Bolshevik Party had led in the establishment of a revolutionary workers' and peasants' republic.

The congress in Baku was an event without precedent. Delegates from more than two dozen peoples of Asia met in joint conference with leaders of workers' parties in Russia, Western Europe, and the United States to hammer out a common policy in the fight against imperialist domination and capitalist exploitation.

Comments of some of the more than two thousand delegates reflected a conviction that a new age had begun for the toilers of the East, ending the epoch in which seemingly blind forces had ruled the lives of oppressed working people. "A new world is awakening to life and struggle: the world of the oppressed nationalities . . . of the East," began greetings from the Azerbaijan Communist Party (see appendix 5). Karl Radek, a leader of the Communist International, reporting to the congress on the world political situation, noted that increasingly the peoples of the East refused to perish in bitter resignation. "They have hope," he stated, "they feel their strength" (session 2). According to Bibinur, a woman delegate from what is now Kazakhstan, the advent of Soviet power meant that "a bright sun has reached us, warming and comforting us

. . . the first we have known." Another woman delegate, Najiye Hanum from Turkey, was confident that present trials were leading to a new day: "To see the dawn one has to pass through the dark night" (session 7).

Previously, struggles aiming to lay the foundations for democracy, independence, and social progress in the East had been stifled by the landlords, moneylenders, petty manufacturers, and other exploiting layers. If the traditional authority and organized violence of the local rulers proved insufficient, then the struggles by peasants, youth, and workers had been crushed by the military might of the colonizing powers. Although traditional social systems were disintegrating under the impact of capitalist economic penetration, the road to industrialization and social advance was blocked off by imperialist rule. Colonial societies remained hopelessly mired in poverty and social decay.

Yet as congress delegates gathered in Baku, capitalism as a world system—shaken by war, economic dislocation, and revolution—was undergoing the most severe crisis it had yet experienced. Workers and peasants in the vast territory of the former tsarist empire of Russia had broken free of capitalist rule. They had organized a number of revolutionary governments of workers and peasants, voluntarily joined in a federative alliance led by the Soviet republic of Russia.

One of the Russian Soviet government's first actions had been to proclaim the right of all the subject peoples within the boundaries of the old tsarist empire, which encompassed many Asian peoples, to "free self-determination up to and including the right to secede" (see appendix 1). Finland, Estonia, and other states had acted on this pledge, establishing their independence.

Another early Soviet appeal pledged to Muslim workers and farmers that "henceforth your beliefs and customs, your national and cultural institutions are declared free and inviolable" (see appendix 2). Declaring null and void all the treaties through which tsarism had lorded it over and looted the Eastern peoples, the appeal called on them to "build your national life freely and without hindrance." This promise was subsequently concretized through treaties with China, Iran, and other countries which, among other provisions, canceled the debts owed the tsarist regime.

The Communist International (or Comintern) was founded in March 1919 on the initiative of the Communist Party (Bolsheviks), which had led the workers and peasants of Russia to victory. In July 1920 the new International convened its Second Congress, held in Petrograd [St. Petersburg] and Moscow, which adopted a line of march for worldwide socialist revolution. Three weeks before the Comintern congress opened, however, on June 29, the International's Executive Committee had issued a call to all peoples of Asia to send representatives to a congress in Baku. Comintern chairman Gregory Zinoviev later told the Baku gathering that its sessions were "the complement, the second part, the second half" of the world congress that had just been held (session 1).

Within the Comintern's predecessor, the Socialist (or Second) International, the idea had been widespread that the relationship of workers in the advanced capitalist countries toward the East consisted chiefly of an obligation to be carried out by a future Socialist government. Such a government would then act to make the fruits of Western progress available to the "backward" peoples of Asia and Africa. This notion, sharply contested by the Bolsheviks, helped to justify the opportunism of the Socialist International's majority leadership, who from 1907 began to advocate a "reformed" colonialism as they led that International to its ignominious collapse in 1914.[1]

In contrast to this view, the Communist International viewed the oppressed peoples as already constituting a decisive battalion in the international class struggle. It was true that mechanized industry and its complement, the industrial proletariat, was small or nearly nonexistent in most of Asia and Africa. But independent organizations of peasants and other urban and rural toilers—including some proletarian and even communist organizations—were found in several countries.

A year before the Baku congress, Bolshevik leader V.I. Lenin observed that the oppressed masses, who until then had been merely "objects of international imperialist policy, existing only as material to fertilize capitalist culture and civilization," would now "rise as independent participants, as builders of a new life."

As a result, Lenin noted, "the socialist revolution will not be solely, or chiefly, a struggle of the revolutionary proletarians in each country against their bourgeoisie. No, it will be a struggle of all the colonies and countries oppressed by imperialism." Lenin's remarks, made to a conference of Communists from Asian countries living in Soviet Russia, are printed in appendix 3.

Through the actions of the Communist International of Lenin's time, revolutionary workers the world over reached out their hands to ally with toiling masses who formerly had no hope of liberation. Moreover, the workers' and peasants' republic in Russia stood ready from the outset to assist peoples struggling to break free of imperialist rule. With these developments in mind, the Baku congress set its sights on nothing less than "a single union of the working people not only of Asia and Europe but of the entire world, so as to put an end to capitalism and begin a new and better life" (opening rally).

In his closing remarks to the conference, Zinoviev stated that it was now possible to supplement and broaden the call with which Karl Marx and Frederick Engels in 1848 closed the Communist Manifesto, the fundamental programmatic document of the modern communist movement. Zinoviev proposed the amended wording, "Workers of all lands and oppressed peoples of the whole world, unite!" Just as the revolution of oppressed peoples needed the support of allies in the imperialist countries, the Communist International asserted, the proletariat in the industrially advanced lands, too, could not triumph except in alliance with the peoples of the colonial and semicolonial countries. For the first time, therefore, urgent necessity had laid the material basis on both sides for an alliance of working people of the East and West in a common international movement.

The message of the Baku congress

The guiding ideas advanced at the Baku congress had been debated and adopted the previous month by delegates—including a number from Asia—to the Comintern's Second Congress. These revolutionary perspectives were codified in the resolution on the colonial and national questions approved by the congress (see appendix 4). Lenin drafted the resolution and reported on it to the congress.[2]

The key points advanced by this resolution and by related Second Congress documents can be summarized as follows:

- There was no truth in the claims of the great capitalist powers to be leading the colonial peoples toward independence and prosperity. In reality, the colonizing powers that had emerged victorious from World War I were moving to consolidate their grip on Asia and Africa and deepen the enslavement of the peoples of the East. As for promises to colonies of independence (usually honored in the breach), the Second Congress resolution explained, "The imperialist powers, with the help of the privileged classes in the oppressed countries, are perpetrating a fraud. They are creating state structures that pose as politically independent states but are economically, financially, and militarily totally dependent upon the imperialist powers."
- The struggle for national liberation was part of an international class struggle against exploitation and oppression by the ruling capitalist families in a handful of imperialist countries, as well as by local landowning and monied classes. The national policy of Communists, the Second Congress resolution explained, should "clearly differentiate between the interests of the oppressed classes, the toilers, the exploited, and the general concept of the so-called interests of the people, which means the interests of the ruling class." Further, it continued, this policy "should with equal precision distinguish between the oppressed, dependent nations that do not have equal rights and the oppressor, exploiting nations that do, in order to counter the bourgeois-democratic lies that conceal the colonial and financial enslavement of the immense majority of the entire world population by a narrow minority of the richest, most advanced capitalist countries."

- No popular mobilization for national freedom could take place in colonial countries unless the peasantry was able to launch an agrarian revolution, which was essential to mobilizing it as an active revolutionary force. The goal of this struggle should be to free the land from burdens of landlordism, indebtedness, and predatory taxation, placing power in the hands of the toilers. The Second Congress adopted programmatic theses on the peasantry and the land question that served as the foundation for the more specific, and to some degree fuller, agrarian resolution adopted by the Baku congress (see session 6).

  "We must particularly strive to give the peasant movement the most revolutionary character possible," the Second Congress resolution on the national and colonial questions said, "organizing the peasants and all the exploited into soviets where feasible, and thereby establishing the closest connection between the Western European Communist proletariat and the revolutionary peasant movement in the East, in the colonies, and in the backward countries in general." Reporting to the Second Congress on this resolution, Lenin stated, "Peasants' soviets, soviets of the exploited, are a weapon that can be employed not only in capitalist countries but also in countries with precapitalist relations."

- Working people could find no salvation in a struggle to preserve their traditional societies, including native exploiters and their institutions of rule. The national ruling classes had ruthlessly enslaved and pillaged their subjects prior to colonial conquest, and they continued to do so as best they could under conditions of foreign domination. Now, under the impact of world capitalism, these societies were in hopeless crisis, unable to defend the toilers from ruin. Local exploiting classes sought to rationalize their own privileges and power—and extort for themselves a few more crumbs from the table of their imperialist overlords—by extolling the alleged virtues of traditional customs, values, and practices that had long been used to keep the producing majority in submission. Working people had no interest in these demagogic efforts.

- Peasants and other working people in colonial countries should support all genuine revolutionary movements for national liberation, even when led by local capitalist forces.[3] But Communists, while actively participating in such movements, should not accept the program and strategic perspectives of the bourgeois leaderships. Instead, they should combat the influence of all the local exploiting layers—both feudalist and bourgeois—and consistently defend their own interests as toilers. In the words of the Second Congress resolution, they should "maintain the independent character of the proletarian movement, even in its embryonic stage."
- A nationalist ideology would obstruct, not aid, the liberation struggle. Peoples of the East should come together on the basis of their common class interests in combating imperialist domination and local exploiters, setting aside any trace of the national exclusiveness or ethnic hostility that had been used for so long by the rulers to keep them weak and divided. Their goal should be to overturn the power of capitalism on a world scale and to join in a world federation of free workers' and peasants' republics. "Federation is a transitional form toward full unity of the toilers of all nations," the Second Congress resolution explained.

- Given the existence of a powerful workers' and peasants' republic, oppressed countries could achieve industrialization and social progress without passing through an epoch of capitalist development. Even in very poor countries, where no separate working class had yet emerged, the struggle must begin for a Soviet system, that is, a state based on revolutionary councils of the peasants and other toilers, where modernization could proceed along a path that would overcome the division between rich and poor.
- Toilers of the East would find an indispensable ally in the revolutionary working class of the advanced capitalist countries. By the time of the Second Congress, the International's affiliates included workers' parties in most countries of Europe, several of them numbering tens of thousands of adherents. The rapid growth of these parties held the promise that colonial peoples could now ally with sizable contingents of revolutionary-minded workers within the colonizing powers. Moreover, the Russian Soviet Republic would render consistent political and material support to all colonized peoples
- The resolution of the Second Congress concluded: "The class-conscious Communist proletariat of all countries therefore has a responsibility to give particular care and attention to the survivals of national feelings in the long-enslaved countries and peoples, while making concessions to overcome more rapidly this mistrust and these prejudices. The victory over capitalism cannot be successfully accomplished without the proletariat and with it all working people of all countries and the nations of the entire world voluntarily coming together in a unified alliance."

- At the Second Congress and the Baku congress, leaders of the Communist International aimed not merely to forge an alliance with liberation fighters from oppressed nations but to win them fully to communism. Revolutionaries from countries imprisoned by imperialism in stagnation and backwardness were now summoned to become equal participants in the Comintern and leaders of the worldwide movement for social revolution.

Upsurge in Europe

In calling the Baku congress, the Comintern spoke in the name of the revolutionary working masses of Europe who, "awakened by the thunder of the World War and driven by hunger . . . have risen up so that they may work not for the rich but for themselves." This revolutionary challenge to the capitalist order in Europe was then the focus of world politics.

In 1914 irrepressible economic and political rivalries among the great capitalist powers plunged them into a world war, resulting in immeasurable destruction of productive wealth, in famine and destitution for working people across Europe, and in the slaughter of millions. The war's impact heightened class antagonisms, driving opposed classes toward a confrontation.

By the end of 1918, revolutions in Russia, Germany, and Austria-Hungary had swept away governments and monarchs across Eastern and Central Europe, forcing an end to the slaughter. Even France, Britain, and the other Allied powers, the military victors in World War I, were deeply shaken by worker and peasant struggles and by the deep discontent among soldiers and sailors. And in Russia, working people achieved a decisive victory in November 1917, establishing the Soviet government.[4]

In 1919 the upsurge in Europe was set back, particularly in Germany, where a murderous war was waged against the workers' movement, and in Hungary, where a revolutionary government formed on the Soviet model was crushed. Yet initial steps were being taken to build Communist parties firmly rooted in the working class that might contribute to victory in further confrontations. Meanwhile, profound economic dislocation continued to undermine the capitalist regimes of Europe. Workers' resistance continued with renewed vigor in 1920, and nationwide struggles took place in Germany, Italy, France, and Britain.

The rebellious ferment faced by the Allied (Entente) powers at home and in their colonies was fed by these governments' campaign to overturn Soviet Russia and the allied Soviet republics. From mid-1918, Soviet territory was invested by a ring of counterrevolutionary White Guard armies, propped up and supported by invading forces of more than a dozen other governments and by a stringent Allied blockade along Soviet borders. During 1919 Red Army forces drove back the White Guards and Allied interventionist armies, but the war still raged on several fronts as the Baku congress convened.

Journey to Baku

The Baku congress was organized by a committee based in Baku that included Azerbaijani Communists Nariman Narimanov and M.D. Guseinov, Said Gabiev of Dagestan, and Turkish Communist leader Mustafa Subhi, as well as G.K. Ordzhonikidze and Yelena Stasova, representing the Central Committee of the Communist Party of Russia.

Delegates from Communist parties in all the major imperialist powers traveled to the congress together with a group of leaders of the Communist Party of Russia aboard a special train from Moscow, taking part in the many meetings and celebrations organized along the route. They crossed areas where White Guard forces were active, passing a major station in Ukraine, Lozovaya, that had just suffered a destructive White attack. On the return journey, their train was blocked at one point because another band of Whites had torn up the tracks, derailing a locomotive; the nearby station at Naurskaya had also been assaulted. For a time the Baku congress train was stranded and in great danger, but the White Guards moved off without attacking.

"Most of the stations had been destroyed, and everywhere the sidings were full of the half-burnt wrecks of coaches," recalls Alfred Rosmer, a delegate from France. "When the Whites had been beaten they destroyed everything they could."[5] The fuel shortage was so acute, Stasova tells us, that on occasion passengers disembarked at stations and took down fences and gathered other wooden materials for the firebox.[6]

Across all the Soviet-held territories of Asia, an extensive campaign of public education took place to provide a basis for the popular election of delegates. Several "agit-trains" were sent out to organize this work, including the "V.I. Lenin," the "Red East," and the "Soviet Caucasia"; some "agit-ships" also served in the campaign. Rallies and meetings were held throughout the Soviet East. As delegates made their way to Baku, they were met by celebrations; in the town of Agadash, a Baku newspaper reported, one hundred sheep and goats were slaughtered in honor of the congress. Another form of participation was the holding at many points in the Soviet East of special Baku congress *subbotniks*—a day of volunteer labor for economic reconstruction. Twenty-five thousand volunteers participated in the largest of the subbotniks in Baku.[7]

The British government did what it could to block delegates' journeys to Baku. A steamship carrying delegates from Enzeli in Iran was attacked by British military airplanes; two delegates were killed and several wounded. Two other delegates were killed at the Azerbaijan border by Iranian police. British warships patrolled the Turkish Black Sea coast to bar delegates from setting sail from Turkey for Soviet territory. But a timely gale blew up, forcing the British flotilla to return to Constantinople [Istanbul]; revolutionaries from Turkey immediately set sail and completed the risky voyage successfully. In the Transcaucasus (between the Caucasus Mountains, Turkey, and Iran), the two bourgeois republics of Armenia and Georgia banned attendance at the Baku congress, but many delegates managed to slip across the borders undetected.

In the months before the Baku congress, thousands of militant Muslims left India and headed west, hoping to prevent the Allied powers from dismembering Turkey, then the seat of the caliph, who was seen as the head of Muslims around the world. Many of these fighters reached Kabul, where about 150 of them formed the pro-Soviet Indian Revolutionary Association at the beginning of 1920. A group of twenty-eight of the most committed members set out for Turkestan. After an arduous journey through the Hindu Kush and Alai mountains, they arrived in Tashkent on July 2. Others soon followed this route. Meanwhile, some Indian soldiers in Britain's Mideast army defected to the Soviet side and made their way to Baku. By the end of 1920, more than two hundred Indian revolutionaries were on Soviet soil. Fourteen of them attended the Baku congress, as did a smaller number of Korean and Chinese workers living in Russia and a delegate from Japan.[8]

Who the delegates were

The delegates present at Baku included a core of leaders of long experience in the Bolshevik movement, such as Narimanov and Ahmed Sultanzadeh, a Communist leader from Iran. Many other leading figures in the congress were fighters against tsarist oppression who had only recently joined the revolutionary movement for Soviet power. Among them were Turar Ryskulov, who led the faction of Communists of Muslim origin in the Turkestan party, and Narbutabekov, a leading spokesman for the nonparty delegates at Baku. The delegation from Khiva [Khorezm] was headed by a Muslim cleric, Bekkhan Rakhmanov, who had recently joined the Khiva Communist Party—a fact that provoked derision from some Western European critics of the Comintern. The delegates in Baku from parties in the West, who came from diverse political backgrounds, were equally recent recruits to communism.

The total number of registered delegates at the congress was about 2,050. The most detailed available political breakdown, taken from congress records, lists 55 percent as Communist Party members, another 20 percent as supporters, and 25 percent as "nonparty" (see Composition of the Congress, p. 289). Yet according to a later report by Zinoviev, participants in meetings of the Communist delegates (the "Communist fraction") were considerably outnumbered by those attending meetings of the non-Communist ("nonparty") fraction. This fraction "broke down in turn into two groups," Zinoviev added. "First there were the genuinely nonparty forces, in which we must include the representatives of the peasantry and the semiproletarian urban population. Then there were those persons who claimed to be nonparty but in fact belonged to bourgeois parties."[9]

Best known among the bourgeois political figures at Baku was Enver Pasha, former leader of the Young Turk movement and of the Turkish government during World War I. In exile following Turkey's surrender, he had arrived in Moscow August 14 seeking Soviet arms and money to build an international Islamic revolutionary organization with the stated goal of driving the Allied invaders from Turkey.

Many working people in Baku looked on Enver as a heroic figure who had led Muslim resistance during the war against the Western powers, especially Britain. But among congress delegates, Enver was widely despised for his government's role in driving the Turkish workers and peasants into World War I and for inciting the slaughter of Turkey's Armenian population. After initially deciding to permit Enver to address the congress, the Presiding Committee ruled to exclude him from the sessions, in view of the likely negative response of most delegates.

Enver took part in discussions on the fringe of the Baku congress that led to the formation of two anti-Communist political parties: ERK (Will), later named the Group of Turkestan Socialists, and the Central Committee of National Muslim Unions. Both groups opposed Russian influence and favored political unification of the Muslim peoples of the former tsarist empire.

Another bourgeois current from Turkey also sent a delegation to Baku: the national independence movement in Anatolia led by Mustafa Kemal. Statements by a representative of this movement and by Enver were read to delegates during session 4.

The course of events at Baku

The city of Baku, one of tsarist Russia's major commercial and industrial centers, was the heart of its oil industry. The modern city center was inhabited by the chiefly Russian and Armenian propertied classes, officials, and skilled workers. Further out was a ring of industrial suburbs, and beyond it the oil fields. The majority of workers were of

Muslim faith, representing both Azerbaijani and other nationalities. Most of these workers lived separated from their families in barrack-like conditions. Beyond the oil fields lay the agricultural countryside of Azerbaijan, economically backward and as yet almost untouched by the political and social struggles of the capital.

The Baku congress brought together representatives of peoples long divided by the structures of tsarist rule, by the shifting boundaries of civil war, and by ethnic and religious mistrust fostered by local exploiting layers and encouraged by the colonial power in Moscow. Indeed in Baku itself, the rivalries of bourgeois nationalist parties had led to assaults in 1918 on first the Muslim and then the Armenian quarters, which left thousands of victims.

The congress, by contrast, took on the colors of a festival celebrating the unity of the nationally oppressed toilers. On Friday, September 3, the congress organized a procession through the streets of Baku and the dedication of a monument to Karl Marx. "The whole organized population of Baku passed in review for hours under the burning sun of the Orient," reports Dutch delegate Henk Sneevliet: "workers, women, youth and the schools, Persians and Turks, all the services of the Red Army . . . and congress delegates from all the nations."[10] On the day following the congress, September 8, a large assembly was held to mark the burial of the remains of twenty-six leaders of the Baku Soviet murdered in 1918 by White Guards with British complicity. A Conference of Youth of Asia, attended by more than one hundred representatives from Armenia, Azerbaijan, Bukhara, Georgia, Iran, Khiva, Turkestan, and Turkey, took place in Baku September 9–10.

Some delegations submitted statements on political questions faced by the peoples they represented. A declaration by delegates from Armenia, found in appendix 6, condemns the Armenian government's responsibility in the "cleansing" operations against minority ethnic groups and in military conflicts in the region. The statement counterposes a course of revolutionary struggle as the road to unity among working people of the Caucasus.

Three statements, published for the first time in English in appendix 7, presented to the congress conflicting views on the Zionist project to settle Jews in Palestine. The first, a declaration by Mountain Jews, was made by revolutionaries from an indigenous, Eastern Jewish community who were influenced by Zionism. The Poale Zion statement (appendix 7b) was written by a Zionist group that supported Soviet power and for a time moved closer to the Communist Party. The response of the Jewish sections of the Russian Communist Party (appendix 7c) presents the Comintern's analysis of Zionism and its impact on Palestine, which the Second Congress resolution on the national question had summed up as "a crass example of Entente imperialism and the bourgeoisie of the relevant country working together to swindle the working classes of an oppressed nation."

Congress sessions resounded with translations into a variety of languages of Asia, many of which had been stifled in the days of the tsars. Most of the delegates from Europe and America also understood no Russian and needed translation. Following each speech, debate halted to permit a rendering into major Asian languages in turn. Sometimes limited to summaries, translations were often far longer than the original speech. John Reed later joshed British Communists about the experience of one of their compatriots, presumably Thomas Quelch. According to Reed, the British delegate's timid and hesitant remarks were translated by Peter Petrov with such enthusiasm and such a spirit of invention that the hall soon erupted with cheers and shouts of "Down with British imperialism!" as swords and rifles were brandished in the air. The dismayed British delegate protested, "I'm sure I never said anything like that; I demand a proper translation."[11]

Soon the proceedings were lagging far behind the planned agenda, and in session 4 stricter rules of order had to be adopted. Translations from the podium were now given only in Farsi (Persian), Azerbaijani, and Russian, and were restricted in length. Delegates gathered in groups for renditions into other languages.

A small but significant number of women—about fifty-five—took part in the congress, and women's struggle for liberation was addressed on several occasions during congress sessions.[12] A proposal to elect three women to the Presiding Committee, Zinoviev later reported, aroused strong objections from some nonparty delegates, and a lengthy debate ensued. When three women were unanimously elected to the committee in session 5, however, the entire congress rose to greet them in a thunderous ovation. In session 7, two women delegates spoke on the liberation of women of the East.

In session 3, Narbutabekov, a non-Communist delegate from Turkestan, called for action against chauvinist abuse of the indigenous peoples by some Soviet officials in Central Asia. A resolution arguing the case against such abuse was submitted by Communist delegate Turar Ryskulov and twenty other delegates from a number of nationalities.

Communist leaders repeatedly denounced such chauvinist practices, which had been carried over from the former tsarist administration, where they were rampant. In December 1922 Lenin warned of the danger that "the 'freedom to secede from the union' by which we justify ourselves will be a mere scrap of paper, unable to defend the non-Russians from the onslaught of that really Russian man, the Great-Russian chauvinist—in substance a rascal and a tyrant, such as the typical Russian bureaucrat is."[13]

The problem was exceptionally acute in Turkestan, which from early 1918 had been cut off from Soviet Russia by White Guard forces. The Turkestan government followed a blatantly chauvinist course. Operating under the Soviet banner, the Central Committee of the Russian Communist Party later noted, "old servants of the tsarist regime, adventurers and kulaks [rich peasants] . . . began to persecute the indigenous population in a most brutal manner." As a result, working people in Turkestan had been pushed into the arms of the reactionary ruling layers there.[14] In the fall of 1919, Turkestan soviets broke from this disastrous policy and set out on a revolutionary course. Nonetheless, chauvinist abuses had been far from fully overcome at the time of the Baku congress.

In his closing remarks to the congress, Zinoviev pledged corrective action on the points raised by Narbutabekov. This began immediately, as twenty-seven congress delegates traveled to Moscow, where they discussed their criticisms and proposals with the Communist Party Political Bureau. A resolution was adopted, based on a draft by Lenin and incorporating several points made in the document presented to the Baku congress by the twenty-one delegates. Appendix 8 contains the resolutions of the congress delegates and the Political Bureau along with one of the statements made as part of implementing the Political Bureau decision; all three documents, newly available, lay hidden for many decades in closed Soviet archives.

Resolutions adopted by the congress included a manifesto to the peoples of the East, an appeal to workers of the advanced capitalist countries, and theses on the agrarian question and on Soviet power in the East. The final congress decision was to elect an executive body to continue its work: the Council for Propaganda and Action.

Upsurge in the colonial world

The Baku congress's call for united action against British imperialism corresponded to a vital turning point in the struggle against colonial rule in Asia.

In the years following the Russian revolution of 1905, national-democratic uprisings had shaken Turkey, Iran, and China, signaling what Lenin termed "the awakening of Asia." But these attempts to shatter the old order had been frustrated, and at times soaked in blood, with the aid of imperialist forces.

As World War I ended, the example of the Russian revolution helped unleash a new wave of anticolonial struggles across the Asian continent. Another element feeding this upsurge was popular opposition to the continuation of colonial rule as registered by the war's victors in the Treaty of Versailles, concluded in 1919. The treaty confirmed the partition of almost all of Africa, much of Asia, and substantial territories in the Caribbean and the Pacific into colonial empires ruled by Britain, France, the United States, and other powers. The few independent countries of Asia, such as Turkey, Iran, and China, remained subject to infringements of their sovereignty and economic disabilities imposed by the capitalist powers. Meanwhile, advancing from their bases in Egypt and India, contingents of the British army fanned out over much of the Near East and Central Asia.

By mid-1920 anticolonial struggles had put imperialism on the defensive across much of Asia. Across Turkey, proindependence forces were taking up arms against the

Allied occupation forces. In Iran, much of which was under British occupation, uprisings took place in the northeast and northwest against the Tehran rulers, and a mass movement arose against a treaty that would have made the country a de facto colony of Britain. In the northern province of Gilan, Communists joined in early 1920 with national independence fighters in establishing a revolutionary government. Meanwhile, British and French rule in the Middle East provoked popular uprisings and sharp clashes during 1919–20 in Egypt, Syria, and Mesopotamia [Iraq].

When the congress convened, the British government had been forced by this resistance and by the advance of the Soviet revolution to withdraw from Afghanistan, Turkestan, the Transcaucasus, and part of northern Iran. Adding to London's difficulties, a month before the Baku gathering the Indian National Congress, led by Mohandas Gandhi, launched a campaign of noncooperation with British rule that rapidly assumed mass proportions.

In China, the Versailles settlement sparked a student protest in Beijing on May 4, 1919, which in turn opened up nationwide agitation for China's national sovereignty and a profound radicalization among its youth.

When delegates at Baku spoke of the East, it was Asia and Africa that they usually had in mind.[15] John Reed, however, a delegate from the United States, told the congress of the yoke of U.S. domination in the Caribbean and in Mexico, where a revolution was under way to "keep the wealth of Mexico for the Mexicans," as well as of the mounting antiracist resistance of black people in the United States (see addendum to session 4).

The upsurge among colonially oppressed peoples also found expression within former tsarist Russia, where Asian peoples' support to Soviet rule helped sway the balance in the civil war and push back imperialist invading armies. By early 1919 close to 250,000 working people of Muslim origin were serving in the Red Army under the command of Muslim officers. These troops made up almost half the officers and soldiers of the Soviet Sixth Army, the main force resisting White commander Kolchak on the Siberian front. Red Army contingents were formed from among the more than one million Asian immigrant workers. Tens of thousands of Chinese workers joined the Soviet forces, a development that provoked noisy alarm among anti-Soviet propagandists. Indeed, the Red Army was built not as a Russian but as an international force pledged to serve the cause of world revolution.

During the early months of 1920, the revolution advanced deeper into Asia as the working people of the North Caucasus, Azerbaijan, and Khiva established Soviet republics. Elsewhere in Soviet territory, many Asian and other peoples were setting up autonomous republics. In Turkestan, the Red Army advanced toward the frontiers of Iran, Afghanistan, and China.

Participation in the Baku congress by revolutionaries from across Asia was a tangible act of solidarity with the embattled Soviet republics. Delegates sought to defend the historic gains of the Russian revolution, such as the overthrow of tsarist autocracy, land reform, and the freeing of captive peoples. But the most effective defense, in the delegates' view, would be for workers and peasants of the East to take advantage of the world capitalist crisis to prepare new Soviet revolutions in Iran, Turkey, and elsewhere in Asia.

Impact of the congress

Assessing the joint results of the congress in Baku and of the second Comintern congress that preceded it, Lenin noted that their achievements, while they "cannot be immediately assessed or directly calculated," were "of greater significance than some military victories." The Baku congress showed that the banner and program of Bolshevism "are an emblem of salvation, an emblem of struggle to the workers of all civilized countries and the peasants of all the backward colonial countries," Lenin continued. "That which was achieved in Moscow in July and in Baku in September will for many months to come provide food for thought and assimilation by the workers and peasants of the world."[16]

The call of the congress for a "holy war for the liberation of the peoples of the East . . . for the liberation of all humanity from the yoke of capitalist and imperialist slavery" won an immediate response from toilers in countries close to Baku. The sense of liberation from age-old fetters was recalled decades later by Babayev, who attended the congress as a young Muslim Azerbaijani serving as a guard. When the call to prayer came, he found it natural to set aside his gun during devotions, after which he would "go back to defend with our blood the conference and the revolution." Inspired by the "declaration of holy war against the enemy of revolution," he explains, "thousands of people, convinced there was no contradiction between being a Bolshevik and a Muslim, joined the Bolshevik ranks."[17]

The outstanding achievement of the Baku congress was to speed the formation and development of Communist parties in the East. Many working people in the Caucasus, Iran, Turkey, and the Arab East first heard of the accomplishments of the Baku congress through the work of the ongoing executive body it established, the Council for Propaganda and Action. This body, based in Baku, rapidly published congress decisions in Farsi, Turkish, and

Arabic. In the first ten weeks of its activity, the council trained and sent out 170 educators and organizers. It established a cadre school, whose first class of some fifty students graduated in January 1921. They were backed up with a supply of books and pamphlets; available records of one two-week period show that 1,270 pieces of literature were shipped, of which 433 were in Farsi and 176 in Turkish. One issue of a magazine, *Narody Vostoka* (Peoples of the East) was published in October in Russian and Turkish, bearing the Baku congress slogan, "Workers of the world and oppressed peoples, unite!"[18]

The Baku congress rapidly provoked a sharp protest from the British government, which complained on October 1 of a "real hurricane of propaganda, intrigue, and conspiracy against British interests and British power in Asia."[19] Nonetheless, the Soviet government was able to make rapid progress toward a trade agreement with Britain; its signing in March 1921 forced a decisive breach in the anti-Soviet blockade.

During the year following the congress, Soviet governments were established in Armenia and Georgia, while a pro-Soviet revolution triumphed in Mongolia. Soviet Russia defeated the final White Guard armies, forced the invading Polish government to make peace, and brought the devastating civil war to a close.

In Turkey, however, while national independence was secured, a bourgeois government under Mustafa Kemal quelled the revolutionary upsurge. A similar development took place in Iran, where a new government crushed the uprising in Gilan province; the establishment of the Pahlavi dynasty followed in 1925.

The third Comintern congress, meeting in July 1921, noted a temporary restabilization of capitalism on a world scale. To adjust to changed conditions, and also to better centralize the work of the Comintern, the Council for Propaganda and Action was wound up early in 1922, and its activities were continued as part of the work of the Comintern center in Moscow. A congress of toilers of the Far East was held in Moscow in January 1922.[20] During the year that followed, the deepening of the Chinese revolution opened up for the Communist International the outstanding opportunity and challenge it was to encounter for the application of the ideas of the Baku congress.

The Baku congress today

Over the three years following the Baku congress, capitalist reaction—aided by the proimperialist Social Democratic current that headed a section of the workers' movement—regained the upper hand for the moment across most of Europe. Even more deadly for the prospects of an alliance of workers and oppressed peoples was the growing hold in the Communist Party of Russia and the Comintern of a reactionary petty-bourgeois layer rooted in the party and state bureaucracy. This layer drew strength from the heavy toll of death and destruction that exhausted the working class during years of civil war and imperialist intervention, and from the impact of the Soviet republic's isolation following on defeats of the working class in Europe.

Campaigning against the danger represented by this reactionary layer, Lenin drew particular attention in December 1922 to its bullying attitude toward the peoples of the smaller republics in the Soviet Union that had been oppressed under tsarism. Outlining sweeping corrective measures, Lenin fought against bureaucratic practices that undermined the alliance of workers and the oppressed peoples. He wrote, "It would be unpardonable opportunism if, on the eve of the debut of the East, just as it is awakening, we undermined our prestige with its peoples, even if only by the slightest crudity or injustice towards our own non-Russian nationalities."[21]

In March 1923 Lenin was incapacitated by a stroke, ending his political activity. In the years that followed, the petty-bourgeois forces gained the upper hand in the Communist Party leadership, finding their personification and leader in Joseph Stalin. Increasingly abandoning revolutionary internationalism, these forces put the Communist Party, Comintern, and Soviet state on a counterrevolutionary course. With their triumph, the Soviet working class was driven out of politics, and the opening for a world alliance of the oppressed and exploited was closed off. Ultimately, the continuity of Marxism in the Soviet Union was extinguished.[22]

Under Stalinist rule, the Soviet republics in Asia were subjected to bureaucratic centralization, chauvinist and Russifying policies, forced collectivization, counterrevolutionary terror, and mass murder. Among the victims in the ensuing frame-up purges were Dadash Buniatzadeh, Jalalutdin Korkmasov, Narbutabekov, and Turar Ryskulov—indeed, all the speakers from Asia at the Baku congress who were within Stalin's reach and whose fate is known. All were killed except for Khaver Shabanova, who was jailed but escaped execution. Nariman Narimanov, congress cochairman and first president of the Azerbaijan Soviet republic, died before these purges in 1925. Yet even he was posthumously denounced and vilified. The republics of Central Asia and the Caucasus came to resemble Bantustans, excluded from any role in world politics beyond occasional folkloric display and administered by corrupt and violent chieftains dependent on Moscow's favor.

Comintern policy under Stalin's leadership went over to the nationalist ideology of "socialism in one country."

Revolutionary workers' and peasants' movements were subordinated to bourgeois-nationalist political currents and to the narrow national interests of the bureaucratic caste ruling in the Kremlin. The initial, disastrous results of this policy were recorded in the defeat of the 1925–27 revolution in China.[23]

Six decades later, in late 1989 and early 1990, working people of Baku entered the political arena once more, solidarizing with antibureaucratic struggles across Eastern Europe and the Soviet Union. The Moscow regime unleashed a military counterattack, known as bloody January, to suppress this movement. The people of Baku responded by demonstrating one million strong, dealing a hard blow to the murderous regime. Political life began to open up to working people in Azerbaijan and the other Soviet republics.

On a world scale, the prospects for realization of the goals of the Baku congress are today better than at any other time since the early 1920s. Today the world capitalist economy is gripped in a profound and extended crisis of stagnation and decline. Its world political system is one of growing disorder, marked by increasingly uncontrollable economic conflicts, military interventions, and wars. Working people in oppressed and imperialist countries alike are increasingly confronted with the need to take the path of militant struggle to defend their most elementary class interests. The obstacle posed by Stalinism to taking this path has been decisively weakened.

In these conditions, the conceptions of united world struggle for political and social liberation mapped out at Baku and by other Comintern congresses in Lenin's time will now find new life and expression in the struggles of workers and farmers in Asia, Africa, and Latin America, as well as of those in the imperialist heartlands.

New exponents of revolutionary internationalism will lead working people in taking up and acting on the basic ideas of the early Communist International and the Baku congress. They will stand on the achievements of outstanding internationalist fighters who have proven in life the validity of these principles in the decades since Lenin's death. Among such leaders can be counted Carlos Fonseca, founder of the Marxist movement in Nicaragua; Maurice Bishop, leader of the 1979–83 workers' and farmers' government in Grenada; Thomas Sankara, leader of the 1983–87 revolution in Burkina Faso; Malcolm X, outstanding fighter for revolutionary internationalism; and Nelson Mandela, head of the African National Congress. Key principles proclaimed in Baku have above all been upheld by Fidel Castro, Ernesto Che Guevara, and other leaders of the Cuban revolution, and defended by the Cuban people through more than thirty years of defiant struggle.

A note on this edition

The present text of the congress proceedings is an edited version of a translation by Brian Pearce, made from the original Russian edition and checked against the French text published in 1921.[24] Pearce's annotation has also been utilized in the preparation of notes and a glossary. These materials have been used by permission of Index Books and Brian Pearce.

The text of appendixes 3 and 4, taken from the most recent English edition of Lenin's *Collected Works*, have been checked against the original Russian text, and a small number of corrections have been made. The other appendixes are newly translated from Russian. Appendixes 5 and 8 are printed by permission of the Russian Institute for the Preservation and Study of Documents of Contemporary History (hereinafter cited as Russian Documents Center).

A glossary has been provided, containing biographical information on leading participants in the Baku congress and others mentioned in the text, as well as explanations of unfamiliar terms.

Robert Des Verney, Rachel Gomme, Jeff Hamill, and Doug Hord translated for this volume. Brian Pearce made helpful suggestions regarding translation and annotation.

The Russian Documents Center helped locate documents in Moscow used in preparing this book. Most of the photographs were provided by the Municipal Library in La Chaux-de-Fonds, Switzerland. Mete Tunçay advised on a wide variety of questions of Turkish working-class history.

The Central State Archives of Political Parties and Social Movements of the Republic of Azerbaijan (Bakhtiar Rafiyev, director) provided important documentation relating to the congress and carried out the painstaking work required to make this material available for the present edition. Solmaz Rustamova Tohidi of the Azerbaijan Academy of Sciences assisted in completing this work.

The Communist International in Lenin's Time

To See the Dawn is the fifth installment in the Pathfinder series, The Communist International in Lenin's Time. This series presents the example and lessons of the international communist movement in the first years after the October 1917 revolution, before Lenin's death in January 1924.

This series traces the historical continuity of Marxist leadership in the workers' movement, starting with the struggle led by Lenin, following the 1905 uprising in Russia, to revolutionize the Socialist International. It follows this continuity to the launching of the Communist (Third) International and through the first five years of its activity. Previously published installments in this series are:

- Lenin's Struggle for a Revolutionary International: Documents, 1907–1916, The Preparatory Years.
- The German Revolution and the Debate on Soviet Power: Documents, 1918–1919, Preparing the Founding Congress.
- Founding the Communist International: Proceedings and Documents of the First Congress, March 1919.
- Workers of the World and Oppressed Peoples, Unite! Proceedings and Documents of the Second Congress, 1920. 2 volumes.

Forthcoming installments of the series will include the proceedings of the third and fourth congresses of the Comintern, held in 1921 and 1922 respectively.

John Riddell
and
Ma'mud Shirvani
JULY 15, 1993

CALL
JUNE 29, 1920

Call to the Baku congress

To the enslaved popular masses of Persia [Iran], Armenia, and Turkey:[1]

On August 15, 1920,[2] the Executive Committee of the Communist International will convene *a congress in Baku of the workers and peasants of Persia, Armenia, and Turkey.*

What is the Communist International? It is the organization of the revolutionary working masses of Russia, Poland, Germany, France, Britain, and America. Awakened by the thunder of the World War and driven by hunger, these masses have risen up so that they may work not for the rich but for themselves. They have risen up so that they may never again take up arms against their own suffering and deprived brothers, but instead bear arms to defend themselves against the exploiters. These working masses have understood that their only strength lies in unity and organization; these alone can guarantee their victory. Last year they formed a mighty organization: the Third International. Despite all persecution by capitalist governments, this International has in its eighteen months of existence become the moving spirit of all the revolutionary workers and peasants striving for liberation around the world.

Why is the Communist International convening a congress of Persian, Armenian, and Turkish workers and peasants at this time? What has it to offer them? What does it want from them? In their fight against capital, the workers and peasants in Europe and America turn to you because you, like them, suffer under the yoke of world capitalism. Like them, you are obliged to fight against the world's exploiters. If you join with the workers and peasants of Europe and America, this will hasten the downfall of world capitalism and ensure the liberation of workers and peasants throughout the world.

Peasants and workers of Persia! The government of the Qajars in Tehran and its underlings, the provincial khans, have robbed and exploited you for centuries. The land that according to the shariat [Islamic law] was common property has been seized by the lackeys of the Tehran government.[3] They deal as they will with this land and impose taxes and dues upon you as they see fit. After sucking the lifeblood out of the country and reducing it to poverty and ruin, *they sold Persia last year to the British capitalists for £2 million.*[4] They did this to form an army in Persia that will oppress you even more than before, squeezing taxes and tribute out of you for the khans and the Tehran government. They have sold Britain the rich oil fields of southern Persia, thereby cooperating in the plundering of your country.

Peasants of Mesopotamia [Iraq]! The British proclaimed the independence of your country, but eighty thousand British soldiers stand upon your soil, robbing and killing you and violating your women.

Peasants of Anatolia![5] The British, Italian, and French governments hold Constantinople under the muzzles of their guns. They have taken the sultan prisoner and forced him to agree to the partitioning off of exclusively Turkish territory and the placing of Turkey's finances at the disposal of foreign financiers, so they may more easily plunder a Turkish people already impoverished by six years of war. They have taken the coal mines of Heraclea [Eregli] and your seaports. They have sent their troops into your country, trampling your fields. They dictate their alien laws to the peaceful Turkish peasant, seeking to make you their beasts of burden, onto whose backs they put whatever loads they choose.

Some of your beys and effendis have sold out to the foreign capitalists. Others summon you to arms to fight against the foreign invader—but without allowing you to take power for yourselves in your own country. They do not let you take over the lands and fields that the sultan presented to various parasites, so that you may sow these fields for yourselves. And tomorrow, if the foreign capitalists should come to an agreement with your oppressors on less severe peace terms, your present leaders will use this opportunity to lay new chains upon you, just as is being done by the landlords and former officials in regions permanently occupied by the foreign armies.

Peasants and workers of Armenia! For years you have been victims of foreign capital. Talking at length about the slaughter of the Armenians by the Kurds, it stirred you up to fight against the sultan, a fight that continually brought it new advantages. During the war the foreign capitalists not only promised you independence but also incited your teachers, priests, and merchants to lay claim to the land of Turkish peasants, so that unending war might rage between the Turkish and Armenian peoples, from which they might extract unending profit.[6] *So long as this discord persists between you, the foreign capitalists will profit by it, frightening Turkey with the threat of an Armenian rising and frightening the Armenians with the threat of pogroms by the Kurds.*

Peasants of Syria and Arabia! The British and French promised you independence, but today their armies have occupied your country and are dictating their laws to you. After liberating yourselves from the Turkish sultan and his government, you have now been made slaves of the governments of Paris and London, which differ from the sultan's only in that they hold you down more firmly and plunder you more severely.

You understand all this very well. The Persian peasants and workers rose up against the treacherous government of Tehran. The peasants of Mesopotamia have rebelled against the British occupation force, and the British press reports on losses suffered by the British army fighting the rebels near Baghdad.

Peasants of Anatolia! You are being urgently summoned to rally under the flag of Kemal Pasha, to fight against the foreign invaders. But at the same time we know that you are trying to form your own people's party, your own peasants' party, which will be able to carry forward the fight in the event that the pashas make peace with the predators of the Entente.

It has not been possible to establish peace in Syria. As for you, peasants of Armenia—the Entente, despite all its promises, allows you to starve, so as better to control you. You are coming to understand more and more clearly that hope of salvation through help from the capitalists of the Entente is utterly senseless. Even your bourgeois ruling party, the Dashnaktsutiun—those lackeys of the Entente—

has been forced to turn to the workers' and peasants' government of Russia with a request for a peace treaty and for assistance.

Now we see that you yourselves are beginning to understand your needs. And so we address ourselves to you, in our capacity as representatives of the European proletariat, possessing great experience accumulated in our struggle, in order to help you achieve your emancipation. We say to you: *The time when the European and American capitalists could suppress you by the force of their guns has passed, never to return. Everywhere in Europe and America the workers are rising up in arms against the capitalists, waging bloody war against them.*

While we have not yet vanquished world capitalism, already the capitalists are no longer able to dispose of their people's blood at their own discretion. For two and a half years the Russian revolution has been struggling against the entire world. The French, British, and American capitalists have tried by every means—armed force, famine—to conquer the Russian workers and peasants, tighten a noose round their necks, and make them their slaves. They have not succeeded. *The Russian workers and peasants have staunchly defended their government and formed an army of their own that has utterly smashed the reactionary forces supported by the Entente capitalists.*

Workers and peasants of the Near East! If you organize yourselves and set up your own workers' and peasants' government, if you arm yourselves, uniting with the Russian workers' and peasants' army, you will subdue the British, French, and American capitalists, get rid of your oppressors, and find freedom. You will be able to create a free world republic of the working people. You will use the riches of your native land in your own interests and those of the rest of working mankind, which will be glad to take them in exchange for the products you need and will joyfully come to your aid. We want to talk with you about all this at the congress.

The Executive Committee of the Communist International, as the representative of the British, French, American, German, and Italian workers, is coming to Baku in order to discuss with you how to unite the efforts of the European proletariat with yours in order to struggle against the common enemy.

Spare no effort to ensure that as many as possible may be present on September 1 in Baku. Formerly you traveled across deserts to reach the holy places. Now make your way over mountains and rivers, through forests and deserts, to meet and discuss how to free yourselves from the chains of servitude and unite in fraternal alliance, so as to live a life based on equality, freedom, and brotherhood.

We appeal first and foremost to the workers and peasants of the Near East, but we will also be glad to see among the delegates representatives of the popular masses who live much farther off—representatives of India as well as of the Muslim people who are developing freely in association with Soviet Russia. On September 2 thousands of Turkish, Armenian, and Persian workers and peasants must peacefully come together in Baku for the liberation of the Near East.

May the congress proclaim to your enemies in Europe and America and in your own countries that the age of slavery is past, that you are rising in revolt, and that you will be victorious.

May this congress proclaim to the workers around the world that you are defending your rights, that you are uniting with the mighty revolutionary army that is now fighting against all injustice and exploitation.

May your congress bring strength and faith to millions and millions of the enslaved throughout the world. May it instill in them confidence in their power. May it bring nearer the day of final triumph and liberation.

The Executive Committee of the Communist International
CHAIRMAN: *G. Zinoviev*
SECRETARY: *K. Radek*

For the British Socialist Party:
W. McLaine, Tom Quelch

For the British Shop Stewards' committee:
J. Tanner, J.T. Murphy

For the French delegation to the congress of the Communist International:
A. Rosmer, Delinières, J. Sadoul

For the Italian delegation to the congress of the Communist International:
Bombacci, A. Graziadei

For the Communist Party of America:
L. Fraina, A. Stoklitsky

For the Communist Labor Party of America:
A. Bilan

For the Spanish Federation of Labor:
Angel Pestaña

For the Central Committee of the Communist Party of Russia:
N. Bukharin, V. Vorovsky, A. Balabanoff, G. Klinger

For the All-Russia Central Trade Union Council:
S.A. Lozovsky

For the Communist Party of Poland:
J. Marchlewski (Karski)

For the Communist Party of Bulgaria and the Balkan Communist Federation:
N. Shablin

For the Communist Party of Austria:
Reisler

For the Communist Party of Hungary:
Rákosi, Rudnyánszky

For the Communist Party of Holland:
D. Wijnkoop

First congress of the peoples of the East

Proceedings

OPENING RALLY
AUGUST 31, 1920

Joint celebration of the Baku soviet and the Azerbaijan trade union congress

(*The meeting opened at 1:25 a.m. with the participation of the members of the Congress of the Peoples of the East.*)

CHAIRMAN: Comrades, let us now proceed with our meeting. I call the meeting to order.

Allow me, comrades, to address in your name a warm fraternal greeting to our dear guests. (*Applause*)

The enlarged Soviet of Workers', Red Army Men's, and Sailors' Deputies of Baku, together with the district soviets and the entire Trade Union Congress of Azerbaijan, is glad to see at this celebration of theirs representatives and leaders of world communism, (*Applause*) as well as representatives of the Baku proletariat and of the working masses of Azerbaijan. Those present here hope and believe that under the experienced leadership of the comrades who have come to visit us, at a time when we have begun to forge a mighty weapon for the struggle against world imperialism, we shall fulfill with honor the task that has fallen to our lot. (*Applause*)

We hope, comrades, that their brief visit will help us unite our scattered forces and rapidly find the ways and means to achieve the victory we desire as soon as possible. Under their leadership we shall perhaps enter sooner than we expect into the realm of communism. Long live our leader who has come to visit us here, Comrade Zinoviev, (*Applause*) leader of world communism! (*Ovation. The orchestra plays the "Internationale."*) Long live Comrade Radek, leader of the international proletariat! (*Ovation. The orchestra plays the "Internationale."*)

Comrades, together with Comrades Zinoviev and Radek, we have among our visitors the leader of the Communist Party and of the communist revolution in Hungary, which has suffered so much under the yoke of the White Guard tyrants, a comrade known to you, Comrade Béla Kun. (*Ovation. The orchestra plays the "Internationale."*)

Comrades, present here besides our own delegates are representatives of the Communist parties of Britain, Germany, France, Italy, and other countries of Western Europe and America. (*Applause. The orchestra plays the "Internationale."*)

Comrades, present at our celebration today along with the representatives of the proletariat of the West are delegates, assembled in congress, from the oppressed masses of the East. This alliance is for us a symbol of our fraternal unity and a pledge of lasting victory, the basis for which we are laying here today. Long live the representatives of the proletariat of the West and the representatives of the working masses of the East! (*Applause. The orchestra plays the "Internationale."*)

Comrades, let us shout together a greeting to all present and to all our visitors. Hurrah! (*A loud "Hurrah!" The orchestra plays the "Internationale."*) I call upon Comrade Karayev to translate my remarks into Turkic.[1]

(*Karayev translates into Turkic. The "Internationale."*)

CHAIRMAN: Comrade Narimanov has the floor, to bring greetings from the Azerbaijan Revolutionary Committee. (*The "Internationale."*)

NARIMANOV: Dear comrades, I am happy to greet you in the name of the workers' and peasants' government of Red Azerbaijan and of the Central Committee. (*Applause*)

Dear guests, this significant occasion shows that we are close to our aim, the triumph of the Third International. (*Applause*)

Victory to the Third International! (*Loud applause. The "Internationale."*)

CHAIRMAN: Comrade Kasumov will give the Turkic translation.

(*Kasumov translates into Turkic. The "Internationale."*)

CHAIRMAN: The next speaker will be the chairman of the Executive Committee of the Communist International, Comrade Zinoviev. (*Loud applause, growing into an ovation. The "Internationale."*)

ZINOVIEV: Comrades! It is not without emotion that I address this gathering of ours today.

Comrades, we who are no newcomers to the revolutionary movement naturally recall the first years of the struggle, which united the workers of all the peoples of Russia in close, unbreakable fraternity with the sections of the working people who live and fight in Baku. I greet you in the name not only of the Executive Committee of the Communist International, not only of the Central Executive Committee of our Soviet republic, but also of the workers of a city of the Soviet republic who cherish an especially warm feeling of fraternal friendship for you—the workers of the city of Petrograd. (*Loud applause. The "Internationale."*)

Comrades, in those dark years, now so far off and yet at the same time so near to us, we were all held in the iron grip of tsarism, and all the peoples of Russia lived in our country as though in one great prison. In those years, among the first proletarian centers to come out against tsarism, the city of Baku was far from the least outstanding.

Every old revolutionary knows that next to Petrograd and Moscow we usually named Baku, Warsaw, and Riga as leading cities in our strikes, demonstrations, and risings in the revolutionary struggle. Everyone remembers how, on the eve of 1905, during the bourgeois revolution of 1917, and at the beginning of the October events,[2] the detachment of our workers living and fighting in the smoke-blackened city of Baku faithfully carried out its proletarian duty to the revolution, to the working class of Russia, and to the working class of the entire world.

Today we remember tens and hundreds of our best friends who came from the ranks of the workers of Baku, worked in a number of other cities, took on responsible posts in the revolution, and sometimes—when the heavy paw of the tsarist gendarmes lay too weightily upon us—brought back life to our all-Russia organizations.

We remember our best friends and brothers: Shaumyan and Dzhaparidze, with whom many of us were connected by years of common revolutionary work, common fraternal friendship. As you all know, they were torn from our ranks by the violent hands of hangmen and traitors to the working class.[3] The names of such fighters of yours as Shaumyan and Dzhaparidze are on the lips of all the workers of Petrograd, Moscow, and Russia as a whole. The children in Soviet schools are taught to hold in respect those who, standing at a post of glory at a hard moment of betrayal and perfidy, bravely defended the red flag.

Those were the months, comrades, difficult both for you and for us, when you were cut off from your fraternal family of the working peoples inhabiting Russia. At that time the workers of Petrograd, the workers of Moscow, and the workers of all Russia received no news from you. The British press lied about you; you were slandered by the traitor press of the Mensheviks, the Socialist Revolutionaries, and all the other Judases who have betrayed the workers' cause. But we knew very well that these slanders were not true. We knew very well that here the workers of Baku were not surrendering; they were awaiting the moment when they could get back what was theirs and stretch out once more a fraternal hand to the workers of all Russia and the world as a whole.

And, comrades, we were not deceived. We know that in the few short months and weeks that have passed since you were liberated, you have again taken your place in the ranks, again assumed your rightful place, one of the most honorable, among the world's proletarians, among the peoples of Russia. (*Applause*)

I mentioned Warsaw. Comrades, at the present time the White Guard flag still flies over Warsaw. Many of us, along with the workers of other peoples, were worried at the setbacks our Red Army suffered before the walls of Warsaw. You know that our army swept forward almost to those very walls. But Polish capitalism, helped by the British, whom you know well, helped by French officers, whom you also know, helped by the bourgeoisie of the entire world, whom we all hate, dealt a blow to our Red Army and forced it briefly to retreat. But, comrades, our forces have again gathered strength.[4] Unless all the signs are deceptive, and if it is possible to speak on the basis of previous experience, we can say that not months but only weeks will be needed before our Red Army stretches out its red hand once more toward Warsaw.[5] (*Loud applause. The "Internationale."*)

Formally speaking, comrades, the war against White Poland is being waged by the Russian Soviet Federated Republic. In reality, however, it is not merely a war between the Russian socialist republic and the White Polish republic, but a war of labor against capital.

The Second World Congress of the Communist International, at which thirty-seven countries were represented, recently ended its sessions in Moscow. It declared to the whole world that the war of the Russian Soviet Republic against White Poland is our war, the war of the Communist International against the bourgeoisie, against the imperialists around the world.[6]

And I am profoundly convinced, comrades, that our congress of the working masses of the Eastern peoples will support this call and say: Yes, the war of the Russian Soviet Republic against White Poland is the war not only of the proletarians of the West but also of the working masses of the peoples of the East against our common oppressors. (*Loud applause. The "Internationale."*)

Comrades, the Communist International was founded only a year and a half ago. At the First Congress we were still a propaganda society, we were only a group of people who were beginning to make propaganda for our ideas. There were already Communist currents in a variety of countries, but as yet there were no strong Communist parties.

After a mere year and a half, at the Second Congress of the Communist International in Moscow—as I have already told you—we had representatives of organized Communist parties and groups from thirty-seven countries in Europe and America.[7] With us we have all those who are honest and steeled in battle, all who are strong and ready to come to grips with the bourgeoisie throughout Europe and America.

And now, here in Baku, we are taking a second step forward. We do not want to become like the heroes of the Second International—traitors who sold the flag to the enemy. We are mindful that in this world live not only people with white skin; not only the Europeans, whom the Second International was particularly concerned with. In addition, there are also in the world hundreds of millions of people who live in Asia and Africa. We want to put an end to the rule of capital everywhere in the world. And this will become possible only when we have lit the fire of revolution not merely in Europe and America but throughout the world, and when all the working people of Asia and Africa march with us.

The Communist International wants to unite under its banners speakers of all the languages of the world. The Communist International is sure that under its flag will rally not only the proletarians of Europe but also the mighty mass of our reserves, our infantry—the hundreds of millions of peasants who live in Asia, our Near and Far East.

To your city has fallen the great honor of serving as the gate through which the Western proletariat is passing in order to extend its hand to the peasantry of the East. Your city is now the scene of new events, previously unknown in the history of mankind. Representatives have assembled here from the hundreds of millions of peasants of the East who have learned the lessons of the war and have understood that it is necessary to seize capital by the throat—with our knee on its chest! We must put an end, once and for all, to the infamy of capitalism.

Many peasants today, who are still illiterate and do not yet know our program, know very well that they have been slaughtered for hundreds of years for the greater glory of capital. We are sure that those tens and hundreds of millions of peasants of Asia will now take up the call that has reached them from the organized vanguard of the Western European and American proletariat. The peoples of the East will come together in fraternal unity and forget everything that formerly divided them. They will forget the hatred artificially fostered among them by the capitalists. They will remember that we need a single union of the working people not only of Asia and Europe but of the entire world, so as to put an end to capitalism and begin a new and better life.

At the present time the Communist International could not choose a more appropriate place than Baku for the embattled peoples of the West to meet the awakening peoples of the East.

The Baku soviet is certainly well aware of the historic importance of this moment and is doing everything in its power to create the atmosphere of unanimity and brotherhood in which a fraternal union of the proletarians of Europe with the peoples of the East will come into being.

I am sure that the workers of Baku, who have made so many sacrifices, will be glad that the Congress of the Peoples of the East is being held in their city, in Baku. They are thereby rewarded for the many trials they have suffered, over and above those that have been the lot of the workers of other cities.

And the Second Congress of the Communist International made no mistake when it fixed this congress to be held in Baku. Its voice will be heard in London, in Paris, in Constantinople, and in New York. At first, perhaps, the imperialist gentlemen, who habitually stop up their ears, will try to hush it up. But the East will know how to speak out so loudly that all the wadding will fall out of the diplomatic ears of the British and French imperialists. They will have to learn that the East wants to serve no longer as a field for exploitation by the world's beasts of prey, and that historically decisive days have arrived.

Comrades, you are honored to be living through a moment when millions of workers and peasants from all the Western countries are uniting with the hundreds of millions who make up the peoples of the East. Upon this moment depends the destiny of the world in the years that lie ahead. Let us give all that we can for the success of this alliance!

Let us get down to the work of organizing this congress. May the Eastern peoples realize that a new era has dawned, that a new page has been turned in the history of mankind, that the sun of communism shines not only for the proletarians of the West but also for the working peasants of the whole world.

Long live the fraternal union of the peoples of the East!

Long live the unity of the hundreds of millions of peasants of the East with the millions of proletarians of the West!

May this alliance prove unbreakable. May the rule of capital perish forever. And may the order soon prevail, the bearer of which is the Communist International, created by the working people of the whole world! (*Loud applause*)

CHAIRMAN: Comrade Radek will deliver a speech of welcome.

RADEK: The Congress of the Peoples of the East has been convened at a historical moment of exceptional gravity. The duel between the workers and peasants of Russia and the capitalist world—first and foremost British capital—has passed through many stages, corresponding to the strength of Soviet Russia.

British capitalism thought to crush us either by armed force or through diplomatic negotiations. During the past year we experienced a massive wave of intervention by the Entente. Paid by the British capitalists, the armies of Denikin, Yudenich, and Kolchak tried to crush Soviet Russia. But just as capital, lord of the world, thought this victory was within its grasp, it was wrested away by the consciousness of Soviet Russia's working-class masses and advanced peasants, acting through the Red Army.

Then they began to talk with us, to conduct peaceful negotiations, while at the same time unleashing against Soviet Russia a new bloodhound—White Poland. When the Red Army began to drive back White Poland, peace for Soviet Russia seemed to draw near once more, but since our first setbacks we have seen that British imperialism is again trying to terrorize us.

Warsaw seemed to be the nodal point of the struggle between Moscow and London. The Red Army is preparing for a fresh offensive, which will show British imperialism that it still exists, that Soviet Russia is still strong, and stronger than ever. But at that very moment we are showing here, at the Congress of the Peoples of the East here in Baku, that Soviet Russia—that is, the world proletariat represented by Soviet Russia—possesses a second sword as well. That sword is the revolt of the peoples who have lived under the tyranny of world capitalism—British capitalism first and foremost. Soviet Russia approaches these peoples with fraternal words, it approaches them as brothers, as comrades in struggle.[8] The voice of the representatives assembled here—of the Red working masses of the entire East—will tell British capitalism, will tell world capital, that the proletariat in revolt will strike at it not only in the streets of Europe's metropolitan cities but also in the villages and towns of Asia.

These millions in chains, who were looked on as slaves to be denied human rights, see that we, comrades, approach them differently from the way the bourgeoisie once approached them. As you know, after the Great French Revolution, when the France of Napoleon went to war against Britain, young French imperialism approached the peoples of the East and turned to Persia and India. But it addressed only the governments of those countries, which exploited the masses of the people. Later on in the nineteenth century, the governments of Britain and Germany turned their eyes toward the East in the course of the struggle between themselves; however, they did so with one guiding idea: to strengthen their forces for this struggle. And the peoples of the East shed their blood, but they shed it not for themselves but so that one of the imperialist scoundrels might be victorious over the other.

We do not approach these peoples in order to use their strength for our struggle against capitalism. We do so in order to help them escape from the yoke not only of capital but also of medieval relations, from the yoke of feudalism and ignorance, and to give them the opportunity to begin living as human beings. We approach them knowing that the young communist world being born amid unheard-of suffering cannot yet bring them the wealth of the West—that has still to be created. But we approach them so as to free them from the yoke of capital, to help them build a new, free life in whatever way they consider corresponds to the interests of their working masses.

It was not by accident that in planning the Congress of the Peoples of the East we chose the city of Baku. Here in Baku, where Persians, Turks, and Tatars have worked for many years, here in Baku where capitalism bullied and exploited these workers, socialist ideas came to them at the same time and found a common response in their hearts.

We know how the socialist revolution was born here in Baku. The idea of struggle against Russian tsarism spread outward from here. Workers returning to Persia took with them this idea of struggle not only against tsarism but against capitalism too, for the emancipation of all peoples from every kind of yoke. This workers' city saw both unprecedented luxury on the part of the bourgeoisie and the most miserable conditions of existence for the workers and the people as a whole. We are certain that this city will be an arena of international revolution. From here will flow an electric current of political awareness. Here will be planted the banner of struggle for the liberation of the East that the Communist International has entrusted to the Baku proletariat, an experienced fighter for the liberation of the working people.

Long live the Baku proletariat! Long live these front-rank fighters for the liberation of the peoples of the East! (*Applause*)

CHAIRMAN: Comrade Karayev will give the Turkic translation. (*Karayev translates into Turkic. Applause.*)

CHAIRMAN: I call upon the leader of Soviet Hungary, which was born amid the fires of the terrible World War, Comrade Béla Kun. (*Applause. The orchestra plays the "Internationale." Shouts of: "Long live Soviet Hungary! Hurrah!" The orchestra plays the "Internationale." Shouts of "Vivat [may it live]! Hurrah!" Applause.*)

BÉLA KUN: Comrades, though I speak Russian very badly, please allow me to greet you in the language of the international revolution—in the Russian language. (*Applause*)

Comrades, I greet you in the name of the most oppressed of proletarians, those of White Hungary. When Soviet power arose in Hungary, you very probably knew little about us. Few people in the East knew about those who stood in the advanced positions of the international revolution. For during the period of Soviet power in Hungary you were being oppressed by Denikin, by the British and French imperialists and their hirelings—our enemies, your oppressors. You did not know all that was happening. Recall, comrades, what was done in Baku by Denikin's men and by the British generals and officers who ruled in this place at that time and are now in prison here. Then you will know what our Denikinites did, under the leadership of Horthy, the straw man of American businessmen,[9] and of British and French generals and officers.

Just as happened here, comrades, so too in Hungary thousands and thousands of workers were slaughtered. Just as here, our proletarians and peasants too were crushed. And just as you, during the White Terror in Azerbaijan, looked forward to receiving help, so too our workers and peasants looked forward to receiving help from the international proletariat, to being liberated by them.

Comrades, in White Hungary the revolution will rise again, the proletarian revolution will live again. We, the Hungarian proletarians, hope that this congress in Baku will secure the rear of the international revolution in the West. May the fraternal alliance of the proletarians and peasants of East and West—may this Red Army of the East also go forward along with us against all the imperialists and capitalists, against the hirelings of imperialism and capitalism.

Long live this fraternal alliance of the peoples of East and West! Long live the Communist International! Long live Red Azerbaijan! (*Ovation. Applause. The orchestra plays the "Internationale."*)

CHAIRMAN: Comrade Sultanov will translate. (*Sultanov translates into Turkic.*)

CHAIRMAN: I call upon the representative of the Communist Party of Great Britain, Comrade Quelch. (*Applause. The orchestra plays the "Internationale."*)

QUELCH: (*Speaks in English. Loud applause. The "Internationale."*)

CHAIRMAN: Comrade Petrov will translate into Russian.

PETROV: Comrade Quelch expresses his gratitude for the reception you have given him as the representative of the British Communist Party. For his part, he greets you on behalf of the British Communists and the British working class. (*Loud applause*)

The British working class, says Comrade Quelch, is very slow to get going, but once it starts to move there is no force on earth capable of stopping it. (*Loud applause*)

At a certain moment, says Comrade Quelch, the British capitalists, the British government, threatened Soviet Russia with war. And what happened? The British working class formed a Council of Action, and we have heard no more of that threat from the British government.[10] The British working class is against war, the British working class is on the side of Soviet Russia. It knows very well that the British capitalists, the British imperialists, have oppressed Ireland, Egypt, and a number of other countries, and do so still. But the British working class is advancing hand in hand with the working class of Russia and other countries, and its struggle portends the downfall of British imperialism in the near future. (*Loud applause*)

The social revolution in Britain is near at hand. The congress of representatives of the Eastern peoples in Baku gives it a fresh spur. The movement of the Eastern peoples will also contribute to sweeping away the British imperialists. (*Loud applause*)

Long live Soviet Russia! Long live the world revolution! (*Loud applause. The "Internationale."*)

CHAIRMAN: Comrade Karayev will translate into Turkic. (*Karavev gives the Turkic translation.*)

CHAIRMAN: I call upon the representative of the Balkan Communist Federation, Comrade Shablin. (*Loud applause. The "Internationale."*)

SHABLIN: (*Speaks in Bulgarian. Loud applause. The "Internationale."*)

CHAIRMAN: I think everyone understood, and so no translation [into Russian] is required. Comrade Karayev will translate into Turkic.

(*Karayev gives the Turkic translation.*)

CHAIRMAN: I call upon the representative of the French Communist Party, Comrade Rosmer. (*Loud applause. The "Internationale."*)

ROSMER: (*Speaks in French.*)

PAVLOVICH: Comrade Rosmer says: The cordial greeting you have given me will touch the hearts of the proletarians of France.

Until now you have known and felt the consequences of only one alliance, that between the French bourgeoisie and the Russian counterrevolution. But now the French proletariat has begun to rouse itself. It is groaning beneath the oppression of the bourgeoisie, which strives to prevent it from allying with the Russian proletariat.

Comrade Rosmer refers to the example of the French sailors who were sent to bombard the maritime cities of Soviet Russia. They refused to carry out this order, and for that 46 of them were shot, while 340 are still languishing in the dungeons of France's convict prisons.[11]

The news of the heroic exploit of these sailors rang like a tocsin all through France, arousing vigor and revolutionary initiative in tens of thousands of workers and finding a passionate response in the towns and in the villages.

The workers of France know and feel that Soviet Russia is the friend and ally of the world proletariat. And today Soviet Russia is the country the French proletariat love best.

When the French railwaymen went on strike recently,[12] they said: We want to leave capitalist France; we ask to be sent to Soviet Russia; we will starve, ache, and suffer there along with the Russian proletarians, but at least we will know that we are suffering so that Soviet Russia may flourish.

Ruined by the war and on the brink of economic bankruptcy, capitalist France nevertheless dreams of strengthening its position by an alliance with the counterrevolutionary clique of agents of the Entente—Wrangel and others. But this alliance has been smashed, the link has been broken, and in place of this alliance a new one is developing—between the proletariat of Russia and that of France and all countries.

Long live the international proletariat! Long live the Communist International!

(*Loud shouts of "Hurrah!" and applause.*)

CHAIRMAN: I call upon the representative of America, John Reed. (*Applause*)

REED: (*Speaks in English but ends in Russian.*) Long live the international Red Army! (*Applause*)

CHAIRMAN: Comrade Petrov will translate.

PETROV: Comrade Reed began his speech with the words: Do you know how "Baku" is pronounced in American? It is pronounced "*oil*"![13] And American capitalism is striving to establish a world monopoly of oil. On account of oil, blood is being shed. On account of oil, a struggle is being waged, in which the American bankers and the American capitalists attempt everywhere to conquer the places and enslave the peoples where oil is found.

Comrade Reed says that he would have liked to see Mexico too represented at this congress in Baku.[14] For Mexico is now almost entirely in the grip of American capitalism, which has seized Mexico's oil. But Comrade Reed says that in Baku there are no more capitalists, and this oil no longer belongs to the capitalists. If this can be done in Baku, in Russia, why cannot such a social order be achieved in America and around the world? (*Applause*) The East will help us overthrow capitalism in Western Europe and America, whose foundations lie in the exploitation of the East. As soon as the Eastern peoples rise in revolt, the last foundations of capitalism will collapse, and then the peoples will endeavor to create a social order in which not only oil but everything produced by human hands will belong to the toilers. (*Applause*)

CHAIRMAN: The translation into Turkic will be given by Comrade Sultanzadeh.

(*Sultanzadeh translates into Turkic. Applause.*)

CHAIRMAN: I call upon the representative of the Communist Party of Austria, Comrade Steinhardt.

STEINHARDT: (*Speaks in German.*)

CHAIRMAN: Comrade Steinhardt greets you in the name of the Austrian workers. He says that the working class in Austria, as also in Germany, has had great opportunities for using cultural knowledge for the benefit of the working class. It has been in a much better position there. But neither in Germany nor in Austria have they yet achieved what has been done by the Russian workers in the Soviet republic. The bourgeoisie in Germany and also in Austria is better organized, it is stronger, and so the struggle of the working class is much more difficult there. The working class of Austria has fought resolutely and is still fighting. It has shed a great amount of blood—but it has not yet won victory over the bourgeoisie.

Just recently, in Moscow, from where Comrade Steinhardt came to Baku, world events of the greatest importance took place. The Second Congress of the Communist International was held there. At that congress the basis was laid for an international army of the proletarian revolution.

The world revolution and the working class march under the banner of the teaching of Karl Marx. Leading a detachment of the armed forces of this army is Comrade Trotsky. Incidentally, I forgot to say that Comrade Steinhardt spoke of the general staff of this world proletarian army, whose chairman you comrades in Baku have the pleasure of seeing in the person of Comrade Zinoviev.

Today, says Comrade Steinhardt, the Congress of the Peoples of the East in Baku is a new form of this world struggle of the oppressed against capitalism. It is a blow struck directly at the British and French imperialists, who oppress the Eastern peoples in particular. The sun of freedom has risen in the East and is casting its beams westward. In the East, decisions of the general international congress of the Communist International will be realized. Comrade Steinhardt concludes his speech with: Long live the world Soviet republic! Long live Red Azerbaijan!

CHAIRMAN: Comrades, the list of the speakers is concluded. We are rather tired. Our esteemed guests are also weary from their journey. I think we can close the meeting.

Comrades, allow me on your behalf to thank our comrades who have arrived among us here after a long and hard trip, in order to pour new strength into our veins and help us, when we have absorbed this new strength, to carry on still further with our gigantic, stubborn, and difficult struggle.

Here in Red, revolutionary Baku, which is now lighting up the paths of revolution for the entire East, I greet you, comrades: you, the inciters of Communist revolution—and its leaders, our comrades Zinoviev, Radek, Béla Kun, and the rest who are present here. (*Applause. The orchestra plays the "Internationale."*)

Comrades, let us disperse to the sound of our anthem, the "Internationale"! (*They sing the "Internationale."*)

(*The meeting ends at 3:30 a.m.*)

SESSION 1
SEPTEMBER 1, 1920

Tasks of the Congress of the Peoples of the East

(*The meeting opened at 9:40 p.m.*)

NARIMANOV: In the name of the Central Committee of the Communist International, I declare that the First Congress of the Peoples of the East is in session. (*Loud applause. The "Internationale."*)

Comrades, it is today my happy lot to open a congress that is the first of its kind, something unprecedented and unheard-of in the world—the Congress of the Peoples of the East.

The gray-haired East, which gave us our first notion of morality and culture, will today shed tears, telling of her sorrow, of the grievous wounds inflicted upon her by capital of the bourgeois countries.

These peoples of the East, each living its own distinct life, could not be unaware of the terrible, oppressive effects produced here by capital.

But today, as we learn here about each other's situations, the whole picture will unfold before us. Only then will these peoples of the East realize all the terrible, oppressive effects produced by capital. And this knowledge will impel all these peoples to unite. They will come to one conclusion: to use their united strength to throw off and smash the chains of capital.

The speeches we heard yesterday, however, enable me to stress another significant aspect of this first congress. It seems to me that two worlds are meeting here today: the world of the oppressed and the world of the oppressors. We can be sure that if the representatives of the world of the oppressors were delegates of the bourgeois class, the tears of the gray-haired East would have perhaps no influence at all. But it is our good fortune that the delegates who are here represent the working class of the bourgeois countries. Their hearts are keen and noble, and they will understand what these tears mean. They will hasten the course of events, making it possible for us to announce triumphantly, in the near future, the reign of the Third International. (*Loud applause. Translation into Turkic.*)

NARIMANOV: The Communist fraction at the congress and the fraction of nonparty delegates are represented on the Presiding Committee of the Congress of the Peoples of the East by the following persons:

From the Communist fraction:
   Ryskulov, Abdur Rashidov, and Kariyev, from
      Turkestan
   Mustafa Subhi, from Turkey
   Wang, from China
   Acharya, from India
   Mullah Bekkhan Rakhmanov, from Khiva
   Muhamedov, from Bukhara
   Korkmasov, from Dagestan
   Digurov, from the Terek region

Aliyev, from Northern Caucasia
Kastonyan, from Armenia
Narimanov, from Azerbaijan
Yenikeyev, from the Tatar republic
Amur Sanan, from the Kalmyk republic
Filipe Makharadze, from Georgia
Haydar Khan, from Persia
Agazadeh, from Afghanistan

From the nonparty fraction:
Narbutabekov, from Tashkent
Mahmudov, from Fergana
Takhsim Baari, from Anatolia
Haavis Mahomed, from Anatolia
Wang, from Chinese Turkestan
Kubeyev, from Mangyshlak district
Niyas Kuli, from Turkmenia
Kari Tajiyev, from Samarkand
Nazir Sidiq, from India
Sidajedin Kardash Ogly, from Dagestan
Yelchiyev, from Azerbaijan
Musayev, from Azerbaijan
Azim, from Afghanistan
Abdulayev, from Khiva

Secretaries:
From the Communist fraction: Ostrovsky (in Russian)
From the nonparty fraction: Abdul Hamid Yumusov (for the Muslims); Melikov (in Russian); Mahmud Khan and Ahmed Khan (for the Muslims).

All fractions at the congress have proposed Comrade Zinoviev as chairman of the Congress of the Peoples of the East. (*Prolonged applause and shouts of "Hurrah!"*) The

Communist and nonparty fractions have proposed that the following comrades be elected as honorary chairmen of the congress: Lenin (*Applause. The orchestra plays the "Internationale."*), Zinoviev (*Applause. The "Internationale."*), and Trotsky. (*Applause. The "Internationale."*)

As honorary members of the Presiding Committee, the following esteemed guests have been nominated: Comrades Quelch (Britain), Rosmer (France), Shablin (Bulgaria), Jansen (Holland), Reed (USA), Béla Kun (Hungary), (*Applause. The orchestra plays the "Internationale."*) Radek, (*Applause*) Hodo-Yoshiharo [Yoshiwara Gentaro] (Japan), Steinhardt (Austria), and also our esteemed Comrade Stalin, whom we all know.

Let us now take the vote. (*A voice: "Translation."*)

Do you think it necessary to translate the list of comrades who have been nominated? (*A voice: "Only into Turkic."*)

(*An interpreter translates into Turkic.*)

CHAIRMAN: Those in favor of the proposed list, please raise your hands. Anyone against? Almost unanimously in favor.

I call on Comrade Zinoviev. (*Loud applause. All rise and greet Zinoviev.*) Please resume your seats.

ZINOVIEV: Comrades, my task is to explain to you how the Communist International sees the aims and tasks of this Congress of the Peoples of the East.

The idea of holding this congress was conceived during the preparation of the Second World Congress of the Communist International, when some of the delegates here at this congress came to Moscow. Together with the Executive Committee of the Communist International and in the name of a number of countries, they issued an appeal to you, to the peoples of the East, proposing to organize at Baku the congress at which, today, we have the pleasure of being present.

The Second World Congress of the Communist International was attended by representatives of the Communist workers and peasants of thirty-seven countries in Europe and America. A few representatives of the East were also present at the congress in Moscow. Today, however, we have succeeded in assembling a fuller, mass representation of the working people of the entire East. We consider that the Baku congress will go down in the history of the struggle for freedom as the complement, the second part, the second half of the congress that recently finished its work in Moscow.

We take very great pride in the fact that the Communist International has succeeded, for the first time in the history of mankind, in bringing together today under one roof representatives of more than one-fifth of the peoples of the East. Some of these peoples have lived until now in mutual enmity; some have known little about each other and, in any case, have never had the chance to sit down together and discuss all the burning questions that confront us.

We regard this congress as a major historical event because it shows that now it is not merely the advanced workers and working peasants of Europe and America who are awakening. Rather we have all lived to see the day at last of the awakening not just of individuals but of tens and hundreds of thousands, millions of toilers of the peoples of the East. These peoples make up the majority of the population of the entire globe; by themselves, therefore, they are in a position to settle the dispute between labor and capital once and for all.

Comrades, today's congress was convened, as you know, by the Communist International, a party organization. We have here with us today, however, not only Communists but also hundreds of delegates who do not yet belong to the Communist Party, who regard themselves as nonparty people, and also groups that may well belong to other parties.

At first sight this may seem contradictory. How, indeed, can the party organization have convened a congress not made up strictly of party members but containing, perhaps, a majority of nonparty people?

But this contradiction is merely formal in character. Actually, it is in complete conformity with the policy, aspirations, ideals, and strivings of the Communist International. It has convened the peoples of the East without asking each of the representatives, "Do you, at this moment, belong to the Communist International, to a Communist Party, or do you not?" We did not ask you, "What party do you belong to?" We asked each one, "Do you live by your labor? Do you belong to the working masses? Do you want to put a stop to strife between the peoples? Do you want to organize a struggle against the oppressors? That is enough. Nothing more is required; you will not be asked for any party card. Let us gather together in order to discuss the questions that confront the entire world today."

Comrades, the dispute between the Second International, which has died, and the Third International, which is now growing stronger with each day, is not a narrow dispute internal to the party. It is not a question of interest only to those who already belong to a particular party. No, it is a dispute between labor and capital, a dispute that concerns everyone who lives by his labor.

In Russia as well there are very many illiterate, ignorant, half-crushed peasants who are only now awakening to political life. Today there is already not a single village there, certainly not a single rural district, where the peasants have not heard that the Third International exists and is working to free the toilers from the yoke of the rich. And we are sure that in the East, too, the time will soon come when it will be impossible to find a single district, or a single large capital city, or a single large settlement where the best and most conscious peasants will not know that the Third International exists and that it is working to free the peoples of the East. For life, comrades, has now raised sharply the question of the emancipation of labor, and life is compelling every peasant to take stock of this question.

I can give you a graphic example. If you want to know what the Second International is, look at Georgia, which you all know well enough. There you have the embodiment of the Second International! In Georgia, power is held by a government of Mensheviks, who belong to the Second International. The leaders of present-day Georgia are important representatives of this Second International. And every peasant in Georgia now knows from his own hard experience what it means when a party belonging to the Second International is in power.

It means that the peasants do not get the land. It means there is freedom of the press only for the bourgeoisie, that this freedom does not exist for the workers and peasants. It means that the best leaders of the working-class masses are under arrest. It means that power belongs to a gang who defend, like house dogs, the rule of the rich. It means that Georgia is governed by men who are ready at any moment to offer the sweat and blood of the proletariat on a plate to British capitalism. (*Applause*)

It means that Georgia is governed by men who are ready at any moment to crawl on their bellies before any British, French, or Italian general who seems to them to be powerful. It means that power is in the hands of men who are always ready to wink, if only with one eye, at the tsarist General Denikin when he seems to be the stronger and when it seems to them that Soviet power in Russia is going to perish. In Germany the most prominent representative of the Second International is Noske, the executioner who has shot down thousands of German workers. In Georgia the most prominent representatives of the Second International are Mr. Noe Zhordania and his associates, who are also executioners of the people, ready to cut thongs from the peasants' skins. (*Loud applause*)

Naturally, Zhordania's policy is always presented to the Georgian peasants in the name of the "independence of Georgia" and the defense of that country's "national interests." But comrades, what sense does it make to a Georgian peasant if Mr. Gegechkori and other such gentlemen sing like nightingales about the "independence of Georgia," when the same old landowners still own the land, when the same old oppression continues, and when at any moment some jackbooted British general can trample on the throat and on the chest of the Georgian peasant and worker?

That, comrades, is what is meant by the dispute between the Second and Third Internationals. It is no dispute of bookmen or scholars; it is a question of life and death for the workers and peasants.

Even in its best days the Second International took the view that "civilized" Europe can and must act as tutor to "barbarous" Asia.

Already in 1907, at the international congress held in Stuttgart, the majority of the official Social Democrats (Mensheviks) expressed themselves in favor of the need for a so-called "progressive" colonial policy.[1] In words, the Social Democrats declared that this would be a humane colonial policy—human, mild, and civilized. In fact, however, what they had in mind was support for the capitalists in their robber colonial policy, the policy that endowed the colonies with syphilis, opium, and a debauched caste of officers; the policy that turned these countries into the bourgeoisie's rubbish dump and that plundered them relentlessly, right and left.

And when the war of 1914 came, this Second International, rotten through and through—already in 1907 it had declared for helping the bourgeoisie with white skin to oppress the peoples with black and yellow skin—this Second International naturally sold itself to the bourgeoisie. But then it collapsed at once like a house of cards.

From the first day of its existence, the Communist International said: In Asia live four times as many people as in Europe; there are 800 million people in Asia. And we want to free all the peoples, all the toilers, regardless of the color of their skin, regardless of whether they are white, black, or yellow.

We want to do away with every kind of exploitation of man by man. In our view, anyone who does not understand this stands outside the ranks of socialism. We fight against those who help the bourgeoisie or stand aside when the task is to help the oppressed peoples. We are for organizing the blacks and all others who live by their labor, for organizing all the working people and all suffering and weary humanity, for struggle against the capitalists, the world's oppressors.

This was why, when we concluded our work at the Second Congress of the Communist International, we swore an oath and issued a manifesto in the name of the Communists of thirty-seven countries.

In this manifesto, addressed to the workers and peasants of the entire world, we wrote these words: "The Socialist who directly or indirectly supports the privileged position of one nation at the cost of others, who has made his peace with colonial slavery, who makes a distinction between peoples of different races and skin colors, who helps the bourgeoisie of the metropolis to preserve its domination over the colonies instead of helping the cause of the armed rebellion of the colonies, the British Socialist who fails to support by all possible means the rebellion in Ireland, Egypt, and India against the London plutocracy—such a Socialist deserves, if not the bullet, then certainly the mark of infamy, and no mandate or confidence from the proletariat."[2]

This was our declaration, this was the solemn oath that we took before the workers of Europe and America, and that we solemnly repeat in Baku before the representatives of the laboring masses of the entire East assembled here.

We shall fight to the death against those who forget, even for one moment, their duty to the oppressed nations, to the laboring masses of countries that are being plundered and exploited by capital.

Comrades, I told you that the Communist International wants a bond of brotherhood with all the peoples of the East, with all the oppressed masses. I think that you, comrades, want this alliance too, and cannot but want it. The European proletariat sees now, at every step, that the course of history has united the working people of the East with the workers of the West. Together they can conquer, or together perish. At every step the workers of Germany and other countries see how the bourgeoisie, when it finds itself in special difficulties, brings in colored troops for use against the European workers. The bourgeoisie has brought black troops into Germany and into other countries as well.[3] The Italian bourgeoisie is now threatening its workers that, if they should revolt, Italian capital will move colored troops against them.

The workers of Europe are today learning by harsh experience what they did not understand in the days when they trusted the Second International. The workers are learning that they must, at any cost, form a close alliance with the working masses of the entire East, of the entire world. But it is now necessary that this be understood also by the many-millioned masses of the East as a whole. Your first task when you return home must be to explain to every peasant, man and woman, to every shepherd, to everyone who lives by his labor, to explain to everyone who will listen to you that today we cannot take a single step without each other. The proletarian forces of the West must now be united with the working masses of the entire East, of the entire world, so as, together, to defeat and finally smash our terrible foe, who is still quite powerful even today.

The first task of our congress is to rouse the millions of peasants, to explain to them that it is necessary to plough the land more deeply, to raise up fresh layers of peasants and tell them that unless an alliance of brotherhood and friendship is forged with the whole organized working class of the world, there is no way out. If this is not done they face only ruin. But given such an alliance, the complete victory of labor, its complete victory over the plunderers and oppressors of the world—over the British and French who have oppressed you for decades—this complete victory will be assured.

Comrades, in its very first statements the Third International pointed out that today the world is divided into nations with power and nations without power, into oppressed and oppressor nations.

The Second International avoided saying this. It spoke about equality, in a general way, without explaining precisely the actual situation. At the Second Congress of the

Communist International in Moscow we pointed out once again that the world is divided into powerful nations and oppressed nations.

Comrades, we had occasion to point this out even before the war began and then again during its course. In one of our writings (those interested can read it in my book *The War and the Crisis of Socialism*)[4] we showed, statistics in hand, that before the war the world was divided up like this: six so-called great powers, with a population of 437 million, oppressed all the other countries and states, whose population amounted to 1.22 billion. That was the situation down to the end of the war.

Now, the situation is changed for the worse. As you know, some of the so-called great powers did not make the grade. The number of great powers, the number of plunderers, is now smaller. According to the calculation made by Comrade Lenin at our congress, America, Britain, France, and Japan, these four great robbers, with a total population of barely a quarter of a billion, oppress a billion and a quarter people in the dependent nations.[5]

In the book I mentioned, I worked out that 5 percent of the British people are large-scale property-owners in Britain. And these five men out of every hundred oppress not only the rest of the British but also 890 members of various other peoples: Indians, Persians, Chinese, and so on. Each British capitalist compels nearly a hundred British workers and several hundred working people in the colonies and oppressed countries to work for his benefit. That's how it was before the war, and that's how it is today.

The task before this congress is above all to take account of this fact and explain it to every toiler. Remember this: every large-scale British capitalist compels not only tens and hundreds of British workers to work for him but also hundreds and thousands of peasants in Persia, Turkey, India, and many other countries subject to British capital.

From this it follows that these one and a half billion oppressed people must above all unite. Then there will be no power in the world capable of compelling you to submit to these robbers, the British capitalists. And the representatives of the worker-Communists of the whole world appeal to you and stretch out to you the hand of fraternal aid in this hard but necessary struggle. We are passionately convinced that you will grasp honestly this hand extended to you by the worker of Europe and America, that you will respond with a handshake of friendship. (*Applause*)

We know that the working masses of the East are in some places, through no fault of their own, very backward. Illiterate, ignorant, they are sunk in superstition and believe in spirits. They are unable to read newspapers. They do not know what is going on in the world at large. They do not understand the most elementary principles of hygiene. Only the lackeys of imperialism can mock them for this. The unfortunate Turkish and Persian toilers are not to blame for being illiterate. That is their misfortune. The "civilized" bourgeoisie sitting in Paris and London have devised all sorts of methods for keeping the Indian peasants, the Persian and Turkish toilers, in a state of ignorance.

The task of the more civilized, more literate, more organized workers of Europe and America is to help the backward toilers of the East. Not to mock them, not to put on airs, not to swank about their superiority over the backward Eastern peasants, but to be concerned about their ignorance and backwardness, to extend the hand of aid to them, and to help them in the only way possible: by teaching them to master weapons and to direct these against the white, civilized beasts of prey who sit in the countinghouses and banks of London and Paris. This will help the peasant of the East take the land for himself. It will help him carry further the great revolution initiated by the Russian peasants, after such heavy labors.

We know that in some countries the clergy and feudal lords of the East know how to play tricks on the peasant, raising false hopes, so that he thinks he has obtained land when in fact he has not. They know how to set up legal traps to catch the backward, ignorant peasant. We must expose this deception. We must raise up the peoples of the East so that they will carry out an agrarian revolution like that effected by the peasants of Russia, the Russian peasants who only half a century ago were still serfs and who still today are largely illiterate. Why should the peasants of Turkey, Persia, India, China, Armenia, and so on not do what has been done by the Russian peasants who so recently were serfs? We are sure that the peasants of the entire East, under the wise leadership of the organized workers of the West, will now be able to rise up in their hundreds of millions in order to carry out a real, thoroughgoing agrarian revolution. They will be able to clear the soil so that no large landowners are left, no debt slavery, no taxes, dues, or any other variety of the devices used by the rich are left, and the land passes into the hands of the laboring masses. This is what the Communist International brings to you.

The proletariat wants to help you take the land and create a free union of all the peoples of the world. This is the simple, straightforward program that is written in the heart of every honest worker in Europe and must now be adopted by you, as representatives of the toilers of the East.

Comrades, our congress in Moscow discussed whether the socialist revolution could take place in the countries of the Far East before they have passed through the stage of capitalism.⁶ You know that for a long time the view existed that each country must first pass through the capitalist stage, creating big factories and large-scale property owners. It was thought indispensable for the workers to be massed together in cities, and only then could there be any question of socialism.

We now think that this is not so. From the moment that even one country has broken loose from the chain of capitalism, as Russia has done, from the moment that the workers have put the question of the proletarian revolution on the agenda, we can say that it is possible and necessary in China, India, Turkey, Persia, and Armenia to begin fighting directly for a Soviet system. The workers of Europe will take power, of course, not in order to plunder Turkey, Persia, and other countries, but to help them.

Given this fact, these countries can and must prepare now for a Soviet revolution. They can and must prepare to put an end to the division within them between rich and poor, so as to create a state of the working people and conclude a close alliance with the organized workers of the world as a whole.

In this connection we ask you a question: What will be the form of the state in the East, the form of its organization? We have come to the conclusion that it is necessary to set up soviets even where there are no urban workers. In such cases we can create a state of soviets of the working peasants. Not toy "soviets" such as they now sometimes palm off on you in Turkey, but real ones, in which every working peasant has the right to vote.

I read in the journal *Krasnyy Dagestan* [Red Dagestan] that the law governing elections to soviets is now being codified there. The right to elect members to the peasants' soviets is to be reserved to honest working peasants possessing no more than a certain number of animals. I will not undertake to decide whether or not the figures are what they should be, but the approach is right. Whoever possesses livestock, horned or otherwise, in greater numbers than are needed to work his holding and keep his family in comfort, and who profits by others' need, must be denied access to our peasant soviets. They must be truly soviets of the working people, organized by people who live by their labor and who are concerned not with profit making and speculation but with the common good. We must organize soviets that will be genuine transmitters of the will of the working masses.

We address our appeal not only to those who take the standpoint of communism but also to the nonparty people. We have two streams. One is very fast, impetuous, and strong—the stream of the workers' proletarian Communist struggle in Russia, Germany, France, and Italy, which is broadening out everywhere. But there is also another stream. As yet it is not strong enough; in some places it takes a zigzag course. This is the movement of the oppressed nationalities that have not yet chosen the road they will follow, do not yet know exactly what they want, but feel a strap chafing their backs, feel French and British capitalism sitting astride their necks.

We want these two streams to draw closer and closer together, so that the second stream may be cleansed of national prejudices, so that they may be merged into one single tumultuous, powerful stream that, like the sea, will sweep all obstacles from its path, clearing the land of all the evil from which we have suffered so long.

And so I say that we patiently support groups that are not yet with us and are even against us on some questions. For example, in Turkey, comrades, you know that the Soviet government supports Kemal. We do not forget for one moment that the movement headed by Kemal is not a Communist movement. We know this. I have before me some extracts from the stenographic report of the first meeting of the Turkish people's government in Ankara. Kemal himself says that "the person of the caliph and sultan is sacred and inviolable."[7]

The movement headed by Kemal wants to rescue the "sacred" person of the caliph from enemy hands—this is the viewpoint of that party. Is it a Communist viewpoint? No, it is not. We respect the religious feelings of the masses, and we know how to reeducate the masses. That requires many years' work. We approach the religious beliefs of the working masses of the East and of other countries with caution. However, it is our duty to tell this congress: what Kemal's government is now doing in Turkey—supporting the power of the sultans—you ought not to do, even if this line may be dictated by religious considerations.

You must go forward and not let yourselves be dragged back. We think that the day of the sultans is over, and that you should not put up with autocracy. You should dispel and destroy faith in the sultan, and establish genuine soviets. The Russian peasants also had great faith in the tsar. When a real people's revolution caught fire, however, hardly a trace was left of this faith in the tsar.

It will be the same in Turkey and in the whole East when a real peasants' revolution flares up, rooted in the soil. Then the people will very quickly cast aside their faith in the sultan and in their masters. Consequently, we repeat that the policy pursued by the present people's government in Turkey is not the policy of the Communist International; it is not our policy. And at the same time we say that we are ready to help any revolutionary struggle against the British government. Today the scales of the balance in Turkey are still tipped in favor of the wealthier, but the time will come when this will change.

In Turkey, in Persia, everywhere that peasants are to be found, they are beginning to understand what Bolshevism means.

Recently I asked a prominent Turkish public figure of liberal views what the Turkish peasant understood by the word "Bolshevik." This prominent personage answered: "In our country people usually understand by this someone who wants to fight against Britain and who wants to help us do this."

I asked a second question: "And what does the ordinary peasant in Turkey think about the fact that the Bolshevik is not only against Britain but against the rich in general, including both Russian and Turkish?" To this he did not answer, being inclined to think that the peasant in question would not understand this point.[8]

Based on what I know, however, I would say that the word "Bolshevik" does not need to be translated anywhere in the world, not into Persian [Farsi] or any other language. (*Applause*) I am convinced that the working masses will have need of this word in the struggle not only against Britain but against the rich generally. Yes, we are moving against bourgeois Britain "to take the British imperialists by the throat and set our knee on their chest." British capitalism must be dealt a most powerful blow, aimed at its very heart. That is true. But at the same time we must educate the working masses of the East to hate the rich in general—Russian, Jewish, German, French—and to desire to fight them.

The enormous significance of the revolution that is beginning in the East does not consist in requesting the British imperialist gentlemen to take their feet off the table, only to then permit the Turkish rich to stretch out their feet comfortably on the table. No—we want to ask, ever so politely, that *all* the rich take their dirty feet off the table, so that there may reign among us not luxury, not charlatanry, not mockery of the people, and not idleness, but so that the world may be ruled by the toiler with toil-hardened hands. (*Loud applause*)

Accordingly, we speak directly and definitely to the nonparty delegates here. Pan-Islamism, Musavatism, all these trends are not ours. We have a different policy. We can support a democratic policy such as has now taken shape in Turkey and will perhaps make its appearance tomorrow in other countries. It is not out of some mercenary calculation that we support national movements like those in Turkey, Persia, India, and China. Rather we support them because a conscious worker will tell himself that the Turks who today do not yet understand where all their interests lie will understand this tomorrow. We must support this Turk and help him, and wait for a real people's revolution to arise in Turkey, when veneration for sultans and other obsolete notions will vanish from his mind.

Like an elder brother, says the advanced worker, I must hasten this movement. I will support the present national-democratic movement of the Turks, says the Communist worker. At the same time I consider it my sacred duty to call upon the oppressed Turkish peasants, the Persian peasants, and the downtrodden, oppressed working peasants of the entire East, to hate all the rich, all the oppressors, and to teach these peasants the simple truth that we need real economic equality between all men and real brotherly unity between all who live by their labor.

That, comrades, is our frank statement. We think that none of us should address the Congress of the Peoples of the East in the style of a diplomat. We must put aside despicable diplomacy of every kind on this occasion, when peoples have gathered together who have been oppressed more than any others, and who number in the hundreds of millions—the peoples upon whom, in the last analysis, depends the future of all humankind.

Comrades, when the East truly begins to move, not only Russia but all of Europe will seem only a small corner of this vast scene. The real revolution will flare up only when we are joined by the 800 million people who live in Asia, when the African continent joins us, when we see hundreds of millions of people in motion.

At this historic gathering no one need hide behind diplomacy and reticence. Let all present open their hearts, so that they may hear from each other words of truth, genuine and pure; so that we may choose the real path to victory. We hide nothing from you. We tell you frankly what separates us from the representatives of the current national movement and what we have in common with them.

We say to you that the task of this movement is to help the East free itself from British imperialism. But we have a task of our own to carry out, no less great—to help the toilers of the East in their struggle against the rich, to help them build their own Communist organizations here and now, to explain to them what communism means, and to prepare them for a real revolution of the toilers, for real equality, for the emancipation of mankind from every form of oppression.

Comrades, I think that the fact that I told you frankly what we think about these difficult matters and about our differences in relation to them has brought us closer to those whose views differ from ours. For it is better to openly conclude definite agreements than to approach each other with hostility hidden in our hearts.

I say that we now face the task of kindling a real holy war against the British and French capitalists. Comrades, remember what is being done, northward from here, by these bandits even at this moment.⁹ I will not speak about the peoples who are particularly well represented here. You yourselves know the situation that British and French capital has created in Turkey, the situation British capital has created in Persia, the situation of Armenia, which yesterday all the governments of the Entente wanted to defend and which is today defended by no one.

I will say a little more only about those countries that are poorly represented here—India and China.

Comrades, you know how many hundreds of millions of people live in India, which is being so ruthlessly pillaged by British capital. Perhaps you have heard about the latest events there. Quite recently there was another case in India of Indians being fired on for only a feeble attempt at resistance—what has become known as the Dyer affair. An unarmed crowd was lured to within range of machine guns and mowed down.¹⁰

And when a parliamentary inquiry into this affair was made, newspapers published in London had to write about a scene, immortalized by photography, showing how the British enjoyed themselves when order had been restored: armed British soldiers forcing Indians to crawl on their bellies through the city streets. This is the method used by the civilized British imperialists and their sons, who have attended several universities. They send out their officers in order that by putting a rifle muzzle to the ear of an Indian and making him crawl on his belly they may gladden the heart of a British officer.

And the correspondent of an Italian newspaper has sent similar pictures from China, with the caption, "A matinee in south China."

Comrades, these little pictures, which are to be seen in considerable numbers in any issue of a foreign newspaper, depict for us the unheard-of horrors endured by the peoples of India and China.

Comrades, do not forget that the white British capitalist beasts of prey who so shamelessly oppress the Indian people have also contrived to enlist tens of thousands of Indian soldiers, whom they send to suppress the proletarian movement. Indian soldiers at the present time are fighting on no less than seven fronts under the conductor's baton of British generals. Indian soldiers are in action in the Constantinople theater of war, in Arabia, in Mesopotamia, in Egypt, in Palestine, in northeastern and northwestern Persia.

There, comrades, you see the accursed situation of our oppressed class: they seize Indians by the throat and force them to crawl on their bellies in order to amuse a British officer. And at the same time our brothers, the oppressed peasants of India, are so ignorant that the same British can enlist Indians in their army, provide a few hundred officers drawn from the landed gentry to command them, and send them off to suppress the national-revolutionary movement in Egypt or Persia. That, comrades, is what is horrible about the position we are in. We are helping our executioners with our own hands, helping the British and French capitalists. This is what we must put an end to!

We must at last slam shut this book of the accursed past, so that it may never return. We must open a new page of history, when the oppressed peoples of the East will no longer be slaves, when they will not allow British officers to shamelessly plunder the Indians and the Persians, killing, insulting, and mocking at everyone.

Comrades! Much has been said about "holy war" in recent years. The capitalists, when they were waging their accursed imperialist war, tried to present that slaughter as a holy war and made many people believe this. When they spoke in 1914–18 of a "holy war," that was a monstrous deception. But now, comrades, you, assembled here for the first time in a congress of peoples of the East, must proclaim a genuine holy war against the robbers, the Anglo-French capitalists. Now we must say that the hour has sounded when the workers of the entire world can arouse and raise up tens and hundreds of millions of peasants, can form a Red Army in the East as well, can arm and organize a revolt in the rear of the British, can hurl fire against the bandits, can poison the existence of every insolent British officer who is lording it in Turkey, Persia, India, and China.

Comrades! Brothers! The time has now come when you can set about organizing a true people's holy war against the robbers and oppressors. The Communist International turns today to the peoples of the East and says to them: "Brothers, we summon you to a holy war, above all against British imperialism!" (*Loud applause. Prolonged shouts of "Hurrah!" Members of the congress stand up, brandishing their weapons. The speaker is unable to continue for some time. All the delegates stand up and applaud. Shouts: "We swear it!"*)

May this declaration made today be heard in London, in Paris, and in all the cities where the capitalists are still in power. May they heed this solemn oath sworn by the representatives of tens of millions of toilers of the East, that the rule of the British oppressors in the East shall be no more, that the oppression of the toilers of the East by the capitalists shall cease!

Long live the fraternal alliance of the peoples of the East with the Communist International! May capital perish; long live the reign of labor! (*Burst of applause*)

VOICES: "Long live the rebirth of the East!" (*Shouts of "Hurrah!" Applause.*)

VOICES: "Long live the Third, Communist International!" (*Shouts of "Hurrah!" Applause.*)

VOICES: "Long live those who have united the East, our honored leaders, our dear Red Army!" (*Shouts of "Hurrah!" Applause.*)

CHAIRMAN: Please be quiet and resume your seats. Comrade Buniatzadeh will translate Comrade Zinoviev's speech.

(*Buniatzadeh translates into Turkic and another interpreter translates into Persian.*)

CHAIRMAN: It has been reported that the Kabardian comrades want a translation into their language. Is there an interpreter here who can do that? No.

(*An interpreter translates into Turkish. At 11:50 p.m. there is a break, and the congress reassembles at 12:15 a.m.*)

CHAIRMAN: Tomorrow at 10:00 a.m. sharp there will be a meeting of the nonparty comrades at the Workers' Club. Everyone is to attend. Some very important questions will be decided. Please pass this on to those who are not present; this request applies to both nonparty and party comrades. (*Translation*)

Tomorrow at 10:00 a.m. there will be a Communist fraction meeting at the [Red] Army Club. Everyone is to attend.

The Congress of the Peoples of the East will resume at 5:00 p.m. tomorrow. (*Translation*)

(*The session concluded at 1:10 a.m.*)

SESSION 2
SEPTEMBER 2, 1920

World political situation

(The session opened at 6:55 p.m. Comrade Zinoviev took the chair.)

CHAIRMAN: I declare the second session of the Congress of the Peoples of the East open. In agreement with the Communist and nonparty fractions, we propose to merge two agenda points and proceed immediately to hear reports on the second of these questions: the international situation and the tasks of the Eastern peoples. Then after this we propose to open the discussion on yesterday's and today's reports, taken together. Since this has been agreed by the overwhelming majority of congress delegates, I will allow myself to treat the decision as adopted without further discussion, and give the floor to the reporter. Please translate. (*Translations*)

So we will proceed to the report on the international situation and the tasks of the working masses in the East. The reporter is Comrade Radek.

RADEK: Comrades, yesterday we witnessed a scene that deserves to be called historic, in the full sense of the word. The representatives assembled here of the laboring masses of the Near East heard from the representatives of the European workers in revolt that the proletariat of Europe is ready to fight to the death against the capitalists of the entire world—who have until now oppressed not only the workers of Europe but also the masses of the people of the East. On hearing this, the representatives of those masses here present, moved by a common emotion, rose and swore an oath to wage a holy war, shoulder to shoulder with the workers of Europe, against the oppressors of the world of labor.

But, comrades, this war that now faces us requires more than enthusiasm, more than hatred of the oppressors. The popular masses of the East need to be well informed about the direction taken by world politics. They need to know with precision the enemy's strength and also his weak sides. They need to know how to utilize every fissure that appears in the enemy's ranks so as to carry the struggle against him into his own camp.

The international proletariat keeps a sharp eye on the shifts in world politics. This familiarity with the international situation renders the proletariat a tremendous service in its developing war against capital. In this regard, the working masses of the Near East must attain the same level as the masses of workers in Europe. They must watch the enemy vigilantly and be able to choose the moment for attack. And that is why, rather than resting content with your common urge to fight against world capital, we have put on the agenda a report on the international situation and the tasks facing you.

The gray-haired East, of which Comrade Narimanov spoke with sorrow, has been suffering from the oppression of the capitalists of Europe for more than a few decades. For over a hundred years the peoples of the East have been victims of exploitation, political oppression, and war by the capitalist powers, the capitalist plunderers. Until now they have been only victims; until now they have not been able with their own forces to deal a rebuff to the cravings of these world-class bandits.

The entire history of the nineteenth century is filled with the struggle between British capitalism and the landlord-capitalist tsarist government of Russia for mastery of Turkey, Persia, and Central Asia. Russian tsarism tried to seize Persia and Turkey. It wanted to capture and enslave the peasants of Turkey and find an outlet to the Mediterranean, in order to measure its strength there against British capital.

It went into Persia and enslaved the Persian peasants so as to be able through Persia to get at India, a pillar of the rule of British capital. Fabulous India, the country that nourishes the capitalists of Britain, the London Stock Exchange, with the blood of the Indian peasantry. It enables the younger sons of the British bourgeoisie to acquire millions and then, thanks to these millions, to lead the life of a parasite back in their own country.

In this struggle, "humane" British capitalism, the British lords, were fully the equals of barbarous Russian tsarism. When it suited the British capitalists, they came forward in defense of Turkey and Persia against tsarism. This they did under the banner of humaneness and a human attitude to the peoples of the East, reproaching tsarism for wanting to swallow up these peoples in order to coerce and exploit them. But no sooner had British capitalism reached an agreement with tsarism than it raised the slogan of the annihilation of Turkey, raised the old slogan of Gladstone, the British minister: "Dismember Turkey!"

Let me recall just one fact, comrades. The Anglo-Russian struggle for Persia, the struggle between tsarism and British capitalism, ended in 1907 with an amicable agreement to partition Persia. After that the British capitalists stood by while the tsarist cossack general Lyakhov destroyed the infant freedom of Persia. The cossack brigades dispersed the majlis [parliament], and the representatives of the revolutionary Persian people were hanged in the streets of Tehran and Tabriz.[1] The British capitalists washed their hands of this, saying that it all had nothing to do with them.

But despite the fact that the British capitalists held tsarism in their grip—for Russian tsarism was completely dependent financially on British capital—they did not lift a finger to defend the Persian people. Furthermore, the British foreign minister, Lord Grey, instructed Buchanan, the British ambassador in Petrograd, to inform the tsarist government that Britain would not oppose the Russian aggression provided that tsarism did not send its troops beyond the limits of northern Persia.

The rival robbers agreed to divide Persia into two parts. Northern Persia was handed over to Lyakhov's hangmen, while the south was to be held by the British, serving as a barrier against a Russian incursion into India.

The struggle between Britain and Russia over the peoples of the East was replaced in the last ten years by a different worldwide struggle, that between the Entente group—British and French capital, going arm in arm with tsarism—and a group headed by Germany. And once again we have seen, this time too, how both the British and the German capitalists said their purpose in going into the Near East was to bring civilization to that region, bring literacy to the people, and teach them to use machinery. In fact the struggle between these groups was being waged for conquest of the people's wealth in Turkey and Persia. It was a struggle between common robbers.

The British decided to strike down and partition Turkey before it could gain strength following the Young Turk revolt.[2] Seeing that the Young Turk government was trying to forge an army and introduce a progressive system of taxation and administration, the British capitalists resolved to break Turkey into pieces as soon as possible. For Turkey was enormously important to them.

The world power of Britain extends all over the globe. British capital rules in Africa, holding in its grip both the mines of South Africa and the fertile fields of Egypt. Meanwhile the second pillar of British world domination is India, where more than 300 million peasants work for the British capitalists. Between India and British capitalism's African possessions lay Turkey. Therefore Turkey had to be destroyed, so that the British capitalists, by means of a railway across Arabia and Mesopotamia, might unite their possessions in Africa with those in Egypt and in India. In this way British capital, ruling over the African and Asian nationalities in their hundreds of millions, might freely transfer its troops from one part of the world to another, ruthlessly suppressing the slightest attempt at resistance by the peoples of the East. British capital condemned Turkey to death so as to be able freely to put down the revolutionary movement that was beginning in India.

German capital, on the other hand, appeared as a liberator, a defender of the popular masses, merely because it was opposed to an open partition of Turkey—since it was hard for Germany to get at you from the North Sea. German capitalism did not want to dismember Persia, because it had no free access to that country. What it strove for was to take all of Turkey and all of Persia into its economic grasp, exploiting these peoples under cover of the Young Turk and Persian governments.

The World War of 1914, which led to the deaths of tens of millions of workers and peasants and left behind millions of cripples and tens of millions of widows and orphans, was fought to decide which group—the Anglo-French one or the German one—would rule the world, would be in a position to enslave hundreds of millions of workers and peasants of the peoples of Asia. This war was waged by both sides under the slogan of liberation for oppressed nations.

In 1908 the British capitalists had hailed the advent of the Young Turks, expecting to be able to proceed in alliance with them. Now they suddenly discovered in their hearts a tremendous hatred for the Young Turks, and declared that the Turkish government must be destroyed and the Turkish people torn in pieces, that it was necessary to liberate the cultured peoples of the East—the Arabs, Syrians, and Armenians. The war was fought in the name of smashing the absolutism of the sultan and the Young Turks and liberating the cultured peoples of the East!

How did this war end? Comrades, it ended with the rout of German capitalism, something for which no worker or peasant of the East need shed a tear. But it also ended in the victory of British imperialism. What does this victory mean? The peoples of the East have already found this out. It means that the British navy has seized Constantinople and is holding the Straits [Dardanelles and Bosporus]. It means that a British expeditionary force has occupied Arabia and Mesopotamia, French forces have occupied Syria, and Greek forces have occupied the western part of Asia Minor [Anatolia], including Smyrna [Izmir]. It means that French and Italian troops have occupied southern Anatolia—not just for the moment, not just until the sultan's absolutism has been eliminated, but in order to stay there and dismember Turkey in the guise of creating free, independent states of Syria, Mesopotamia, and Arabia.

As to what this freedom looks like, comrades, we have very good evidence in the French and British press. France promised to establish a free Syria, and found her hireling in the person of the Emir Faisal. However, as soon as he stopped dancing to the tune of the French capitalists, French troops occupied Damascus and drove Faisal away. Now they hold Syria quite openly, expelling everyone whom the French capitalists dislike and dictating their laws to the Syrian people.

The British talked about independence for Mesopotamia, and what a spectacle we behold. In order to create an independent state with a population of two and a half million, British capital has spent a quarter of a million pounds sterling in a single year. The question arose: Why this generosity on the part of the British? A quarrel between French and British capital revealed the answer. Lloyd George, the British prime minister, was asked in Parliament whether Britain was taking over the wealth of Mesopotamia and whether British capital held concessions in Mesopotamia that might have impelled the British government to spend such huge sums. Lloyd George replied that Britain had no concessions and asked for nothing from the Mesopotamians. It was keeping only the concessions that had already been granted to British capitalists by the sultan's government. But when it was explained what this means (a task undertaken by none other than the French foreign minister, Mr. Pichon), it turned out that the British capitalists control all the petroleum in Mesopotamia—the only wealth belonging to the Arabs of that country. This petroleum had been the property of German capitalists and the Turkish government. Now, the British have allowed the French 25 percent of the petroleum, keeping 75 percent for themselves.

The peoples of the East are known to be very courteous, so I will not say at this Congress of the Peoples of the East that Mr. Lloyd George is a liar and a cheat. I will say merely that he does not regard it as a statesman's duty to reestablish the truth, when that truth is that British capitalism has grabbed Mesopotamia not to liberate the Arabs from Turkish oppression but to liberate the Arabs from the petroleum that could have made them a rich nationality in the East. (*Applause*)

How have the British, French, and Americans liberated the unfortunate Armenians, whom they ceaselessly incited for so many decades to fight against the Turks and Kurds, and to whom they promised freedom and cultural development? If we ask how they have stood up for the rights of Armenia, I can refer for the answer to the official organ of the Armenians in America, which recounts quite authoritatively the history of this liberation. This organ, *New Armenia*, published in New York, tells how the French induced the Armenians to send volunteers to Marash [Maras] to defend that province alongside the French against the Turks, promising them that in return they should have Alexandretta [Iskenderun]. But when the decisive battle took place, the French expeditionary force abandoned Marash, and twenty thousand Armenians were left at the mercy of the army of Kemal Pasha. Seeing them as so many enemies of Turkey fighting on the French side, that army spared the life of not a single one of them.[3]

As you know, the Armenian republic, led as it is by bourgeois intriguers in the service of the Entente, is filled with hatred for the Bolshevism of Soviet Russia. This Armenian republic has now been obliged to make peace with Soviet

Russia, for it realizes that no salvation is to be expected from the Entente. Why is it that the British, who keep eighty thousand soldiers in Mesopotamia to liberate the Arabs from their petroleum, do not send their troops to Armenia? A leading British newspaper, the *Manchester Guardian*, spoke frankly about this in an article published on May 12. There is no petroleum in Armenia, it said, nothing from which the Armenians can be "liberated." It is impossible to rob the Armenians, so one can leave them to be robbed. Further, it said, a comparison of the attitude of the British government to Mesopotamian petroleum with its attitude to Armenian blood covers the British government with shame and infamy. That was said by a British bourgeois newspaper—not a newspaper of British workers in revolt, but one that, despite the weight of its criticism, is close to Lloyd George.

How are the British capitalists liberating Persia, now that Russian tsarism and Russian capitalism, despite all the efforts of the Allies, were destroyed at the hands of the Russian workers and peasants? The British capitalists always said their task in relation to Persia was solely to liberate that country. And Britain's present foreign minister, Lord Curzon, in his book on Persia published thirty years ago,[4] said that the task of British policy toward Persia is to uphold Persia's independence and freedom. The Anglo-Persian treaty of August last year shows the sort of freedom British capitalism wants to bring to Persia. For £2 million in gold the British capitalist government has bought the whole of Persia from the Persian government—that is, from its own lackeys. For this £2.5 million in gold the British have secured control of Persia's finances and customs and of the organization of the Persian army. And regarding this policy I can again quote very authoritative testimony, that of the French government newspaper *Le*

Temps of August 17 last year. "Since the Persian government handed over its army command to British officers and its finances to British specialists," it said, "it has no longer any independent force or independent resources by which it could exercise sovereignty." Those are the words of the French government's paper.

Comrades, what does all this mean? It means no more and no less than that Entente capital, headed by France, having struck down its German competitor, the German brigand, has obtained control of the hundreds of millions who make up the peoples of the East in order to enslave them. For the peasant in the East it means that, where previously he had to pay tribute in order to maintain the sultan's clique and all manner of shahs, emirs, and khans, now he has to pay twice as much. He must pay his own exploiters and pay for the bayonets of the French and British forces who will defend his exploitation by the local exploiters.

In Turkey there are natural resources whose development would enable the Turkish people to replace the wooden ploughs they now use with iron ploughs and steam ploughs and would enable them to have their own schools. But now that the British and French capitalists have grabbed the riches of the Near East, the riches of Turkey and Persia, they will exploit them not to develop the civilization of the Eastern peoples but for their own profit, so that the bankers of London and Paris may obtain even bigger profits than they enjoy already thanks to their exploitation of the European workers. (*Applause*)

Comrades, as a result of the victory of the Entente there is danger that hundreds of millions in the East may be reduced to absolute slavery. The dream may be dreadful, but God is merciful. This danger will pass away like a bad dream if the toiling masses of the East rise up together with the workers of Europe. For the victors of the World War are themselves covered with wounds from which they are dying.

Comrades, look at the situation of victorious capital, look at the economic situation of the principal victors of this war. You will see that, in order to vanquish German capital, they have taken upon their shoulders and backs such huge burdens that their spines too must crack. (*Applause*) I have figures here showing the size of the state debts incurred by the victorious countries. The French government borrowed 200 billion francs during the war. The British government borrowed 160 billion. The Italian government borrowed 200 billion. This means that, with the exception of America, all the victorious capitalist countries have lost in the war between a half and three-quarters of all the national wealth of these very rich countries by firing it off into the air. This means that none of these governments is able to find the resources to save itself from financial bankruptcy.

If these governments wanted to pay their debts they would have to confiscate as much as two-thirds of the wealth that exists in their countries. That would mean leaving the mass of the people in those countries only one-third of what they have had to live on. This they cannot do. And we see how the victorious powers are arguing among themselves how to get out of the difficulty. The weakest of the victor powers—the Italian and French governments—are calling on the British and American capitalists to lump all these debts together and pay them jointly, so that whichever power is richest will be the one to pay first and foremost. But the British and American capitalists decline to pay the debts of the Italian and French capitalists—they are unable to pay even their own debts.

The British and American capitalists were very willing to shed other people's blood, ordering the Russian peasants, the French peasants, and the Italian workers to go and die in a war for the benefit of the British capitalists. But when the question of paying debts arises, they now say: Friendship is friendship, but a ledger is quite another matter, so pay your own debts. (*Applause*) And we see, comrades, how the victorious capitalists are trying to crush Russia, which until now was a principal outlet for their goods and supplied them with an enormous quantity of raw material. They are trying to destroy the technically most advanced nation in Europe, namely, Germany. And in so doing, they are tearing up the roots of their own existence.

As we know, the British and American capitalists face a situation where the Eastern peoples, in their millions, are hungry for goods of all kinds, are hungry for manufactures and machines. The British and American capitalists are looking for markets, but they are not in a position to sell because these peoples have nothing with which to pay for the goods. As a result, the whole of world imperialism is choking in the process of a tremendous crisis, gripped by frightful convulsions. Hundreds of millions of people are unable to buy trousers and boots. And at the same time, in America and Britain products are piling up, and America and Britain are threatened with the closing of their factories.

For four long years they hounded the worker masses to the slaughter, telling them: In this war you are destroying the absolutism of the kaiser and the sultan of Turkey, and you will gain from it justice, bread, and freedom. And the masses of the people, who see all this happening, now stand face to face with the threat of hunger and cold. These masses are rising in revolt and advancing their demands.

And never in its long history has Britain seen such a huge wave of strikes and mighty workers' demonstrations as we are now witnessing. None other than the British prime minister, the shrewdest of bourgeois politicians, Lloyd George, frankly declared in an April speech to the British Parliament that Britain faces the threat of social revolution.[5] This is not a statement made by the British Communists, whose hearts long for such a revolution. It is a warning from the British prime minister, calling on the bourgeoisie to unite against the workers.

In America we also see a wave of strikes. In Italy, in one of the Allied countries, we see not only a mounting struggle—we see Italy literally on the threshold of revolution. The Italian government maintains itself only by the power of its bayonets; every day it must shoot down workers in the streets of its cities.[6]

After the victory over German absolutism, Mr. Clemenceau said that Bolshevism was not a danger to France, which had emerged victorious from the war; it was a disease affecting defeated peoples only. Yet now we see the French government filling its prisons with French Communists. We see the French government shooting its sailors, using the threat of death to hold back its armed forces from mutiny and revolution.[7]

The proletarians of Europe and America are rising in revolt to overthrow capitalism and establish the reign of freedom, brotherhood, and labor. And at the same time, comrades, right under the nose of British imperialism, in Ireland, in Egypt, and in India, we see a growing movement of revolutionary struggle of the peoples whom Britain has enslaved.

Comrades, in Ireland, a conquered country, the British government has been obliged to set up a fortress against the Irish people. In Ireland dozens of British policemen and soldiers of the expeditionary force are killed every day in the streets of the cities. In Egypt it is not only professional and intellectual workers, not only students, not only civil servants who are taking to the streets. The demonstrations have led to strikes by the fellahin [peasants], whom the British used as beasts of burden during the war, and by railway workers and telegraph workers. And India is seeing not only a terrorist struggle, not only tremendous agitation among the intelligentsia, but also tremendous strikes involving 300,000 people. These are strikes by Indian workers who unite the struggle for their emancipation from the yoke of capital with the struggle for their national emancipation.

Comrades, there is a book that is a sort of Koran for British imperialism, a book by Professor Seeley published many years ago, which is used in the education of British officers sent to India, and used to educate British governors. In this book, Seeley, a learned advocate of British imperialism, discusses how it is that a little handful of British are able to keep under their heel hundreds of millions of Indians. And he answers that there is no magic in this. In India one part of the population fights against another on behalf of the rule of British capital. If a revolt breaks out in the north, we mobilize the Indian peasants in the south, make soldiers of them, and with their aid suppress the revolt in the north. If the Indians in the west revolt, we throw in Indians from the east, and thus, by using some Indians against others, we keep them all under our control. When people say that there is bound to be a revolution because the Indians are dying of hunger, adds this advocate of British imperialism, this is quite unconvincing. "If they cannot live," he replies, "they die." But it does not follow from this that there will be a revolution. Everyone in Britain has freedom to die of hunger, and if people do not want to do this, that does not mean that there will be a revolution. For a revolution to take place it is necessary, he says, that the people "look to the future," that they have hope of liberation, and that they feel their strength.[8]

Comrades, we are sure that the moment is coming when the peoples of the East will prove to the British capitalists, the British vampires, that they do not want to die, that they have hope, and that they feel their strength. Comrades, until now every people that revolted has felt its weakness, for no one had yet seen workers and peasants conquering their exploiters, no one had seen workers and peasants setting their foot on the chest of British imperialism. But you, comrades, have seen that it is possible to conquer even British imperialism.

When the workers and peasants of Russia rose up, when they overthrew the power of the tsar, overthrew the power of the bourgeoisie and landlords, and established a workers' and peasants' government, the bourgeois of all countries were sure that they would crush Soviet Russia and place their yoke once more on the neck of the Russian workers and peasants. They set about hiring Russian officers, capitalists, and landlords; sent them uniforms, equipment, and military instructors; and launched one campaign after another against Soviet Russia. You remember how they bought the deceived Czechoslovak soldiers and hurled fifty thousand of them against Soviet Russia.[9] You remember how they sent against Soviet Russia Kaledin and Kornilov, and then Kolchak, Yudenich, and Denikin. With the help of British tanks, gas bombs, and shells, Denikin and Kolchak formed an army half a million strong and waged a campaign against Soviet Russia. All capitalist Europe had its eyes on Kolchak and helped him with all its power. Russia was cut off, unable to get a single shell from abroad, unable even to get medical supplies with which to care for its maimed sons.

In spite of all this, the workers and peasants of Russia rose up, arms in hand, and created the victorious Red Army. (*Applause*) They smashed Yudenich, Kolchak, and Denikin. I remember the day when, in a German prison in Berlin, I read in a newspaper: "Tomorrow, Tuesday, in the chapel of the former Russian embassy, a solemn service of prayer will be held for General Yudenich, who has set out for Petrograd." But Yudenich was defeated outside Petrograd, and Denikin was beaten outside Orel. The workers' and peasants' army drove them back. Now Kolchak, Denikin, Yudenich are all gone. And now the workers' and peasants' government is finishing its business with the last of these detachments—with Wrangel and with White Poland. And in all this it has given a powerful example to the peoples of the East who are rising in revolt.

If the workers and peasants of the East want to be free from exploitation, they too can win victory, because their adversary is breaking up, is suffering economic collapse, and because their adversary has been beaten by the Red workers' and peasants' Soviet Russia. Victory for the workers and peasants of the Near East depends only upon their own consciousness and will. No enemy will daunt you, no one will hold back the flood of the workers and peasants of Persia, Turkey, and India, if they unite with Soviet Russia. Soviet Russia was surrounded by enemies, but now it can produce weapons with which to arm not only its own workers and peasants but also the peasants of India, Persia, and Anatolia, all the oppressed, and lead them to a common struggle and a common victory. (*Applause*)

When the capitalists came to the East to exploit the masses, they talked to them about "liberation." So we understand why there is a certain distrust among the backward sections of the workers and peasants, who have learned from harsh experience about deception. They ask themselves: Are the precepts of Soviet Russia sincere, will it carry out its promises? Comrades, it is useless to answer such questions with protestations; they have to be answered with rational arguments.

Soviet Russia arose so that there might be no more slaves and masters, no more rich and poor. Soviet Russia is a huge, well-endowed country, which can feed itself, now that it has thrown out the lice, parasites, and vampires that sucked the blood of Russian peasants and workers. It has the strength to raise the Russian people to a height never before known. The Russian peasant and the Russian worker do not need to seek bread in other lands, for their own produces enough of it. They do not need to go in search of metals, which are found in the depths of their own land: an unheard-of treasure-house.

The Russian worker and peasant, who are moved by desire for freedom for themselves, have no need to enslave other peoples. They know very well that either they will crush world capital or world capital will crush them. They know it is impossible for workers' and peasants' Soviet Russia to exist for a long time side by side with the capitalist countries. The Russian workers and peasants know that if they do not strike down the British capitalists, if they do not crush the French capitalists, they themselves will be crushed. The Russian worker can seek peace and concord with them for a time, he can try to obtain a breathing spell in which the revolution will grow stronger in other countries, but permanent peace between the country of labor and the countries of exploitation is impossible. And the Eastern policy of the Soviet government is therefore no diplomatic maneuver, no pushing of the peoples of the East into the firing line so that the Russian Soviet Republic may gain some advantage by betraying them.

We sacrificed our own territory, our own peasants and workers when, at Brest-Litovsk, German imperialism, armed from head to foot, dictated its terms to us.[10] We were then unable to defend ourselves. Workers and peasants of the East, the time may come when we ourselves will advise you not to go forward to utter defeat but instead to throw a sop to the wild beast that seeks to tear you in pieces. We ourselves may experience such moments, but we are bound to you by destiny. Either we unite with the peoples of the East and hasten the victory of the Western European proletariat, or we will perish and you will be slaves.

Therefore, comrades, what is at issue here is not an alliance like that concluded by people who may tomorrow break with each other and become enemies, but rather a fight in common and to the death. Yesterday you swore an oath to conduct that fight. With our combined efforts we must win. For this common victory, comrades, common sacrifices are needed. The worker masses of Russia have been starving for three years, waiting for victory over world capital. And so, when you greet the Red Army, when you hail its victory, do you think about the fact that its victory and its weapons were forged by the blood and sweat of millions of Russian workers and peasants who sacrificed themselves in these last years?

Understand that your own victory will not be won without sacrifices. Many will have to go hungry or shed their blood. You will have to look on Soviet Russia and your countries in revolt as forming a single army that must gain strength together, arm themselves together, and make sacrifices together for their common cause. And whoever says that this is Bolshevik "imperialism," that we are going to the East for conquest and to feed our army, is consciously spreading lies among the workers and peasants so as to divide them, so that the lords of the world may crush them separately. For us it is a matter of common sacrifices, common burdens, and the victory will be common to us all. This will be a victory not of one people over another but of the laboring masses of all peoples over the handful who have hitherto exploited the entire world.

Comrades, in issuing the call for a holy war against the Entente, above all against British capital, we know that victory will not be ours today. We will have to go on fighting for a long time yet, precisely because the masses of the East will develop slowly. News of the victories of the Red Army, of the struggle of the British, French and Italian proletariat must wander for a long time over plains and desert hills before it reaches the peasant in India and Egypt, and brings him its message: Stand up, arise, working people!

In entering upon this hard struggle, we strive to enable these huge countries, these peoples, to develop their strength, their capacity for collective work to reconstruct mankind on a new basis of freedom, where there will not be people of different-colored skin with different rights and duties, where everyone will share the same rights and duties.

Capitalists around the world talk of the menace from the East, saying that when 300 million Indian and 400 million Chinese peasants revolt, that will be the moment of doom for human civilization. We have seen that civilization, seen it in the glare of shrapnel bursts over battlefields, in ruined homes and cities. Capitalist civilization means death to civilization of every kind. Capitalism is unable to ensure us even the lot of an animal that is at least fed. The sooner that that civilization perishes, the better. (*Applause*) And, comrades, when we hand you the banner of common struggle against a common enemy, we know very well that, together with you, we shall create a civilization a hundred times better than the one created by the slave owners of the West.

The East, subjected to oppression by capitalists and property owners, has developed a philosophy of resignation. We appeal, comrades, to the warlike feelings that once inspired the peoples of the East when these peoples, led by their great conquerors, advanced upon Europe. We know, comrades, that our enemies will say that we are appealing to the memory of Genghis Khan and the great conquering caliphs of Islam. But we are convinced that when you drew your daggers and your revolvers yesterday, it was not for aims of conquest, not to turn Europe into a graveyard. You raised them in order, together with workers around the world, to create a new civilization, a civilization of the free worker. And so, when the capitalists of Europe say that a new wave of barbarism threatens, a new horde of Huns, we answer them: Long live the Red East, which together with the workers of Europe will create a new civilization under the banner of communism! (*Loud applause*)

CHAIRMAN: We shall proceed to the translations. The first will be into Turkic. Comrade Buniatzadeh will give it.

(*A five-minute recess is announced. The session resumes at 8:40 p.m.*)

NARIMANOV: The session will continue. Let the translations be given.

(*Interpreters translate into Turkic, Uzbek, and Chechen. Kartmyzov translates into Kumyk, and, from the Communist fraction, Buniatzadeh speaks in Turkic.*)

CHAIRMAN [NARIMANOV]: Please be seated.

VOICES: Comrade Chairman, please let us have a translation into Uzbek.

(*The chairman speaks in Uzbek.*)

VOICES: We have understood. Please continue.

CHAIRMAN: Will the Uzbek comrades who understood please raise their hands.

VOICES: A majority. A minority. Please go on. Call an interpreter. (*An interpreter translates into Uzbek. Artmasov speaks in Turkic.*)

CHAIRMAN: Comrades, the Communist and nonparty fractions propose that a general discussion be opened on the two reports we have heard. But to prevent the discussion from taking up too much time, we need to decide straight away that only six speakers will be heard. In addition, the representatives of the parties of Britain, France, Bulgaria, America, and a few others, should be given the opportunity to speak on these reports, so that we hear not only from the peoples of the East but also from the workers of the countries whose bourgeoisies oppress the peoples of the East. We put this proposal to you and hope that the congress will give its approval. (*Applause*)

CHAIRMAN: I call on Comrade Buniatzadeh, from the Communist fraction.

BUNIATZADEH: (*Speaks in Turkic. The interpreters translate.*) (*Narimanov also speaks in Turkic.*)

CHAIRMAN: Comrade Musazadeh will give the translation.

MUSAZADEH: Regarding Comrade Radek's report, Comrade Buniatzadeh says that the East has been an apple of discord between the imperialists of the West for a very long time. In order to get control of the East and to exploit it, the predators of Europe have set about forming a comprehensive alliance. This was the context that gave rise to the Triple Entente and the Triple Alliance, both of which had the same aspiration to become masters of the East, to exploit the peoples of the East for the benefit of the plunderers. A result of this Alliance, or of this Triple Entente, was the Italo-Turkish War, which was promoted by Britain. The unprovoked attack by Italy upon Karakalise was prepared by the British cabinet.[11] Hardly had this war in Tripolitania [Libya] ended than Russia promoted and formed an alliance between the Balkan states and started a new war in the Balkans with the same aim as before, to get control of the Turkish Straits. Furthermore, the Triple Alliance and the Triple Entente sent their troops for the same purpose into ancient and unfortunate Persia, where they pursued the same aim of subjecting the country and exploiting it.

After the Russian revolution of 1905 the revolution made its way into Persia. The oppressed peoples rose up, as the Russian workers had done, and proclaimed the power of the soviets.[12] But the defeat of the Russian revolution entailed the burial of the Persian revolution as well by the hand of General Lyakhov and the other generals sent by [Tsar] Nicholas into Persia. The Persian revolution was crushed along with the Russian.

Comrade Buniatzadeh described vividly how the first Persian revolutionaries, expelled from their country by the Persian tyrant Muhammad Ali Shah, were executed here. Tireless activity was carried on by the Western powers and the plunderers with the aim of partitioning the unfortunate, benighted East. At the same time as war was being waged in Tripoli [Libya] and in the Balkans, France was pushing into Morocco and strangling that unfortunate independent Eastern state. These aggressive strivings and actions were, of course, the work of the Triple Entente, which the Triple Alliance—the German group—could not look on with indifference. At the same time, unprecedented intrigue aimed against the Entente was being carried on by the German group in the countries of the East.

And then came the international war of 1914, aimed at completely subjugating the East. It ended with the great Russian revolution. After the fall of the bourgeois republic of Kerensky, power in Russia passed into the hands of the proletarians, the peasants and workers. On taking power, the peasants and workers of Russia addressed the peoples of the world, and especially the peoples of the East, as follows: "We have stopped the war, we extend the hand of brotherhood to you, and we urge you to end the war that has been started against us." From that moment the Russian workers and peasants began to turn their attention toward the East.

In concluding his speech, the comrade said that this Eastern orientation has now been crowned with success. The East has risen up. Today it is advancing hand in hand with the Russian proletariat, with combined forces. It will put an end to all the outrages that have been committed up to now. (*Uproar. Voices: "The translations are incomplete, we want a full translation."*)

CHAIRMAN: Comrade Efendiyev will now deal with the parts of the speech that were omitted by the first interpreter.

EFENDIYEV: Comrade Buniatzadeh said a good deal more about what has happened since 1917 in the Caucasus, and this is what was mainly omitted in the translation by the previous interpreter. Buniatzadeh said that the imperialists of Turkey, various Enver Pashas and the like, gave in to incitement by Germany, which looked upon Turkey and the East as a tasty morsel that it wanted to enjoy and treat itself to. This was already part of Bismarck's program. In bringing about independence in the East, the Germans were guided by the well-known slogan: *Drang nach Osten* [drive to the east].

And so with the help of German bayonets, with the help of the German imperialists, the Turkish army conquered Azerbaijan, the richest part of the Transcaucasus, with its wells of oil, the precious fluid that enticed the imperialists to come here. But there were groups and parties in the Caucasus that understood the war differently. They considered that Turkey, with Enver Pasha at its head, had come here to save the people, to deliver the Azerbaijanis from Russian imperialism, and to endow this region with a republic, self-determination, independence, and so on.

This is not true, said Comrade Buniatzadeh. It is a lie. For Turkey, in liberating Azerbaijan from one imperialism—Russian imperialism—thereby handed it over to another imperialism. This one-sided liberation chased away the British only to seat itself in their place and suck up the lifeblood of these countries.

This was a mistake. It was a delusion that is now passing. Today this intoxication is passing, and the masses of Transcaucasia, of Azerbaijan, are waking up and beginning to understand things better and more correctly. Today the Soviet armed forces and the Communist Party have taken the initiative in liberating the Caucasus from the groups promoted by the Turkish and German imperialists. Immediately the masses have begun to get a better grasp of the past and a more accurate evaluation of what is happening now. Today Soviet Azerbaijan has been freed from the groups, the parties, the puppets put up by Turkish and German imperialism. Azerbaijan stands today as the bridge to Soviet politics in the East. Azerbaijan is bound to play a key role in this regard. Culturally and materially it is one of the best and richest countries in the East.

Simultaneously the masses have wholly gone over to the Soviet government. Their experience during the last few years has taught them something and is a political guarantee that in the future they will close ranks tightly with the Communist Party. They will align themselves politically with the course of the Soviets, and make every effort to ensure that Soviet power triumphs throughout the East.

CHAIRMAN: The second speaker will be Comrade Bahaeddin Shakir.

INTERPRETER (*rendering Comrade Shakir's [Turkish] speech into Russian*): I begin without comments and give only the essentials. When the European war began, Turkey went to war with no intention of conquest. It entered the war of necessity, to defend itself. For Turkey there was only one issue at stake: to safeguard its freedom—or to fall under the yoke of one of the coalitions, either the German or the British. Before joining in the war, the Turks thought the matter over for a long time. If they did not enter the war, then, when one of the contending sides proved victorious, that would mean the end of Turkey's freedom. Even earlier Turkey did not follow a policy of conquest and had no predatory aims.

In our country, Turkey, the officers belong to a different category than the Russian or European officers. The Turkish officer is a genuine proletarian. He has not been brought up in the same spirit as officers in Europe and Russia. It is incorrect to hold that Turkey had a plan worked out beforehand and had already come to an understanding with Germany.

The agrarian question in our country, in Anatolia, also has special features. It is a very simple question. There are no landlords there, no large landowners. Turkey has, in general, no powerful bourgeois class, and so neither the Turkish government nor the Turkish people could pursue a solely aggressive policy. They had only one policy: Don't trouble us and we won't trouble you.

Comrades, I will prove this by the fact that when the war had continued for a long time, and the German coalition felt that it was winning, the Turkish people and the Turkish government wanted to establish buffer states, that is to say, an Armenian, an Azerbaijani, and a Georgian state. If it is said that Turkey was pursuing an aggressive policy, how can it be explained that the Turkish people and the Turkish government held strictly to a policy of trying to protect themselves by establishing buffer states between Russia and Turkey? No, neither in the west nor in the east did Turkey intend to annex other people's lands, and, in general, Turkey did not pursue an aggressive policy.

That is what Comrade Shakir said in his long speech. I have translated the essence of it.

(*The same interpreter translates the speech into other languages.*)

VOICE FROM THE HALL (*in Turkic*): The comrade interpreter did not warn us that he was translating the speech of the previous speaker; it was as though he was expressing his own views.

NARIMANOV: Yes, it was a translation. Where is the Persian interpreter?

(*An interpreter translates the speech into Persian.*)

ZINOVIEV: The next speaker will be Comrade Haydar Khan from the Communist fraction.

HAYDAR KHAN: (*Speaks in Turkic and translates his own speech into Persian. An interpreter translates the speech into Russian.*)

INTERPRETER: Comrades, first and foremost I call your attention to the part of the speeches by Comrades Zinoviev and Radek in which Comrade Zinoviev said that we have come here frankly and sincerely to extend our hands to our brothers in the East, and we do not want to employ any diplomacy here. Comrade Radek also said that we have come here to offer our hand, and if we die, we die along with you, and if we live we live along with you. This is of the greatest importance to the peoples of the East, for the peoples of the East have not heard this in two hundred years. All that time they saw and heard how European capital was slaughtering them.

I want to give you a few examples of how European capital sought to stifle the liberation movement of the Eastern peoples. Let us take Persia. A revolution broke out there, and this revolution was put down by the European capitalists, with tsarist Russia and British imperialism in the lead. In the same way, India too, with its 350 million inhabitants, does not have even a penknife in its pocket; it was deprived of the ability to defend itself and is subject to ongoing inhuman exploitation by British capital. The Indians are dying of hunger, but the British capitalists are living in splendid palaces at their expense.

I want to say the same thing about Turkey. A comrade spoke here saying that Turkey waged a defensive war, that Turkey was not a tool in the hands of German imperialism and had no imperialist aspirations of its own. This does not square with the facts, comrades. Turkey had great imperialist aspirations. It acted wholly as a tool in the hands of European imperialists. If Turkey had not been drawn into this war by the imperialists, who were striving for conquest, the European imperialists would not today be tearing to pieces the working peasantry of Turkey.

Comrades, as you see, the East has already woken up, a revolution has broken out in Persia itself against Britain, just as a movement has begun in India and also in Turkey. Gathered here are representatives of these and other peoples who are hostile to British and every other kind of imperialism. I am sure that these peoples will reach agreement here and will organize a rebuff to the British and other imperialists and liberate the East from the yoke of the capitalists. (*Applause*)

CHAIRMAN: We will now end the session, but first there is an announcement. Both fractions have agreed to set up four sections: on the agrarian question, on the national-colonial question, on the question of building soviets, and on the organizational question. These four sections are to be made up as follows: each group of twenty delegates will choose one representative to join each section. This will mean approximately ninety members to a section. It is desirable that the elections take place tomorrow, since the congress will not be meeting then—there will be a parade. The elections will have to take place in the hostels, so that each hostel elects one representative per twenty delegates. If there are any left over, they must be grouped. If any have to be eliminated, the Presiding Committee will see to that. So we ask you to ensure that all these sections are established tomorrow. (*Translation*)

(*The session was closed at 12:02 a.m.*)

SESSION 3
SEPTEMBER 4, 1920

Discussion: Turkestan, Mountain republic

(*The session opened at 12:13 p.m. Comrade Zinoviev took the chair.*)

CHAIRMAN: I declare the third session of the Congress of the Peoples of the East open. We will continue with discussion of the first two reports. Comrade Narbutabekov has the floor.

NARBUTABEKOV: Comrades, before making my speech I must warn you that, having only fifteen minutes—(*Voices: "Can't hear."*)

CHAIRMAN: Please be quiet: the comrade is a bit hoarse.

NARBUTABEKOV: My time is limited. In fifteen minutes it is, of course, impossible to describe fully the international situation of the working masses of the East. I will be brief and I ask you to listen to me with attention and not to interrupt, as I have no voice left.

In his speech, Comrade Zinoviev described the tasks before this congress clearly and distinctly. I will not touch on that. As for the situation of the working masses in the

East, that is an extraordinarily important question not only for us, the peoples of the East, but also for the Soviet government itself. Any government that sets itself the task of achieving certain aims among the many millions of the East where there are so many languages and dialects (about fifty-three) needs to listen to the voice of these peoples. And as delegates, our duty is to put certain demands to the Soviet government precisely and clearly.

We declare that our Muslim peoples and peoples of the East want no government other than that of the soviets. We have no other choice. It is either the British capitalists or the working masses of Russia and the world as a whole. It is an either-or situation, as Comrade Radek said: either Soviet power must perish, and all become slaves, or it must conquer, and then we shall be free.

In order that these words may be put into practice, we the peoples of the East must make it quite clear that there are two worlds: the world of the West and the world of the East. As you know, during the many centuries of its historical development, the West has changed its form of state structure several times, from the most despotic forms to liberal-democratic republics, while in the East the form of the state structure has not altered. Russia is the first of the European states to have brought forward a new form of state structure, that of Soviet power. Comrades, the world of the East and the world of the West are complete opposites in this respect. Psychologically, culturally, economically, and religiously, in its social forms and in the nature of its everyday life, the East is in a special situation, and these peculiarities have got to be reckoned with.

Nicholas II and other plunderers of the working people never took account of these peculiarities. Our interests were always trampled on. In the first days of the revolution, in opposition to Kerensky's capitalist slogan of "War until final victory," the Bolsheviks put forward the slogan of "Self-determination for the nationalities." It found an echo in all fifty-three nations of the Russian state. This was one of the principal reasons why Kerensky's capitalist slogan failed. We, the peoples of the East, had faith in that slogan of "Self-determination for the nationalities." To this day we maintain that faith, faith in the ideological guides and leaders of the world proletariat—Comrades Lenin, Trotsky, Zinoviev, and others. But at the same time we must tell the congress that what we want is for the voice of the Muslim working people and the peoples of the East to be heard. If this voice is heard, the state power will find it easier to carry out its tasks and aims in implementing the great principles of the social revolution in the East.

We demand genuine realization of the principles of freedom, equality, and brotherhood—in fact and not merely on paper. If that is done, I am sure, not a single Muslim will venture to raise his hand against Soviet power.

You all know, comrades, that in the East from time immemorial, beginning with Genghis Khan and Timur and ending with the bloody Abdul Hamid, there has been no other form of government but despotism: "In heaven there is almighty God, and on earth the sultan." The state structure did not alter as in the West. When the great Russian revolution burst upon the world, we were utterly unprepared for it. We were unable to immediately adapt the entire mass of our habits and ways of living to the framework of communism. It must be said that no form of government other than Soviet power is acceptable to the East as a means of saving the working masses of the Eastern peoples from the hands of the capitalists. Everyone knows that the East is utterly different from the West, that its interests are different. Thus a rigid application of the ideas of communism will meet with resistance there.

Accordingly, if we want the 400 million in the Muslim world to join the Soviet power, we need to apply a special yardstick in their case.

The nonparty comrades wish to declare that the diverse interests and special features that exist in the Caucasus and Turkestan and in all the former borderlands of the Russian state must be resolutely defended. It is the duty of the congress to stress them, to say to our government: Comrades, the Muslims will not abandon the Soviet government, but this is on condition that the peculiarities of the Eastern peoples are recognized, and the measures adopted toward them by the Soviet government are implemented not on paper but in fact. (*Applause*)

Comrade Radek said that the Soviet government is accused by the Western European *Kulturträger* [upholders of civilization], the Western European brigands, of carrying out a policy of Red imperialism. In order to refute this charge, our comrades—the leaders of the Communist Party and the Soviet government—must declare that this is not so and will not be so.

We Turkestanis state that we never once saw Comrade Zinoviev, or Comrade Radek, or the other leaders of the revolution. They should come and see for themselves what is happening in Turkestan, what exactly is being done there by the local authorities, whose policy is alienating the working masses from the Soviet government. I regard it as my duty as a delegate to say this, because I am staunchly in favor of the platform of Soviet power.

I will be brief, for time is short. This congress is made up not of creatures of the bourgeoisie but of genuine representatives of the working masses, who must support Soviet power. Whether Chechen, Dagestani, Ajarian, Kirghiz, or Kazakh,[1] everyone at this congress must clearly and definitely tell the government what our needs are.

We must say: "Comrades, do not waver, go straight ahead along the road laid down by the working masses of the people, for there is no other road, no other way out. Even if the Western European proletariat does not support Soviet power it will be supported by the Muslims and the peoples of the East."

For this reason I hold that Soviet power can find no better ally at the present time than the working people of the East. For during the three years that our comrades, the best leaders of the world revolution, have been appealing to them, the Western European proletariat has shown no active support. The well-known failure of the July 21 strike proved that because of the conditions of its political life, the Western European proletariat cannot help.[2] It is necessary, without losing a moment, to organize the East in the proper way, in accordance with its religious and socioeconomic conditions. There is no other road for the Soviet government. (*Applause*)

We Turkestanis point out that from the moment of the October revolution the toiling masses of Turkestan rallied to Soviet power just like their Russian comrades. As we shed our blood on the Turkestan fronts against the enemies of Soviet power, our lives became closely linked with those of the toiling masses of all Russia. Accusations that Turkestani activists display chauvinist tendencies must be rejected, for our workers have proved the contrary with their blood.

For three years the working people of Turkestan have acquitted themselves with honor in this struggle. But what was needed to ensure this? Very little. Only paying close attention to the life of the Eastern peoples and applying the principles advocated by delegates here. There is no question of counterrevolution here, nor of chauvinism, for we, representatives of our working people, have suppressed our narrow nationalist tendencies. And we, the first revolutionaries of Turkestan, have no fear of any ulema [body of Muslim clerics], of any Black Hundreds made up of mullahs. We were the first to raise our banner against them, (*Applause*) and never shall we lower that standard; we shall conquer or perish.

Let me tell you, comrades, our Turkestani masses have to fight on two fronts: against the reactionary mullahs in our own midst, and against the narrow nationalist inclinations of the local Europeans. Neither Comrade Zinoviev, nor Comrade Lenin, nor Comrade Trotsky knows the real situation, what has been going on in Turkestan these last three years. We must speak out frankly and paint a true picture of the state of affairs in Turkestan. Then the eyes of our leaders will be opened. They will come to Turkestan and set things right.

I throw this out to you all, both the nonparty and the party comrades from Turkestan.

In order to prevent what has happened in Turkestan from being repeated in other parts of the Muslim world, I warn our government that we know all the shortcomings of the policy pursued for these three years. Remove your counterrevolutionaries, we say; remove your alien elements who spread national discord; remove your colonizers who are now working behind the mask of communism! (*Loud applause. Cries of "Bravo."*)

Comrades, I will not say much, but will confine myself to recalling the sacred words of the world's leader, Comrade Lenin, when he said that he is on his own and we must help him in every possible way.

You have his famous words before you and you keep them in your heart—and after these words nobody can say that the Soviet government wishes us ill. Within it there may be provocateurs and demagogues, but they must be ruthlessly destroyed, just like counterrevolutionaries.

We are not afraid of open counterrevolutionaries; we have encountered them in battle on the front lines. But, comrades, there are among you persons who, behind the mask of communism, are bringing ruin upon Soviet power as a whole and spoiling the entire Soviet policy in the East. We must fearlessly declare: Down with these provocateurs and demagogues who corrupt the fundamental idea of Soviet power! (*Loud applause. Shouts of "Down with them."*)

Now, in addition to what I have said, I must add the following. The theoretical position of the Soviet government toward the East was set out with the greatest clarity in the appeal to the toiling Muslims of Russia and the East.[3] In November 1917, the Council of People's Commissars issued a special appeal, signed by Comrade Lenin himself, to all the toiling Muslims of Russia and the East. It called for the treaty partitioning Turkey and taking Armenia away from her to be torn up and annulled, and for Constantinople to remain in the hands of the Muslims. This historic appeal also stated, "Henceforth your beliefs and customs, your national and cultural institutions are declared free and inviolable. Build your national life freely and without hindrance. It is your right. You yourselves must be the masters in your own land. You yourselves must build your life as you see fit."

After these words, is it conceivable that we would turn our backs on the Soviet government?

But now, as we travel about, Muslims come up to us and say that our beliefs are being trampled on, that we are not allowed to pray, not allowed to bury our dead in accordance with our customs and religion. What is this? It is nothing but the sowing of counterrevolution among the toiling masses.

It may be that the same thing is happening in other places too, but I declare, in the name of the nonparty delegates—and perhaps the Communists also will join in this—that with the remarkable congress we are holding today our Soviet government should introduce a definite policy in relation to the East. Then the Eastern peoples will rally to the Soviet power not only on paper but in arms, and no power in the world will be able to resist the pressure of the many-millioned masses of the peoples of the East, together with the proletariat and peasantry of Russia.

Long live the oppressed East!

Long live those real Communists who unreservedly want to put these principles into practice!

Long live our leaders, the leaders of the world proletariat—Comrades Lenin, Trotsky, Zinoviev, and the others.

(*Tajiyev translates into Turkic, and other interpreters translate into Turkish, Persian, and Chechen.*)

KORKMASOV: Comrades, I am taking the floor to join in the discussion and will have to speak in Russian and then translate my own words into Kumyk. So for me to translate another speaker now into Kumyk is, owing to my state of health, too much for me. I ask Comrade Aliyev to take my place.

(*Interpreter translates into Kumyk.*)

CHAIRMAN: The last of the speakers on the list, Comrade Korkmasov, will now address us.

KORKMASOV: Comrades, the fervent, inspiring call with which Comrade Zinoviev summoned us to struggle against world imperialism aroused in the hearts of all members of the congress feelings that already earlier had filled the hearts of the Mountain poor. When they drew their sabers and daggers, only lately wiped clean of Volunteers' blood,[4] the Mountain poor showed that today as always they are ready to follow their great leaders into a bloody, decisive, final battle against the brigands and scoundrels of world imperialism for the sake of the emancipation of the oppressed peoples of West and East. (*Loud applause*)

Comrades, what speeches can be made, what discussion can take place after this decisive demonstration you have given? It would be incomprehensible and alien to the Mountain poor. Assembled in their own congress a month ago, the Mountain poor, and even the ulema, issued a call for a ghazavat, a holy war, against all the oppressors of the East: not to lay down our arms until the enemy of all the poor of the world and the working people of all nations has perished! (*Applause*)

The Mountain poor do not need any words. From the beginning of the great social revolution they have waged a ceaseless struggle not only against the internal counter-revolutionaries (the imam, the Mountain government) but also against the external ones, the imperialists: the Turks and the British and their hirelings—Bicherakhov's and Denikin's men.[5] And, naturally, comrades, after experiencing this entire, incredibly hard struggle, the Mountain poor cannot utter any equivocal words here or lodge any complaints.

But let me tell you in a few words, comrades, what has happened in these three years, so that these facts from the life of our region, from the life of the working masses of the North Caucasus, may form a living bridge between East and West, illustrating the great truths of international politics and the struggle against international imperialism expressed here by our comrades Zinoviev and Radek.

Thanks to their self-sacrificing struggle, comrades, after a struggle such as not a single revolution, not a single people has known, the Russian workers and peasants won freedom. They then presented this freedom, as though on a platter, to the peoples of the East.

And what happened? It turned out that the ruling classes—the princes, the khans, the beys, the rich, the mullahs—set out to erect a wall between the great social revolution and the harassed Mountain poor. These parasites, thanks to the intrigues of the Turkish imperialists and the British, brought on to the scene an idol, the imam, as a religious weapon with which to oppress the toiling masses.

What a farce! After the great Shamyl, who defended the Mountain poor against the khans, the agents of the autocracy; Najmuddin Gotsinsky, a common criminal who was put in prison by even the tsarist government, was raised to the dignity of imam.[6] How did the Mountain poor react to this farce? Did they stand for it? No, the Mountain poor launched a civil war.

However, none of the efforts of the pan-Islamists and the pan-Turkists and none of the attempts made by the British and the agents of Nicholas were successful. After less than a year, the imam was overthrown by the very forces that had particularly supported him; he was nicknamed "not imam but Ivan." The poor of Dagestan, led by their socialists, linked up with the Red forces and proclaimed Soviet power there.[7] It is hard to convey to you the joy that was felt by the working people. This power is our own, the power of the poor, they said. After this, is it possible for us to utter words such as those that were uttered here just now? Such complaints are alien to our poor.

The Mountain princes, generals, and landlords were beaten in the mountains in their gamble on the imamate. Nevertheless, comrades, these forces—sustained by the counterrevolution raging in Russia and aware of the strong sympathy with the Turkish people among the masses—turned their gaze to Turkey, where various pashas, beys, and so on ruled, sitting on the backs of the working people. Would they help in crushing the Mountain poor? Turks did actually come in. I am very sorry not to see here a leader who was very active in organizing the counter-revolution in the mountains—Enver Pasha. Sitting in the palace of the old sultans and forgetting the ideals of the original Young Turks, he—along with Chermoyev, Kotsov, and other generals of Nicholas II—organized a counter-revolution to crush Soviet power. (*Applause*)

Turks appeared—and what did they do? The Young Turks Yusuf Izet Pasha, Nuri Pasha, and various other pasha-mashas and beys—who ought to have won victories on various fronts of the imperialist wars dear to their hearts—turned up in Dagestan in order to establish a front against the working people. Thanks to help from Bicherakhov's cossacks and officers of Nicholas's army, they were able for a time to overturn Soviet power in Dagestan.[8]

But what did they give to the poor of Dagestan in place of that power? The one-man dictatorship of Prince Tarkovsky. That was how the ideology of the Young Turks took shape at the great moment of the social revolution. They found no other way of solving their problems. Around this counterrevolutionary, around this traitor to his own people, all sorts of rascals subsequently gathered—Kotsovs, Chermoyevs, and the like—and proclaimed the mythical Mountain republic. They plundered the working people and sold the weapons left behind by the Turks, who had fled for home before the stronger imperialist, the British. But after only a few months, having nothing more left to plunder, this gang of adventurers abandoned the Mountain people, leaving them to be victims of the Volunteer bands. That was how the wretched farce entitled the "Mountain government" was played out.[9]

The Volunteers found that the Turks and their creatures had not finished the job of crushing the Bolsheviks. Backed by the British, they launched a furious campaign against all adherents of Soviet power, both particular individuals and entire communities. The Turks had arrested Bolsheviks and exacted contributions from Bolshevik settlements, but the Volunteers decided that this was not enough, and that counterrevolutionaries must do still more. They unleashed a real war against the Mountain poor. This heroic struggle, which lasted nearly a year, is known to you, comrades; it has dyed Dagestan in the color of its own blood, shed for the glorious red flag. (*A storm of applause*)

You also know, comrades, how the Mountain poor during those same long months of struggle also had to repulse Musavatist agents—as well as Turkish counterrevolutionaries who let loose an internal onslaught, in the person of Nuri Pasha, another counterrevolutionary and the brother of Enver Pasha. The struggle was a tragic one. Comrades, the Mountaineers wanted to make their small contribution to helping the great Red Army, which was also there fighting the counterrevolution on the steppes of Russia. The struggle was crowned with victory. At the end of twelve months the Red Mountaineer partisans had captured the towns of Temir-Khan-Shura [Buinaksk], Derbent, and Petrovsk [Makhachkala], and greeted with red banners the first detachments of the great Red Army.[10]

So for the Mountain poor, comrades, you cannot talk about this or that detail, some parochial matter, such as the Turkestani comrade raised, when what is at stake is the world revolution. What faces us is a great world war. We must tell and do tell those international scoundrels, the imperialists of France, Britain, and America: Even before the Congress of the Peoples of the East, before our leaders' call, we began a ghazavat against you, a holy war. And tomorrow we shall go into action against you, arms in hand! (*Loud applause*) And so, comrades, let me end with the call:

Long live the oppressed peoples of the East!
Long live the oppressed working masses of the West!
Long live their alliance under the red banner of the Third International! (*Shouts and applause*)
Long live their fraternal alliance under the guidance of our great leaders, Comrades Lenin, Trotsky, and Zinoviev—to smash the enemy, world imperialism and capitalism! (*Applause*)

(*Korkmasov translates his own speech into Kumyk.*)

CHAIRMAN: Please pay attention, a Turkic translation will now be given.

VOICE: The Turkic speakers understood—only a Persian translation is needed.

CHAIRMAN: The point is that the previous speech was translated into a Turkic language but delegates told us that they did not understand. So they asked that this speech be translated into Turkic, and we will now have this translation. Please pay attention.

(*Buniatzadeh translates the speech into Turkic.*)

ZINOVIEV: Comrades, I have to announce that we need to complete the elections to the sections. Far from all the hostels have carried out these elections, and this must be done without delay. The next session will begin at 6:00 p.m. And now we shall break for lunch. (*Translation*)

(*The session was closed at 3:00 p.m.*)

SESSION 4
SEPTEMBER 4, 1920

Guest speakers; India; Turkey

(The session opened at 8:00 p.m. Comrade Zinoviev took the chair.)

CHAIRMAN: I declare the fourth session of the Congress of the Peoples of the East open.

Before proceeding to our regular business I wish to inform you of a decision just taken by the Presiding Committee of our congress. The Presiding Committee has discussed a schedule for the work of the congress so that it may be concluded according to a definite plan. The Presiding Committee has decided that our work should be finished by the ninth; we therefore have five days and nights at our disposal.

So that our work may finish within this time, the Presiding Committee finds it necessary to take a number of steps to abbreviate our discussions. It has therefore decided, first of all, to reduce the number of guest speakers. We would be very pleased, of course, if all the comrades who have come here from abroad could address us, but unfortunately the congress has not time enough to hear them all. Accordingly, we shall call on the British and French comrades only, while the speeches of the representatives of America, the Balkans, Spain, Holland, Austria, Japan, and other countries will be printed in the newspapers and included in the report of our congress.[1]

Further, the Presiding Committee proposes that speeches be translated only into the three official languages: Russian, Azerbaijani-Turkish, and Persian. Next, the Presiding Committee requests that comrade delegates who do not understand any of these languages do as we did in Moscow at the congress of the Communist International. Comrades who do not understand the speaker's language should sit together and try to arrange to have among them a comrade who does understand the language in question and can explain to them what is being said. When necessary, while a translation into one of the official languages is being given in the hall, they can give their translations either in the corridors or out in the street. This is awkward, of course, but it would be even more awkward to drag the congress out interminably. Today there were only two speakers, for fifteen minutes each, while the rest of the time has been spent in giving translations, and an entire session has been used up in this way.

In addition, the Presiding Committee has decided that the comrade interpreters should abridge when they translate, conveying what was said in such a way that the translation takes only a quarter of the time taken by the speech itself. Until now matters have proceeded differently: the interpreter's speech has taken a great deal longer than the original. We consider that at such a huge congress as this we must proceed more economically.

I call on the interpreters to translate. (*Translation*)

Comrades, the Presiding Committee has one other announcement to make. It proposes that the congress agree to select from among the members of the Presiding Committee two comrades to act as chairmen. For its part, the Presiding Committee proposes that these comrades be Narbutabekov and Narimanov. In addition, the Presiding Committee asks the congress to confirm the appointment of two women as representatives of the women delegates to the congress.

In order to speed up the proceedings, the Presiding Committee has decided that plenary sessions of the congress will take place each day, starting at 5:00 p.m. and continuing until 11:00 p.m. Then, from 11:00 p.m. to 2:00 a.m., meetings of the sections or of the fractions.

Finally, I want to inform you of a rule proposed by the Presiding Committee. A reporter will be allowed one hour, and a coreporter thirty minutes. For a summary, fifteen minutes, and for other speeches, ten minutes. Speakers will not be allowed to speak more than twice. One will be called upon to speak for, and another against. A reporter will reply at once to all questions that have been handed in. Opportunity to pose questions in person will be given at the end of the session. Speakers will be recognized only on receipt of written requests. Statements will be submitted in writing.

(*Translation*)

CHAIRMAN: Comrades, in view of the fact that all these proposals have been adopted unanimously by the Presiding Committee, I feel able to ask the congress to confirm them. Will those opposed to the Presiding Committee's proposals please raise their hands.

(*An interpreter translates into Turkic.*)

CHAIRMAN: Those in favor of confirming the Presiding Committee's proposals, please raise your hands after the translation. (*Translation*) Thank you. Who is against? No one. Adopted unanimously. We will proceed to the next agenda point. First of all, I call upon the delegate from the United Communist Party of Great Britain, Comrade Quelch.

QUELCH: (*Speaks in English.*)

CHAIRMAN: The Russian translation will be given by Comrade Petrov.

PETROV: Comrade Quelch began his speech with a quotation from Marx. Karl Marx said that the British working class would be free only when the peoples of the British colonies were free. That is why Comrade Quelch is here, representing the British Communist Party—because the party recognizes that the truth of what Karl Marx said is beyond any doubt.

Comrade Quelch says that the enemy of the British working class, the British capitalist class, is at the same time the enemy of the peoples of the East, the oppressed East.

Therefore, the struggle of the British working class against British capitalism is at the same time your struggle, the struggle of the oppressed peoples of the East.

British imperialism is today oppressing and plundering hundreds of millions of people in Ireland, India, and other countries. In Ireland at present there is a serious situation; a decisive struggle is taking place. The Irish people are fighting for their independence. In spite of the presence in Ireland of a huge number of British soldiers, the Irish people are fighting heroically and successfully for their independence. The same thing is happening in India, which has been oppressed by British capitalism for centuries. To this day the British capitalists are sucking all the wealth out of wretched, starving India.

Moreover, so as to safeguard its rule in India, British imperialism is seizing Central Asia, extending its rule over the whole of Asia. British imperialism is like a monster that can never be satiated. Greedy, it grabs more and more territory, oppressing the people who live there.[2]

The British working class knows this, and its congresses have frequently protested this policy of British imperialism. Congresses of Britain's organized workers have demanded and continue to demand that the right of self-determination be accorded to all peoples and nationalities. (*Applause*) They are striving for complete liberation for all peoples oppressed today by British imperialism. The struggle of the British working class is directed against those who are your enemies too, that is, against British imperialism. In recognition of this, the British Communist Party has sent a representative to Russia and to this congress. But the moment will soon be here when the representatives of the British proletariat will be able to render more substantial help in our struggle for liberation from British imperialism.

British imperialism costs the British proletariat very dear. The frontiers of the British Empire are strewn with the bones of British workers killed for the glory of British imperialism.

Standing at the head of all the workers and oppressed peoples, the Russian Soviet Republic is waging a decisive struggle for the complete liberation of mankind.

It is therefore natural that British, French, German, and Austrian workers, and workers in other countries, are rallying in ever greater numbers under the banner of the Russian Soviet Republic, under the banner of communism.

At the present time, Soviet Russia is negotiating with the British capitalist government. But British workers know that these negotiations, and the temporary peace that the Russian republic is trying to obtain, are only intended to win new positions for continuing this struggle. The workers of Britain and the other countries of Western Europe have complete confidence in the Russian Soviet Republic and support it in all the steps it takes, in its entire policy.

This great congress shows that you too, the peoples of the East, are marching behind the Russian Soviet Republic in its struggle for the liberation of mankind. In Britain the working class is getting ready to take political power; social revolution is imminent there. (*Applause*) We can be sure that the peoples of the East will go forward together with the revolutionary proletariat under the banner of the Communist International right up to complete victory and the destruction of the old world, in order to create a new world of freedom and happiness for mankind.

Down with international imperialism! Long live the Russian Soviet Republic! Long live the world Soviet republic! Long live the International! (*Applause. Translations into Turkic and Persian.*)

CHAIRMAN: The next speaker will be the representative of the French workers, the delegate of the Paris Committee for the Third International, Comrade Rosmer. (*Applause*)

ROSMER: (*Speaks in French.*)

CHAIRMAN: I call on Comrade Pavlovich.

PAVLOVICH: I came to Russia, says Comrade Rosmer, to attend the Second Congress of the Communist International. I considered it my duty to come here to Baku to bring greetings from the workers and peasants of France to the oppressed peoples of the East.

When the World War began, the bourgeois press of all countries asserted that this war, in opposition to barbarous Germany, would bring freedom to the oppressed nations. But in that case, why did the great powers not begin by freeing the peoples they themselves oppressed? Why did Britain not give freedom to Ireland? Why did it keep the 300 million people of India under its yoke? Why did France, which said it was fighting against German barbarism, oppress and hold down Morocco, Tunisia, Algeria, and other Muslim countries?[3]

When the war ended, France and Britain tried to take back from these peoples even the miserable crumbs they had given them. When it was necessary to fight the Germans, when hundreds of thousands of Algerians, Tunisians, and Moroccans had to be mobilized, they were promised various freedoms, but the moment that Germany had been defeated all these miserable freedoms were withdrawn. And when a delegation sent to France by representatives of Tunisia pointed out that 45,000 Tunisians had fallen on the battlefield and recalled the promises that had been made to them, these delegates were themselves put in prison. The indigenous newspapers that took the liberty of publishing this fact were closed down and confiscated. That is how they behave in France, and in Britain too. That is how all the great powers treat the countries whose lives they expended in order to defend themselves against German imperialism.

But how are we to account for the fact that now, after the war, the European states are obliged to exploit the population of Africa and Asia as never before? This is very easy to explain. War, bankruptcy, and ruin have led to a fall in the productivity of labor. The French worker does not want to work for the capitalist as he used to, and it is impossible to force him to work. And so they have thought of a way. They want to squeeze the indigenous population of Asia and Africa still harder, turning them into slaves forced to work not only for themselves but also for the French and British workers. The indigenous world must understand the danger that threatens it. It must unite around Soviet Russia, the palladium of the Eastern peoples' independence, and raise the banner of revolt and holy war against the capitalist world.

Long live the Third International! (*Applause*)

CHAIRMAN: Comrade Korkmasov will give a brief translation. (*Korkmasov translates.*)

CHAIRMAN: The last speaker will be the representative of India, Comrade Fazil al-Qadir.

FAZIL AL-QADIR: (*Speaks in Farsi [Persian].*)

INTERPRETER: Comrades, the representative of India greets the First Congress of the Peoples of the East. The Indian peoples languishing under the yoke of British capitalism look for help from you and from Soviet Russia, which carries forward the revolutionary banner of the world proletariat. We have long looked forward to the congress, looked forward to the day when all the peoples of the East would unite and free ourselves from world imperialism.

Long live the world revolution! Long live the unity of all the peoples of the East!

DECLARATION BY THE INDIAN REVOLUTIONARY ASSOCIATION IN TURKESTAN

To the comrade delegates to the Second Congress of the Communist International in Baku.

On behalf of the 300 million oppressed people in India, the Indian Revolutionary Association in Turkestan asks the delegates to this congress and representatives of Soviet Russia, gathered here with the aim of liberating mankind, to help India, which is in such great need of their assistance. All who are striving for liberation hope that this help will be given without any interference in the internal affairs and religious life of those who await liberation from the yoke of capitalism and imperialism. All revolutionaries appeal for help to Russia in their struggle to put their national programs into effect.

With regard to the Eastern question as a whole, one important fact especially stands out, the importance of which cannot be denied. India, and India alone, is the real cause of serious conflicts in this world. History has shown more than once that freedom for India means freedom for the world and an end to all wars. From the huge population of India the brutal British forcibly take men for their army in order to attack other nations.

The Indian Revolutionary Association is in a position to prove this fact, and present this proof to the First Congress of the Peoples of the East in Baku. The association asks that the congress give it as soon as possible the very great help that India so much needs.

> *Mohammed Abdur Rabb Barq,*
> *Chairman of the Indian Revolutionary Association*
> TASHKENT, AUGUST 10, 1920

CHAIRMAN: In conclusion Comrade Shablin will make a brief statement on behalf of the Communist Party of the Balkans.

SHABLIN: Comrades, the Balkan Communist Federation, to which belong the Bulgarian, Yugoslav, Greek, and Romanian Communist parties, has authorized me to tell you, delegates of the peoples of the East, that we, the Balkan peoples, are also oppressed and enslaved just like you by the world bandits of Britain and France. Your struggle means our liberation as well.

The victorious Russian revolution, which is becoming a world revolution, shows us the path of the great struggle for liberation once and for all from exploitation of man by man.

Against the united front of the imperialist oppressors we bring forward the united front of the oppressed and enslaved peoples of the entire world.

Long live the great solidarity of the proletariat!

Long live the liberation of the East!

Long live the alliance of the working people of the whole world!

CHAIRMAN: We have been obliged, unfortunately, to refrain from hearing from the comrade representatives from America, Japan, Spain, Holland, and Austria, owing to lack of time, and we ask permission for their speeches to be printed in the newspapers and also in the report of our congress. (*Voices: "Yes, yes."*)

Next, comrades, two prominent Turkish political leaders, who are not delegates to our congress but are present here in Baku, have sent written statements to the Presiding Committee. As these statements are of great political importance, the Presiding Committee has decided to make them public, both from this podium and in the press. One of these statements is by Enver Pasha and the other by Ibrahim Tali, the representative of the Turkish people's government of Anatolia. We shall now read both of those statements. (*"Yes, yes." Translation.*)

CHAIRMAN: I call upon Comrade Ostrovsky to read the statements. (*Uproar. Exclamations.*) Comrades, please be absolutely quiet.

DECLARATION BY ENVER PASHA

Comrades, on my own behalf and that of my comrades, I thank the Third International and its Presiding Committee, who have enabled us, as fighters against world imperialism and capitalism, to assemble in Baku today.

Imperialism and capitalism are not satisfied with robbing us and stripping us naked but are trying to drink our blood and destroy us. We consider ourselves fortunate, comrades, that in contrast to this, and in opposition to the lying politicians of Europe, we today stand shoulder to shoulder with a true and honest ally, the Third International.

Comrades, when Turkey entered the war, the world was divided into two camps. In one was imperialist and capitalist Russia—old tsarist Russia—and its allies, and in the other Germany, also imperialist and capitalist, with its allies. Of these two groups, we fought against tsarist Russia, Britain, and their friends, who wanted to strangle and destroy us utterly. We took the side of Germany, which at least agreed to let us live.

German imperialism used us for its bandit aims. But our desire was only to safeguard our independence.

Comrades, the sentiment that caused us to leave our comfortable life in Berlin for the burning deserts of Tripoli and the poor tents of the Bedouin, forcing us to spend there the most difficult time of our lives, was no sentiment of imperialism.[4] We were trying to save Tripoli for the Tripolitanians, and we are glad that now, after nine years of war, they have succeeded in driving out the Italian imperialists. Nor did we have any different intention where Azerbaijan was concerned. We consider that Azerbaijan belongs to the Azerbaijanis.[5] If we fell into a false situation, that was our bad luck.

During the World War, comrades, I occupied a very important post. I assure you that I regret that we were obliged to fight on the side of German imperialism. I hate and curse German imperialism and the German imperialists just as much as I hate and curse British imperialism and the British imperialists. In my view, all whose aim is to enrich those who do not work deserve to be destroyed. That is my viewpoint where imperialism is concerned.

Comrades, I assure you that if the Russia of today had been in existence then, fighting the war with its present aims, we would have been fighting on your side, just as today, with all our energy. In order to show more clearly the rightness of my thinking, I will tell you that when we decided to act together with Soviet Russia—and did so—Yudenich's army was near Petrograd, Kolchak held the Urals, and Denikin was approaching Moscow from the south. The Entente, which had set these forces in motion and regarded the game as already won, was showing its fangs and rubbing its hands with glee. That was the situation when we set out to be friends with Russia. Had the Black Sea storms not forced me back, breaking the mast of my vessel, had the bars of the prisons of Kovno and Riga and the forced landing of airplanes in which I was flying not delayed me, I would have been with you in Russia's most difficult hour, and it would not have been necessary to relate these unnecessary details in order to explain matters to certain comrades.[6]

Comrades, you know that in the imperialist conflict of this World War we were defeated. But from the standpoint of the war of the oppressed I do not regard us as having been defeated. For Turkey, due to the closing of her straits, became one of the factors that brought about the collapse of insatiable tsarist Russia and its replacement by the natural ally of all the oppressed, Soviet Russia. Thereby Turkey helped to bring about the opening of a new road for the salvation of the world. From the standpoint of the oppressed, I see this as a victory.

Comrades, as I have said, the army that is now waging a heroic struggle against imperialism—drawing its strength from the peasantry—was not defeated. It laid down its arms only temporarily. And now, after having fought against the same enemy for fifteen years, it is still fighting on, despite the greatest privations, for a second year. It is impossible to compare the present struggle with the previous one. Now that the Eastern world has come forward in alliance with the Third International, and the oppressed of the whole world support its just claims, this struggle is filled with resolute hope of victory.

Comrades, the intense phase of imperialist war began at the time of the Transvaal war,[7] and it continued from 1914 to 1917 as a conflict among imperialists, which has now ended. But at the present time this war has entered a decisive period. And it will certainly end in victory for us—that is, victory for the oppressed—and not just with imperialism and capitalism piling their arms, but with their complete destruction.

The present congress brings fresh strength to the Red Army, which is shedding its blood in defense of the oppressed, and also to the Turkish fighters. In the same way, this congress helps ensure that the struggle will end in our victory, that is, in the victory of justice.

It is not only our endeavor to find support in the struggle we have undertaken that has led us to turn to the Third International. It may be that another factor is the similarity of our principles. We have always drawn our revolutionary strength from the people, that is, from the peasants. If our factory workers had been a strong force, I would have mentioned them first. However, they too were with us. They worked with us, body and soul. That is how it is now, too. Consequently, we base ourselves upon the oppressed section of the people. We feel their pain, and we live and die along with them.

Comrades, we take account of the people's desires and stand for recognizing their right to self-determination.

We consider ourselves bound by the strongest ties for the whole of our lives to those who want to live together with us. As for those who do not want to do this, we are willing to recognize their right to decide their fate for themselves. That is our view on the national question.

Comrades, we are against war, that is, we are against people strangling each other for the sake of power. And in order to achieve permanent peace we march with the Third International. Therefore, despite all obstacles, we are now waging a bloody struggle, one that we will continue.

Comrades, we want happiness for the working people, that is, we are against speculators, whether foreign or native, profiting by the fruits of others' labor. That must be opposed without any hesitation. We want our country to enjoy the fruits of common labor through the development of agriculture and industry on a large scale. That is what we think about the economic question.

Comrades, we are convinced that only a conscious people can achieve happiness and freedom. We want sound knowledge, associated with labor and guaranteeing us genuine freedom, to bring enlightenment to our country, and in this respect we recognize no distinction between men and women. That is what we think about social policy.

Comrades, I declare to you that the Union of Revolutionary Organizations of Morocco, Algeria, Tunisia, Tripoli, Egypt, Arabia, and India, which has sent me here as its representative, is in full solidarity with you in this respect.[8] It is fully convinced that, by using all revolutionary means, it will succeed in breaking the teeth of the wild beasts and depriving them of their strength once and for all.

Comrades, the hands raised for this purpose reach out to each other. I shake the hands of all those who will work with us through to the end of this struggle, which will go on for a long time but will end in our victory. I wish them success.

Long live the alliance of the oppressed!

Down with the oppressors, who tremble before this alliance!

CHAIRMAN: I call upon Comrade Mehmet Emin to translate Enver Pasha's statement into Turkish.

(*Mehmet Emin translates.*)

CHAIRMAN: Comrade Ostrovsky will now read the statement by the representative of the Ankara government, Ibrahim Tali.

STATEMENT BY IBRAHIM TALI

World imperialism, which led Central Europe to an explosion, stretched out its hands to the vital arteries of Turkey, bringing it, in the course of four years, to a state of complete breakdown.

The Turkish peasant took up arms with no aim other than protecting his national frontiers and defending his productive forces from foreign exploitation. Believing the promises of the lying American professor [Woodrow Wilson] who said that now every people would be ensured the right to life and freedom and that all workers would be happy, he laid down his arms.

But then these arms were turned against him. All his sacred rights were beginning to be destroyed for the benefit of the Western capitalists, and they wanted to take from him his last crust of bread. On seeing this, the Turkish peasant straightaway rose up in indignation and rebelled.

Comrades, I will now explain to you the causes and factors that led to this revolt, its essential character, and how the government born of this revolt came into being. The Anatolian revolt was due to causes of two kinds, external and internal. The external ones were these. The Turkish peasant, who had been fighting for four years on more than eleven fronts against the most powerful bourgeois states, at last felt a strong desire to eat in peace the bread he had won with the sweat of his brow and to live in peace in his village. But the Western capitalists decided to send against this Turkish peasant, who had laid down his arms, the stooges in their service—from the west the Venizelist Greeks and from the east the Dashnak Armenians.

The Turkish peasant knew that the imperialists and their hirelings acted with fire, sword, and bombs wherever they went. These were robbers, a handful of whom were seizing by force the fruits of the labor of the working class. But, thinking that this monstrous decision would not be put into practice, the Turkish peasantry remained calm for a while.[9]

France, however, which had said that it was fighting for the freedom of the peoples, was not satisfied with having taken Syria and seized in addition Adana, Marash, and Yurknesh, amid conflagrations and acts of violence. At the same time, once he had made sure of the victory over our country, the French prime minister—who had said that he was acting in the interests of civilization—threw off his mask. He announced in the Palais Bourbon for all to hear: "In order to safeguard her economic interests in the East, France must have control of all the mineral resources situated in the zone extending to Mosul. And so we consider it necessary to continue our advance as far as Mardin. We must take into account the importance to French industry of the natural resources found there."

Comrades, as a result, an offensive was launched against Smyrna, our only outlet to the Mediterranean Sea. This brought about a union of the defenders of national rights, in the west and in the east, against the robbers. After the seizure of Smyrna in the east, opponents of the imperialists, that is, the population of Erzurum and Trebizond, took the initiative in convening a national assembly in Erzurum, which resolved to defend our rights. Subsequently this decision was reiterated and confirmed at congresses in Sivas and Ankara.

The internal causes were as follows. The poor peasant of Anatolia had suffered for centuries from the violence and tyranny of the bourgeoisie. He was oppressed, he was worn out by the disease that came from Stambul [Istanbul]—the bureaucracy, the dictatorship of both the sultan's government and the aristocrats, and also the parasitic officials sent to him by the government. Now a feeling of holy anger awakened in him against the aristocrats and pashas who had never spent a day of their lives with the peasant when he was working in his fields and dying of hunger. Instead, in splendid palaces and villas on the shore of the Bosporus, they had given themselves up to the vilest pleasures, consuming the results of the work of the poor class and always acting provocatively toward the peasantry. By this revolt the peasant made it clear that in the future he would give not a single crust of his bread to Stambul, its pashas and beys, and their parasitic hirelings. These, comrades, are the causes and the main features of the recent revolution in Anatolia. They show that this is not in the least a movement based on the bourgeoisie, as is supposed in the West.

The accomplices of Western capitalism in the East—the Dashnaks, the supporters of Venizelos, and also their stooges, the old courtier pashas, who used the sultan's court in the interests of British capitalism—have thrown themselves into the arms of the Entente. Speaking frankly,

I can tell you that since this development, the Anatolian revolutionaries have turned to the East, where the Red revolution has risen like the dawn. The classes whose interests are endangered by this popular movement have joined forces everywhere to strive to advance the counterrevolution. And the counterrevolutionaries—parasites who prey on the people, such as Sheikh Rejeb in Sivas, Sheikh Eshref in Bayburt, and also the Chabanoglu family (accustomed for centuries to lead a carefree, debauched life at the expense of the poor people) and likewise Yuzgada and other such persons—all these together organized revolts. In Stambul, where it seemed natural to them for the Anatolian peasant to live in slavery, they together with Anzavur Pasha set out to defend religion.[10]

Comrades, the Anatolian peasants and the revolutionaries who had been abandoned to these criminals and brigands reacted with enthusiasm and rejoicing to the international revolution, which they felt sure would bring liberation and happiness to all mankind. They are convinced that their destiny is bound up with that of the Third International.

This was confirmed by the delegation sent to Moscow by the revolutionary people's government (organized by the defenders of the people's rights following the dispersal of the parliament by the imperialists) and by the national congress. They are happy that the hand sincerely extended from Anatolia has been clasped with the same sincerity, and they are ready to utilize the social and moral results of this revolution, whose principles they consider salutary for mankind.

Comrades, it is clear from what has been said that Anatolia, in pursuit of its course of promoting enlightenment, has resolved to defend its fate and its independence to the last breath of the last of its sons. And it accepts with complete sincerity the hand of friendship extended to it by Soviet Russia.

Long live revolutionary Russia, which has set out on this road, and its backer, the revolutionary East!

ZINOVIEV: In connection with the declarations we have just heard, the Presiding Committee proposes that a resolution be adopted. The text of this resolution will be presented to you by our Hungarian comrade, Béla Kun.

BÉLA KUN: The Presiding Committee of the Congress of the Peoples of the East has unanimously resolved to present this resolution to you:

RESOLUTION

Having heard Enver Pasha's statement on the Turkish national movement, the Congress of the Peoples of the East adopts the following resolution:

1. The congress expresses its sympathy with all Turkish fighters in combat against world imperialism—the oppressor and exploiter of the Eastern peoples, which holds in slavery the working people of the entire world—and first and foremost against the British and French imperialist bandits. Like the Second Congress of the Communist International, the First Congress of the Peoples of the East declares that it will support national-revolutionary movements that seek to free the oppressed peoples of the East from the yoke of foreign imperialists.

2. However, the congress notes that the broad national-revolutionary movement in Turkey is directed only against foreign oppressors. Success for this movement would in no way signify the emancipation of the Turkish peasants and workers from oppression and exploitation of every kind. The success of this movement would not entail

resolution of the questions that are most important for the Turkish toiling classes, namely, the agrarian question and the question of taxes, and would not eliminate the principal obstacles to the liberation of the East, namely, national discords.

3. The congress finds it necessary to act with special caution toward leaders of the movement who in the past led the Turkish peasants and workers to the slaughter in the interests of one of the imperialist groups, thereby subjecting the toiling masses of Turkey to twofold ruin in the interests of a small group of rich men and high-ranking officers. The congress proposes to these leaders that they prove in deeds that they are now ready to serve the toiling people and make amends for their false steps in the past.

In calling on the toiling masses of Turkey and the entire East to support the national-revolutionary movement in Turkey, the congress urges the peasants and workers of Turkey to come together in independent organizations and to stand ready to carry the cause of emancipation through to the end. They must not allow the foreign imperialists, who are trying to hinder the work of emancipation, to make use of connections and influence among the Turkish rich—kulaks, bureaucrats, and generals (the pashas, derebeys, and so on). Only in this way can the toiling people of Turkey succeed in freeing themselves from all their oppressors and exploiters. Only then will the land, the factories, the mines, and all the country's wealth be put at the service of the toilers and the toilers alone. Only in this way.

(*Ismail Hakki translates the resolution.*)

CHAIRMAN: I now put to a vote the resolution that the Presiding Committee has unanimously recommended to you. (*Uproar. A voice: "I want to speak."*)

The Presiding Committee proposes that the vote be taken without discussion. According to the rule you should have handed up a note. (*A voice: "I did hand up a note." The vote is taken.*)

All in favor of the resolution that was read to you, please raise your hands. (*Uproar. Voices: "I handed up a note." "Let me reveal the truth."*)

Please do not make a row. There are 1,800 of us here. It is impossible to carry on like this. Please put your hands down. Who is against? Any abstentions? The resolution is adopted. (*Applause*)

Comrades, we have now completed the first two points on the agenda. We propose that the congress empower the Presiding Committee to draw up two appeals. One appeal will be addressed to the peoples of the East. On behalf of our congress, it will describe the situation in the East and the oppression to which the peoples of the East are subjected by British imperialism. This appeal will conclude with a call to a holy war of the toiling masses against the robbers of the East—the French and British imperialists. (*Loud applause. Shouts of "Hurrah!"*)

The second appeal we propose to address to the toiling masses of Europe and America, to the workers, our brothers in labor. In this we will first show, on behalf of the Congress of the Peoples of the East, how vilely the bourgeoisie of their countries have dealt with you. Finally, we will call upon them to pay attention to this situation in the East. We will call upon the British workers to support not only Soviet Russia but also the peoples of the East, oppressed by the British government. We are sure that this appeal in the name of tens of millions of toilers of the East to the workers of Britain, America, and France will be listened to and printed in workers' newspapers throughout the world. Workers around the world will understand what a tremendous duty is incumbent upon them, and they will strive to fulfill this duty to the peoples of the East. (*Applause*)

Comrades! These two appeals have been composed. In a day or two, tomorrow or the day after, proofs of them will be issued to you. These appeals will have to appear over the signatures of all the members of the Presiding Committee you have elected. (*Applause*)

(*An interpreter translates. Applause.*)

CHAIRMAN: Will all those who agree with issuing these two appeals on behalf of the congress please raise their hands. Please put your hands down. Who is against? Any abstentions? None.

Tomorrow the congress will meet at 5:00 p.m.

The next question on the agenda is the colonial-national question. At 11:00 a.m. the agrarian section is due to meet at the Army Club. If the elections have not been carried out, this will have to be seen to, and at 11:00 a.m. the agrarian section will meet at the Army Club. The congress of the peoples will reassemble at 5:00 p.m.

(*The session was closed at 11:00 p.m.*)

ADDENDUM
SPEECH BY JOHN REED

I represent here the revolutionary workers of one of the great imperialist powers, the United States of America, which exploits and oppresses the peoples of the colonies.[11]

You, the peoples of the East, the peoples of Asia, have not yet experienced for yourselves the rule of America. You know and hate the British, French, and Italian imperialists, and probably you think that "free America" will govern better, will liberate the peoples of the colonies, will feed and defend them.

No. The workers and peasants of the Philippines, the peoples of Central America and the islands of the Caribbean—they know what it means to live under the rule of "free America."

Take, for example, the peoples of the Philippines. In 1898 the Filipinos rebelled against the cruel colonial government of Spain, and the Americans helped them. But when the Spaniards had been driven out, the Americans did not want to go away.

Then the Filipinos rose against the Americans, and this time the "liberators" started to kill them, their wives, and children, torturing and eventually conquering them. They seized their land and forced them to work and make profits for American capitalists.

The Americans have promised the Filipinos independence. Soon an independent Filipino republic will be proclaimed.[12] But that does not mean that the American capitalists will leave or that the Filipinos will not continue to work to make profits for them. For the American capitalists have given the Filipino leaders a share of their profits; they have given them government jobs, land, and money. They have created a Filipino capitalist class that also lives on the profits created by the workers—and in whose interest it is to keep the Filipinos in slavery.

This has also happened in Cuba, which was freed from Spanish rule with the help of the Americans. It is now an independent republic. But American millionaire trusts own all the sugar plantations, apart from some small tracts they leave to the Cuban capitalists, who also administer the country. And the moment that the workers of Cuba try to elect a government that is not in the interests of the American capitalists, the United States of America sends soldiers into Cuba to compel the people to vote for their oppressors.[13]

Or take the example of the republics of Haiti and San Domingo [Dominican Republic], where the peoples won freedom a hundred years ago. Since this island was fertile and the people living on it could be put to use by the American capitalists, the United States government sent soldiers and sailors there on the pretext of maintaining order and smashed these two republics, setting up in their place a military dictatorship worse than that of the British tyrants.

Mexico is another rich country close to the United States. In Mexico live a backward people who were enslaved for centuries, first by the Spaniards and then by foreign capitalists. After many years of civil war, the people there formed their own government—not a proletarian government but a democratic one—which wanted to keep the wealth of Mexico for the Mexicans and tax the foreign capitalists. The American capitalists did not concern themselves with sending bread to the hungry Mexicans. No, they initiated a counterrevolution in Mexico, in which Madero, the first revolutionary president, was killed. Then, after a three-year struggle, the revolutionary regime was restored, with Carranza as president. The American capitalists made another counterrevolution and killed Carranza, establishing once more a government friendly to themselves.

In North America itself there are ten million Negroes who possess neither political nor civil rights, despite the fact that by law they are equal citizens. In order to divert the attention of American workers from the capitalists, their exploiters, these workers are incited against the Negroes, provoking war between the white and black races. The Negroes, whom they lawlessly burn alive, are beginning to see that their only hope lies in armed resistance to the white bandits.

Today the American capitalists are addressing friendly words to the peoples of the East, with a promise of aid and food. This applies especially to Armenia. Millions of dollars have been collected by the American millionaires in order to send bread to the starving Armenians. And many Armenians are now looking for help to Uncle Sam.

These same American capitalists incite the American workers and farmers against each other. They starve and exploit the peoples of Cuba and the Philippines. Savagely they kill American Negroes and burn them alive. And in America itself, American workers are obliged to work under frightful conditions, receiving low wages for a long workday. When they are exhausted and used up they are thrown out onto the street, where they die of hunger.

The very gentleman now in charge of bringing aid to the starving Armenians, Mr. Cleveland Dodge, who writes emotional articles about how the Turks have driven the Armenians into the desert, is the owner of big copper mines where thousands of American workers are exploited. When these workers dared to go on strike, the guards protecting Mr. Dodge's mines drove them at bayonet point out into the desert—just as was done to the Armenians.[14]

Many Armenians are grateful to America for its attitude to the Armenians who suffered from the brutality of the Turks during the war. But what has America done for the Armenians apart from issuing hollow declarations? Nothing. I was in Constantinople at that time, in 1915, and I know that the missionaries refused to make any serious protest against the atrocities, saying they had a lot of property in Turkey and so did not want to put pressure on the Turks. The American ambassador, Mr. Straus, himself a millionaire who exploited thousands of workers in his enterprises in America, proposed that the entire Armenian people be shipped to America. He himself donated quite a large sum for this project. But his plan was to make the Armenians work in American factories and provide cheap labor so as to increase the profits of Mr. Straus and his friends.

But why do the American capitalists promise aid and food to Armenia? Is it out of pure philanthropy? If so, let them feed the peoples of Central America and help the Negroes of America itself.

No. The main reason is that there is mineral wealth in Armenia, and that it is a big reservoir of cheap labor for exploitation by American capitalists.

The American capitalists want to win the confidence of the Armenians with a view to getting their claws into Armenia and enslaving the Armenian nation. It is with that aim that American missionaries have established schools in the Near East.

But there is also another very important reason. Together with the other capitalist nations, united in the League of Nations, the American capitalists are afraid that the workers and peasants of Armenia will follow the example of Soviet Russia and Soviet Azerbaijan—take power, take their country's resources into their own hands, and work for themselves, making a united front with workers and peasants around the world against world imperialism. The American capitalists are afraid of a revolution in the East.

Promise food to starving peoples while organizing a blockade of the Soviet republics—that is the policy of the United States. The blockade of Soviet Russia has starved to death thousands of Russian women and children. This method of blockade was applied with the goal of turning the Hungarian people against their Soviet government. The same tactic is now being used with the goal of drawing the people of White Hungary into war against Soviet Russia. This method is also being used on the small countries bordering Russia—Finland, Estonia, Latvia. But now all these small countries have been obliged to make peace with Soviet Russia—they are bankrupt and starving. Now the American government no longer offers them food; they are no longer of any use to America, and so their peoples can starve.

The American capitalists promise bread to Armenia. This is an old trick. They promise bread but never give it. Did Hungary get bread after the fall of the Soviet government? No. The Hungarian people are still starving today. Did the Baltic countries get bread? No. When the starving Estonians had nothing but potatoes, the American capitalists sent them ships laden with rotten potatoes that could not be sold at a profit in America. No, comrades, Uncle Sam never gives anybody something for nothing. He comes along with a sack stuffed with hay in one hand and a whip in the other. Anyone who accepts Uncle Sam's promises at their face value will find that they must be paid for in sweat and blood.

American workers are demanding an ever larger share of the product of their labor. With a view to preventing revolution at home, the American capitalists are forced to seek out colonial peoples to exploit, peoples who will furnish sufficient profits to keep the American workers in obedience and so make them participants in the exploitation of the Armenians. I represent thousands of revolutionary American workers who know this. They understand that, acting together with the Armenian workers and peasants, with the toiling masses around the world, they will overthrow capitalism. World capitalism will be destroyed, and all the peoples will be free.

We appreciate the need for solidarity among all oppressed and toiling peoples, for unity of the revolutionary workers of all the countries of Europe and America under the leadership of the Russian Bolsheviks, in the Communist International. And we say to you, peoples of the East: Do not believe the promises of the American capitalists!

There is only one road to freedom. Unite with the Russian workers and peasants who have overthrown their capitalists and whose Red Army has beaten the foreign imperialists! Follow the red star of the Communist International!

SESSION 5
SEPTEMBER 5, 1920

National and colonial questions

(*The session began at 7:15 p.m. Comrade Zinoviev took the chair.*)

CHAIRMAN: I declare the fifth session of the Congress of the Peoples of the East open. The Presiding Committee proposes that we now deal with the national and colonial questions. Comrade Pavlovich will give the report.

PAVLOVICH: Comrades, questions of colonial and national policy have played a very big part in world history. The last World War was the result of a clash between great world powers in their attempts to gain possession of the black and, above all, the yellow continents. On the eve of the war I formulated the essence of the colonial conflicts between the European powers when I said that these rivalries could be reduced to the conflicts between three groups of letters: B-B-B, C-C-C, and P-P.

Germany was advancing a project for a great Berlin-Byzantium [Istanbul]-Baghdad railway, which was to bind to the German Empire with a steel chain the whole of the

Ottoman Empire, and especially Asia Minor. Through the latter it was to open a road for German imperialism to Persia, India, Egypt—that is, a road to mastery of the black and yellow continents.

To Germany's three Bs, Britain counterposed three Cs: Cape Town-Cairo-Calcutta—a railway that was to unite into one the whole of East Africa from south to north, and then Arabia, Mesopotamia, southern Persia, and India. Against these two projects, Russia put forward its own project of Petersburg to the Persian Gulf. In all of these schemes we see the struggle between the world powers for the mastery of Asia and Africa.

Such questions, which focus mainly on colonial policy, brought about the World War of 1914–18. They now threaten to give rise to armed conflict between the allies of yesterday: America and Japan, America and Britain, and finally, Britain and France.

Revelations in the French press linked to the Senate debates on Clemenceau's resignation show that at the most critical moment of the war with the Triple Alliance, Britain and France were preparing to tear each other's throats out over the division of Asia Minor. Clemenceau had to give up his post in connection with very serious clashes with Britain over Syria.[1] Today relations between France and Britain are extremely strained. Except for fear of Soviet Russia and Bolshevism, we must assume, the World War of 1914–18 would long since have been transformed into a war to the death between the victor powers, as happened with the first Balkan War.[2]

Armed conflict between France and Britain, Britain and America, or America and Japan is not at all out of the question, so long as the fate of the peoples rests in the hands of the bourgeoisie. America and Japan confront each other, armed to the teeth, over the question of hegemony in the Far East. America is expanding its navy with feverish speed, setting the goal of possessing by 1925 a navy equal in strength to that of Britain, the mistress of the seas. It is doing this to deprive Britain of maritime hegemony and strengthen U.S. influence in the East. Britain is taking all possible measures against a strengthening of the maritime power of France, not allowing France to add to its navy the submarines captured from Germany. It is doing this because of the danger that in the event of an armed conflict, France—given its excellent naval bases on the Mediterranean—would be able to, if not completely sever, then at least gravely hamper Britain's communications through this great sea road with Egypt, Asia Minor, the Persian Gulf, India—in short, with the East.

This colonial question, the question of the partition of Asia, is the mainspring of the bitter war that the capitalist world has been waging against Soviet Russia since the first day of the October revolution. Russia alarms the countries of the capitalist world as a beacon, a guiding star, summoning all people of courage to the struggle for a new order. It alarms them because of its many millions of inhabitants and its extraordinary wealth in natural endowments and sources of raw material and because it is no longer content to remain, as under the tsars, a semicolony of Anglo-Franco-Belgian capital. Even beyond this, Soviet Russia also inspires fear and dread in world imperialism as a colony that has freed itself from foreign oppression. By its very example it summons the enslaved East to fight for freedom. Its whole internal policy toward the backward nations contributes to the awakening and development in the East of a striving for national self-determination. And not only this, for it also renders real aid to the backward and oppressed peoples living outside the borders of Russia in their struggle against rapacious international capital. (*Applause*)

One of the nonparty comrades expressed his admiration for the leaders of the Communist Party, Comrades Lenin, Zinoviev, and Trotsky, emphasizing the unbounded confidence placed in these highest representatives and leaders of the Soviet government by all the nationalities inhabiting Russia. He mentioned with bitterness that some representatives of the Communist Party, pseudo-Communists, as he called them, behave in the borderlands otherwise than as they should, discrediting the Soviet power and by their conduct inciting the native population against the very idea of Soviet power.

We are aware of this. All this is possible, or rather, it is inevitable. In the storm and stress of mighty historical events, a social order has collapsed that stood for entire millennia. This involves the abolition of such institutions as capitalist property, which has for many centuries been sinking deep roots in the soil of society. It is natural that this, which one might call a geological revolution—the transition to a new form of life—cannot take place painlessly, without unavoidable deformities and deviations, which bear only a temporary character and are of only transitory significance. But the essence of the matter consists not in the abuses committed by some unworthy individual representatives of the Soviet government and the Communist Party. The essence of the matter consists in the general direction, the basic tendency of Soviet policy in relation to the particular nations that inhabit the territory of the former tsarist empire.

The capitalist world understands very well what this general tendency of Soviet policy is in relation to the nations formerly oppressed by tsarism and now oppressed by the whole capitalist world. The fact that the capitalist powers understand our policy so well is precisely why, in the interests of safeguarding their rule over the peoples they exploit, they have declared a war to the death against Soviet Russia. (*Applause*)

Who cannot see the difference between our workers' and peasants' socialist federation and the brigand capitalist empires? The "free constitution" of Britain holds the 300 million people of India, who have for so long groaned under the British yoke, in harsh slavery, strangling them. Republican France cruelly suppresses the slightest manifestation of desire for freedom and national self-determination in Morocco, in Algeria, in Indochina, in all its colonies. The great transatlantic republic, the United States, still refuses to recognize the independence of Cuba and the Philippines, for whose supposed liberation the war against Spain was launched in 1898.

At the same time the government and the worker and peasant masses of the Russian Socialist Federated Republic joyfully greet the formation of the autonomous Bashkir Soviet Republic, the autonomous Tatar Socialist Soviet Republic, and so forth, on the borders of the former tsarist empire—where, as in all capitalist countries, every striving for national self-determination was stifled and suppressed.

In all capitalist states without exception, both large and small—in France, Britain, Japan, America, Holland, Belgium, Poland, and the rest—we see the use of crude violence against national minorities. Sometimes we see the transformation into nations of slaves and serfs of huge communities of hundreds of millions of people who have fallen under the rule of a more organized, more "civilized" minority, as in the case of the enslaved 300 millions of India, ruled by capitalist Britain, armed to the teeth.

At one pole, in the capitalist countries, there is savage suppression of national minorities—and sometimes of national majorities too, where a national minority holds the reins of government. At the other pole, in the republic of soviets, the most attentive, most fraternal feeling and attitude is shown toward not only more or less substantial national entities but even the very smallest of them.

Under the first Ukrainian People's Republic it was the Austro-German imperialists and General Skoropadsky who ruled in Ukraine. That was the time when, by agreement with the Germans and Austrians, Petlyura's Ukraine was obliged to supply Austria and Germany with 75 million poods [1.3 million tons] of grain, 11 million poods [200,000 tons] of cattle on the hoof, and so on.

Under the second Ukrainian People's Republic, Ukraine was a colony of French capital, in line with the agreement that the mercenary Petlyura signed in Odessa with the French general D'Anselme. By this agreement nearly all Ukraine's railways and financial and military enterprises were handed over to the French stockbrokers.

The third Ukrainian People's Republic, promised by the same Petlyura, was merely a screen for the establishment in Ukraine of the hated evil rule of the Polish gentry.[3]

The entire history of Ukraine cries out against this fresh act of betrayal by Petlyura. That history is one of heroic exploits and great defeats of the Ukrainian peasantry, the Ukrainian "cattle," in a struggle many centuries long against the Polish gentry. The whole history of the Poland of the gentry, on the other hand, is but a long series of wars against Ukraine aimed at enslaving it. Ukrainian literature—the immortal works of Shevchenko, Ukrainian folk-poetry—reflect this page of the long-suffering history of the Ukrainian people, whose entire development proceeded through bloody struggle against the Polish lords. All the cossack revolts, the whole struggle of the Zaporozhian Camp, of Bogdan Khmelnitsky, were fundamentally a fight of the Ukrainian peasants against the yoke of the Polish landowners, against the Polonizers, the enemies of the Ukrainian national language and Ukrainian culture.[4]

And Petlyura, condottiere and hired bandit, offered his bloody services to anyone who would agree to pay him well. He wanted to surrender the Ukrainian land, the Ukrainian language, all Ukrainian culture, to the Polish gendarme, to the insolent Polonizers. They closed Belorussian schools, for example, and proclaimed Polish the state language even in the regions where Poles made up only an insignificant percentage of the population. The Polish gentry, the Polish *Kulturträger*, are already trying to Polonize Belorussia [Belarus], Volhynia, and Podolia, and intend to do the same in all the regions of Ukraine that they manage to conquer.

Tens of hundreds of honest Ukrainians who sincerely desire the national and cultural rebirth of Ukraine, including such pillars of Ukrainian national public opinion as Hrushevsky and Vinnichenko, have become convinced that only Soviet power can now fulfill to the end the role of liberator of Ukraine from all forms of oppression.

On May 27 the Presiding Committee of the All-Russia Central Executive Committee confirmed the decision to establish an autonomous Tatar Socialist Soviet Republic with the city of Kazan as its center. This news evoked a mighty echo throughout the many-millioned Muslim world, in Persia, Afghanistan, Turkey, and India. In the eyes of our Muslim brothers, the workers and peasants of the East, it was a fresh example of the great principles that underlie the national policy of the Russian federated republic. But this is not to the liking of the capitalist governments.

Let two or three decades pass. Let popular education spread in the republic of soviets, including the opening of thousands and thousands of schools, evening courses, academies, etc., including the complete ending of illiteracy in Russia and Ukraine. Alongside the wonderful old monuments of Russian and Ukrainian literature, such as the works of Pushkin, Lermontov, Tolstoy, Gogol, and Shevchenko, we will see great new works appear, composed by brilliant new poets, men of letters, etc., arising from the ranks of the workers and peasants. Tatar, Bashkir, Kirghiz, and other poetry and literature, only now awakening to life, will flourish luxuriantly. All the separate streams, tributaries, rivulets, and great rivers will intermingle in a fantastic and harmonious way, merging and feeding with their living waters one common international ocean of the poetry and learning of toiling humanity, freed for the first time from national and class oppression. This will shine with such unprecedented, incomparable beauty as neither classical Greece, with all its amazing works of art, nor the civilization of the medieval and capitalist epochs, with all their blazing galaxy of immortal poets, artists, thinkers, and scholars, could give the world.

Yes, all this will be! But before we reach this wished-for future, much blood will flow. Many thousands of fighters for the new order will fall beneath the enemy's blows upon the battlefields. Many tens and hundreds of thousands of women and children will die from hunger and cold in their homes or beside ruined auls [villages]. All this is inevitable, alas, and it is not of our making. It results from the criminal will of the capitalists, who do not want to give up their profits. But all fighters for a better future have to suffer in this way, and not merely the representatives of the small nations, not only the population of the borderlands. Come and see what is happening in Petrograd, Moscow, Tula, in a great number of our cities. Because of the criminal blockade and the bloody war that was forced upon us, hundreds of thousands of workers in these cities are faint from hunger and cold. Yet they have not lost heart, but march off in their thousands to the front, to lay down their lives for Soviet power. (*Applause*) They know, these heroes, that they will not die in vain, for they give their blood for their comrades' happiness, for a better future for their children and the generations to come.

The war against Soviet Russia is a war against the East.

In the giant struggle we have begun, the peoples of the East will henceforth be our loyal allies. For a war against Soviet Russia is a war against the revolutionary East, and, vice versa, a war against the East is a war against Soviet Russia. (*Applause*)

Why are Britain and France so interested in supporting Wrangel? As long as Wrangel, the White, holds the Crimea, the rear of revolutionary Turkey is cut off and Soviet Russia cannot bring aid to the Turkish revolutionaries. On the other hand, as long as Asia Minor is occupied by the Allies, by their expeditionary forces, our rear is threatened. The Greek occupation of Thrace and Adrianople [Edirne] is aimed at isolating revolutionary Turkey and Soviet Russia from the revolutionary Balkans. Finally, European imperialism is supporting Dashnak Armenia and Menshevik Georgia with arms, money, and bread, in order to maintain these countries as a barrier separating revolutionary Russia and Caucasia from revolutionary Turkey, Persia, and India. Everywhere imperialism is raising up these artificial barriers against us, but they will all collapse under the blows of the masses in the Crimea, Georgia, Armenia, Thrace, and Greece. Just as the Polish mad dog was unleashed against Soviet Russia, the Greece of Venizelos was let loose on revolutionary Turkey. And now we read in Greek papers that have reached here that an attempt has been made on Venizelos's life and he has been wounded with seven bullets.

Who made this attempt? Turks, Bulgars, Russians? No, two Greeks! (*Applause*)

Does not this act show that in Greece itself, transformed from a poor country of four million people into a big military power with a population of twelve million, discontent is growing against the imperialist policy of Venizelos, which is shoving the country toward the abyss of ultimate ruin? Capitalism is digging its own grave, but in order to hasten its death the peoples of the East, shoulder to shoulder with Soviet Russia, must strike the final blows at the world bourgeoisie. The revolutionary East must conclude a close alliance with Soviet Russia. The transitional form to complete union of the toiling masses is a federation of Soviet states.

In their appeal to Soviet Russia, the Turkish comrades expressed the view that the question of the Dardanelles should be decided by the states bordering on the Black Sea, excluding participation by Wrangel and the Entente. We warmly welcome this idea, the realization of which would be a first and decisive step toward a federation of all the peoples and countries whose territories adjoin the Black Sea. (*Applause*)

In one of his articles defending the Poland of the gentry that has attacked Soviet Russia, the renegade Hervé, howled, "If the first line of defense that European civilization established against Asiatic barbarism by creating Poland is broken, the governments of Europe will have to concentrate all their forces on the second and last defense line, running close to Paris, Brussels, and London, along the Rhine—in order to protect European civilization from the invasion of Asiatic cholera, yellow plague, vodka-inflamed savagery, and fanaticism that is advancing, in the shape of the Red Army, upon the whole civilized world."

The Russian Communists are proud of all these attacks made against them. One of the fundamental features of the Third International is that it sides with the revolutionary movement of the oppressed peoples not in words but in deeds, and makes it a duty for the Communist parties of all countries, especially the oppressor countries, to give most active aid to the national-revolutionary movement in the more backward states and nations. (*Applause*)

The leader of the Georgian Mensheviks, Zhordania, counterposes to the Bolsheviks' "Asiatic" policy the so-called European line of the Mensheviks. The Mensheviks, he says, are European Socialists. We, says Zhordania of himself and his friends, are bearers of culture and civilization, whereas Muscovy means Asia with its inertia born of fanaticism.

We can now reply to Zhordania that the entire Third International today shares the viewpoint of the Bolsheviks. All Communists—Russian, French, British, Italian, and so on—have now become Asians and are resolved to help every revolutionary movement in the East and in Africa. When a decision is taken in Britain regarding Persia, India, or Asia Minor, or merely affecting one province of Turkey, or when what is involved is Anatolia, Syria, or Arabia, workers know that this directly affects the fate of the Italian, British, American, and the whole worldwide working-class movement. All such questions call for their immediate intervention and action.

The French, British, and Italian workers who march under the banner of communism must not allow European troops to be sent to Anatolia, Syria, Mesopotamia, Constantinople, etc. And we can hope that the day is not far off when the whole international proletariat will fight as vigorously against the strangling of the East as it is now fighting against the strangling and blockading of Soviet Russia. (*Applause*) The Third International, that is, the

Communists of the entire world, take as their basic task to explain this simple truth: so long as the yellow and black continents are oppressed, so long as European mercenaries are killing Turks, Persians, Arabs, Egyptians, and others, the European worker will be unable to cast off his own chains and will remain a slave of the capitalist. For this reason the Third International calls on the European workers to fight for the liberation of the East.

This is not the attitude to the colonial question taken by the Second International; this is not the current line of action of the Yellow traitor International headed by Kautsky, Renaudel, Vandervelde, and other agents of imperialism.

By its very nature, that International was incapable of supporting the revolutionary movement among the oppressed peoples in Morocco, Algeria, Tunisia, Asia Minor, Persia, India, Egypt, and so forth. Even less was it capable of taking the initiative in bringing revolution to the black and yellow continents, or even simply in making propaganda for ideas of liberation among the suffering masses of Asia and Africa. The Second International did not and does not want to know the East from that angle.

Of course, the leaders of the Second International have allowed themselves to condemn, in words, the colonial policy of their governments. Sometimes they even publish books and pamphlets on these themes in Paris, London, or Berlin—such as the book by Charles Dumas.[5] But these gentlemen have not translated their books and pamphlets into the indigenous languages. They have written on colonial matters merely to attract attention in the metropolitan countries, either in parliamentary circles generally or in the Socialist parties in particular. In fact all these fervent defenders of the natives support the colonial policies of their governments.

When the news was received of the pogroms against the Armenians in Turkey, the European Socialists eagerly organized demonstrations and big meetings to protest against the bloody sultan. But when the French government, year after year, sent ever-increasing numbers of troops to Morocco and massacred Muslim tribesmen, the Socialists remained silent, as they did also in relation to the cruelties committed in India, the strangling of Persia, the enslavement of Egypt, and the mass exterminations and bloody orgies carried out by the British troops on the black continent.

Moreover, there were Socialists such as Lagrosillière, party members, delegates to all manner of Socialist congresses, national and international, who openly defended colonial policy, justifying it by the need to bring the natives the blessings of civilization and progress.

The Second International did not want to know about the East, was not interested in the fate of the peoples of the black and yellow continents. True, when the news came about the anti-Armenian pogroms in Turkey, the whole press of the Second International printed indignant articles in favor of the Armenians and impressive demonstrations were held. But all this was done merely for the benefit of the capitalist governments, who obtained a fresh excuse for interfering in Turkish affairs. The Socialists had one attitude to the anti-Armenian pogroms and another to the pogroms, slaughter, and extermination of the native population in Morocco, Algeria, India, etc.

We condemn anti-Armenian pogroms and will fight against them. But at the same time we make it a duty of members of the Third International, representatives of the French and British parties, to fight with all their power, not just in words but in deeds, against colonial policy generally, against the oppression and extermination of the inhabitants of Morocco, India, Indochina, Algeria, and Turkestan.

The best illustration of the Second International's policy on the colonial question is the fact that at their congress in Geneva not a single word was uttered about the East.[6]

As Comrade Zinoviev showed you, the World War has resulted in the whole world being divided into two groups of nations, with a small group of privileged, exploiting nations with full rights, numbering a quarter of a billion people, separated off from the rest.

As a consequence of this state of affairs, class contradictions have been still further intensified throughout the world, both in the metropolitan countries and in the colonies.

Poverty has been enormously intensified among the population of the victor countries. The value of money has fallen; goods have become more expensive; the productivity of labor has declined. Britain, France, even America, are going through a profound economic crisis. In America two thousand strikes broke out in one month alone. Throughout the capitalist world the workers are not what they were before. Bourgeois economists complain that the proletariat has been engulfed by a wave of laziness and work-shyness, that the working class is suffering from a paralysis of the will. Yes, in a certain sense that is true. The European worker is already psychologically incapable of working for the capitalist as he used to. He is willing to suffer and undergo torments, like the Russian worker, for his own interests, for the interests of his own class, but not for the sake of the dividends and profits of the exploiting class. (*Applause*)

And so we come to the recent efforts directed at intensified exploitation of black and yellow labor. But the East does not want to be a means of enrichment for the capitalists of Europe. Not only does it not want to be exploited more than before; it does not want to be an object of exploitation at all. (*Applause*) The East is no longer what it used to be, either economically or spiritually.

In some Eastern countries (India, for example) during recent decades and especially during the World War, when the metropolis was unable to cope with the demands of the army and navy, a fairly well-developed industry came into existence. In sugar production India holds a very prominent place on the world market—3 million tons, out of the world's production of 16 million. The tobacco, tea, and jute industries and the textile industry in general are strongly developed in India. All together, there are about 15 million factory workers and weavers in the country. In terms of the length of its railway network India holds fourth place in the world, surpassed only by the United States, Germany, and Russia. Consequently, there is a sizable railway proletariat in India.

Alongside this development of industry in India and some parts of China, we see a more extreme intensification of poverty and of class contradictions throughout the East. In India, China, Persia, Bukhara, and elsewhere, the rich have become still richer and the poor still poorer.

In Bukhara the peasants (dehkhans) drag out a very miserable existence. Their situation recalls the dark days of serfdom. They are robbed by everyone, from the mirza to the emir, and in recent years the burden of taxation in Bukhara has grown markedly heavier. Not long ago, fifty dehkhans sold all their cattle and farm implements in order to pay their taxes. Many sold their houses and their plots of land. Cotton is sown only by the rich, and owing to their lack of seed the poor peasants have this year sown only one-tenth of the area they sowed previously.

In Persia all the peasants are landless and all the land belongs to two or three thousand big landowners (molkdars).

Many have claimed that the Eastern peoples must necessarily pass through the stage of capitalism before reaching communism. The Third International has come to the conclusion—through the debates at its Second Congress—that, with the aid of the advanced proletarian countries, the backward peoples can go over to the Soviet system and proceed through a certain stage to communism, missing out the capitalist phase of development. (*Applause*)

The popular masses of the East are not as well educated as the working masses of the West. But in the East, people's hearts, awakened by the thunder of the revolutionary events in Russia, are filled with self-sacrificing zeal and burn with a bright fire of hatred for the oppressors, a sacred fire of struggle.

The entire East is saturated with the bacteria of revolution. Millions of the suffering masses of the East are gripped by the spirit of protest and are straining to go into battle.

If we introduce into this compound—densely saturated with revolutionary bacteria—a crystal in the form of peasant soviets, soviets of the toilers, the resulting crystallization will proceed with rapid strides. We will significantly advance the cause of the revolutionary education and organization of the masses of the East in the struggle against the world of the exploiters, the struggle for a new social order. (*Applause*)

The idea of soviet organization, as Comrade Lenin has rightly said, can be applied not only to proletarian but also to feudal and semifeudal relations. Peasant soviets, toilers' soviets, are a means appropriate not only for capitalist countries but also for countries where precapitalist relations prevail.

Formation of such soviets facilitates the struggle of the toiling masses both against their own exploiters—the landlords, capitalists, and speculators—and world imperialism, which finds its agents and accomplices in all these molkdars, zamindars, khans, beys, pashas, and the like. (*Applause*)

The working masses of the East must rise up against their enemies, both internal and external. But the Eastern peoples cannot liberate themselves from the yoke of the aggressors by their own strength, without the help of the revolutionary world proletariat.

The Russian revolution of 1905 and the Persian, Turkish, and Chinese revolutions of 1908–10 were suppressed by the power of international capitalism.[7] The Russian revolution of 1905 was overcome thanks to the French Bourse, which supplied the tsar with billions of francs. Soviet Russia, on the other hand, defended itself victoriously against the onslaught of world imperialism. This history shows, at one and the same time, all the difficulties of the struggle against world capitalism and also the conditions required for victory over it.

Comrades, we must not lose sight of the simple truth that the peoples of the East will not achieve their freedom unless they unite with the proletariat of all countries. Britain, a mighty military and economic organism against which we are beginning a decisive war with our joint efforts, can be overcome only with the cooperation of the British proletariat itself.

What makes Soviet Russia strong in its struggle against the capitalist powers? How is it possible that this country, shackled by hunger and cold, blockaded on all sides, has for three years sustained a war against the most powerful states in the world? The answer is that a considerable part of the British, Spanish, French, and Italian proletariat—its best forces, whose representatives you see here—is with us, refusing to help its capitalist governments strangle Soviet Russia.

The source of Soviet Russia's might is the sympathy of the international proletariat. And what is the reason for this sympathy? The fact that Russia is the land of the proletariat, the land of Soviet power. The European governments are no longer able to send their own troops against Russia and have to hire mercenaries in the shape of the Polish landlords, the Czechoslovaks, and so on.

If the Eastern peoples want to benefit from the sympathy of the international proletariat, they too must fight for Soviet power, for the principles proclaimed by Soviet Russia.

If the capitalist states, which have millions of men under arms, are not in a position to dispatch troops against Russia, it is because of the European workers. For them, fighting against Soviet Russia means fighting against the proletariat not only of Russia but also of their own countries. From the standpoint of the French and British workers, fighting against Russia means committing class suicide. (*Applause*)

But the same British workers who organize Councils of Action to oppose their own government in its fight against Soviet Russia react very feebly to the events in Ireland, where a war to the death for national self-determination is being waged against the British bourgeoisie.

At best the rank-and-file British worker feels only sympathy with the Irish in their hard fight for self-determination. The Irish epic does not kindle enthusiasm in the breast of the British, French, and Italian proletariat. It does not touch the same strings that are plucked by the gigantic struggle of the Russian people against world imperialism.

Indeed, suppose the Irish separatists succeed in their aim and realize their cherished ideal of an independent Irish people. The very next day, independent Ireland would fall under the yoke of American capital or of the French

Bourse. Perhaps within a year or two Ireland would be fighting against Britain or some other states in alliance with one of the world predators—for markets, for coal mines, for iron mines, for bits of territory in Africa. And once again hundreds of thousands of British, Irish, American, and other workers would die in this war.

Take the example of Poland, whose bourgeois and landlord representatives bewailed for decades, up and down the scale, the partition of the old *rzeczpospolita* [republic],[8] writing ardent articles about respect for the national rights of peoples. Take this bourgeois Poland, which is now acting as hangman toward the national minorities on its own territory and serving as the gendarme of international capitalism in the struggle against the workers and peasants of Russia. Or take the example of the Balkan states—Bulgaria, Serbia, Montenegro, Greece—squabbling among themselves over division of the booty and over their desire to annex to their own territory some nation that was only yesterday under the Turkish yoke. A large number of other facts of this type show that the formation of national states in the East, in which power has passed from the foreign rulers, who have been driven out, into the hands of the local capitalists and landlords, does not in itself constitute a great step forward in improving the lot of the popular masses.

Within the framework of the capitalist system, any newly formed state that does not express the interests of the toiling masses but serves the interests of the bourgeoisie is a new instrument of oppression and coercion, a new factor of war and violence.

If the struggle in Persia, India, and Turkey were merely to bring to power the capitalists and landlords of those countries, with their national parliaments and senates, the masses of the people would have gained nothing.

Every newly formed state would be rapidly drawn, by the very course of events and the iron logic of the laws of capitalist economy, into the vicious circle of militarism and imperialist politics. After a few decades we would witness another world war, the horrors of which would make the war of 1914–18 pale into insignificance. For not tens but hundreds of millions of soldiers from the black, yellow, and white continents would take part in it, armed to the teeth, in yet another war for the interests of the French, German, British, Indian, Chinese, Persian, and Turkish bankers and factory owners. (*Applause*)

What will be the result of the formation of a reborn, powerful Turkey, if power remains in the hands of the rich, the speculators, and the landlords? The examples provided by the recent past—the warlike policy of Enver's Turkey and the behavior of newly free and independent bourgeois states such as Georgia and Armenia—provide abundant illustrations of what I have said.

The Turkey of Enver Pasha made an alliance with the Germany of the same Wilhelm who proclaimed the need for a union of all the Western peoples for war against the East. The behavior of the Turkish representatives at the Brest conference was disgraceful. Yet the Turkish nationalists were not content with the conditions of the monstrous Brest peace. Turkey seized Ardahan, Kars, and Batum [Batumi]. Moreover, the Turkish forces advanced still further and seized Akhaltsikhe and Alexandropol [Gyumri]. Georgia was spared only through the intervention of Germany. Then the Turks threw themselves upon Azerbaijan and seized Baku. The two-month rule of the Turks in Baku was the blackest page in the history of that long-suffering city, the stronghold of the proletariat in Caucasia.

The Georgia of Noe Ramishvili and Zhordania is ravaging and plundering Southern Ossetia, razing its auls to the ground, and terrorizing the population, forcing them to flee into Soviet Russia. Georgian punitive expeditions under the command of the monarchist Colonel Tukhareli are burning entire villages in Abkhazia. Georgia lays claim to Azerbaijani territory, and in 1918 it began a war with Armenia that was stopped only by the intervention of Britain.

Armenia claims Karabakh and Zangezur (the secret letter of General Dro about the occupation of these territories, dated August 4, 1920, has become well known).[9] Furthermore, the Georgian imperialists have put forward truly megalomaniac plans for the annexation of Van, Trebizond [Trabzon], Bitlis, Erzurum, and Diyarbakir, with outlets to the sea. Armenia wants to become a great Mediterranean power, ruling over territories in which Armenians constitute at most 50 percent of the population. The Armenian papers invite the Greece of Venizelos to occupy Trebizond—an utter provocation.

The masses must rise up against their enslavers, both native and foreign. If the national-revolutionary movement leads merely to the formation of new, powerful, Eastern states in which the local bourgeoisie rules, with Indian, Persian, and other parliaments, within decades we will see another frightful world war, in comparison with which all the horrors of the war of 1914–18 will seem trivial.

From all this we may draw the following conclusions. The Communist International recognizes no colonial policy of any sort. The peoples of the East will take this proposition of the Third International and put it into effect by force of arms. There must be no colonies. All nations have equal rights. Out with the British aggressors from India, Egypt, Persia, and Mesopotamia! Out with the French bandits from Syria, and with the Greek bandits from Cilicia, Smyrna, and the rest!

The peoples of the East will brand the Second International with shame and will join with the Third International in saying: "Traitors, renegades, hirelings of capital, get out of the ranks of the International!"

Up to now, the entire world has been divided into two groups of nations—the oppressors and the oppressed. This fact is due, first, to the crude violence of the bourgeois governments, which have put down with fire and sword any manifestation of striving for national self-determination; second, to dissension among the toiling masses of the East; and, third, to the traitorous, rapacious conduct of the native rich, the landlords, of whom there are plenty in any Eastern country. All these Moroccan, Algerian, Persian, Turkish, Indian, and Bukharan rich men and landowners—mulaygafis, hajis, pashas, beys, mirzas, emirs, shahs, khans, maharajas, molkdars, zamindars—are agents of international imperialism, supporting the power of foreign capitalists, of the world bourgeoisie.

The revolutionary national movement will improve the position of the masses of the people only if it constitutes a decisive stage toward a profound and far-reaching socialist movement.

The main guarantee of victory for the Eastern peoples in the struggle against the monster of world imperialism—a fire-breathing dragon compared with which all the fantastic, fabulous creatures of terror created by folk imagination seem but wretched pygmies and dwarfs—is unity of the toiling masses not only of the entire East but also of the West. This war can end successfully only if it is waged on both fronts—against foreign capital and against one's own bourgeoisie.

For the revolutionary masses of the East to fulfill this condition, they must organize around peasant soviets, soviets of the working people.

The Eastern masses can win victory in the freedom struggle only through a rapprochement with the working masses of the West. How can this rapprochement be hastened? The first step toward it must be a close alliance between all the peoples of the East and Soviet Russia, which is seen by the entire international proletariat as the advance guard, the pioneer of the world revolution. The transitional form to full unity of the toiling masses of different nations is a federation of Soviet states of the East for struggle against both the plans of conquest of the imperialist powers and the machinations of internal enemies.

Accordingly, in order to end the fratricidal war between Georgian, Armenian, and Turkish workers and peasants it is necessary, first and foremost, to establish Soviet power in all these countries, and then to form a federation of the peoples who inhabit them. In order to settle the question of the Dardanelles it is necessary to form a Black Sea federation. The principle of federation has shown its viability in external relations through the example of the former Red Hungary, of Ukraine, and so on, and in internal policy in connection with the Tatar and Bashkir republics.[10]

Only the dictatorship of the proletariat and of the working masses in general, who have won liberation from foreign oppression and overthrown capital completely, will provide the backward countries with a guarantee that they will not become new instruments for war, plunder, and coercion, as have the states formed from fragments of the Austro-Hungarian empire and tsarist Russia—Poland, White Hungary, Czechoslovakia, Georgia, Armenia—or from fragments of Turkey—Venizelist Greece and the rest.

Only if labor triumphs completely over capital and reduces it to dust will peace between the toilers of all countries be guaranteed.

Arise, peoples of the East! The Third International summons you to a holy war against capitalist vultures. Comrade delegates, develop the class consciousness of the popular masses, organize them around peasant soviets, soviets of the toilers, summon all the toilers to ally themselves with Soviet Russia, propagate the idea of a federation of oppressed nations, and, finally, create a union of the proletarians and peasants of all countries, religions, and languages.

By the united efforts of the working people of all lands, we must put an end to world imperialism and the coercion of one nation by another. We must put an end to the colonial politics of the capitalist powers and enable all countries to live in freedom and independence.

For this we must take the revolutionary road and prepare for the decisive battle, prepare the masses for immediate armed offensive, in serried ranks and close columns. Make haste, for the revolution cannot be postponed! Delay means death! (*Applause*)

Otherwise, economic ruin will spread, the economic abyss will become wider and deeper, want will increase, decay will be intensified.

For six years now the bourgeoisie has been occupied exclusively with war and plunder. Transformed into a highway robber, it will not cease from this work of destruction. There was a time when the bourgeoisie, in spite of everything, carried mankind forward, at least as regards industrial progress and the growth of the productive forces. Now it is taking mankind backward in every field, pushing it toward final destruction.

Postwar capitalism has all the robber habits of the newly rich upstart, while at the same time it shivers with the feverish fits and spasms of an organism undermined by every sort of excess and standing on the brink of death. Even the most moderate and recently peace-loving bourgeois of the prewar epoch are poisoned by all the miasmas that teem in the atmosphere of imaginary wealth and merely outward-seeming prosperity, and tremble before the specter of imminent bankruptcy that rises up at every moment. Is it surprising that they have literally lost their heads and have become transformed into raging beasts, capable only of hurling themselves upon the creatures around them, biting and tearing them to pieces?

The world bourgeoisie, like a badly wounded beast, is thrashing about in convulsions, in fury, striking blows with its teeth and claws not only at living creatures but at whatever inanimate objects it can reach in its convulsive leaps.

This badly wounded beast must not be allowed to recover. The working masses of the East must rise as one man and, in alliance with the proletariat of Russia and the revolutionary elements of all Europe and America, launch an attack upon the imperialist predator, the evil vampire that holds in slavery hundreds and hundreds of millions of people in the white, yellow, and black continents.

To us revolutionaries there is no one more contemptible, after the hangman, than the latter's victim who submissively and without a struggle yields himself to suffering and torture.

This final duel that we are entering into will require bloody sacrifices and hard efforts. But we will win. We will march forward, never looking back.

Comrades, oriental fantasy has created a fable that shows symbolically, so to speak, the conditions under which a man or a people that has undertaken a certain task can succeed in accomplishing it. This fable tells of three wonders of nature situated on the summit of a magic mountain.

Many brave heroes have set out to win these treasures, but as soon as anyone approaches the magic mountain, voices begin to resound, calling on the brave man to turn back. The plaintive moans and cries of children, wives, fathers, and mothers appeal to the bold spirit to return and not risk his life for a chimera. Or else terrible shouts resound, like the frightful howling of a storm or claps of thunder. Thousands upon thousands of daring fellows failed the test—they looked back to where these sounds were coming from and were transformed into stone statues. And the whole mountain, from foot to summit, became strewn with these lifeless figures of stone into which living men had been transformed.

But then a courageous and strong-willed man came along. He began to climb the mountain, paying no attention either to the tender prayers of his kinsfolk or to the terrible shouts and frightening voices that sounded from behind him, threatening him with all the plagues of Egypt and a most painful death. He did not look back, but marched forward, fastening his gaze upon the summit of the mountain. And he achieved his aim, gaining possession of the treasures that were on the mountaintop.

And now comrades, you are beginning your ascent of the mountain in order to win all the treasures of the world. And you will hear the voices of those near to you, appealing to you not to risk your lives. You will hear the terrifying cries of all sorts of Muslim bigots, pan-Turkic and pan-Islamic fanatics, Georgian and Armenian Mensheviks and Dashnaks, who will threaten you with all sorts of bogies. But you will march forward, ignoring these cries; you will climb the mountain, arms in hand, without looking back—otherwise you will be transformed into statues of stone. (*Applause*)

But you will reach the mountaintop, you will take possession of the wonders of the world, you will see the realm of brotherhood, freedom, real equality of nations, the realm of labor. (*Applause*)

Long live the military alliance for the offensive of the working masses of East and West!

Long live the international Soviet republic of labor, in which there will be no enslaved, no oppressed peoples!

Long live Soviet power throughout the world!

Long live the Third, Communist International! (*Applause*)

CHAIRMAN: Comrades, before proceeding to the translation, we should like to put a proposal to you. In order to underline the aspirations of the congress and hasten the emancipation of women in the East, we ask you to confirm the inclusion in the Presiding Committee of three women. They are Bulach, from Dagestan; Najiye Hanum, from Turkey; and Shabanova, from Azerbaijan. (*Voices: "Yes, yes." Applause, rising to an ovation.*)

Comrade Najiye Hanum will say a few words.

NAJIYA HANUM: (*Speaks in Turkish. Loud and prolonged applause.*)[11]

CHAIRMAN: Long live the emancipation of the women of the East! (*Loud applause. Shouts of "Hurrah!" All stand. Ovation.*)

CHAIRMAN: *Yashasun shargin azad hanum Lari!* [Long live the free women of the East!]

SHABANOVA: Long live our comrades Lenin, Zinoviev, and Trotsky! (*Shouts of "Hurrah!" Applause. Ovation. Exclamations in various languages resound through the hall, covered by the roar of clapping.*)

CHAIRMAN: I call for the translation of Comrade Pavlovich's speech. The translation must be brief, in accordance with our decision of yesterday. I call on Comrade Sultanzadeh to give the translation.

(*Sultanzadeh translates.*)

ZINOVIEV: In view of the fact that the congress is very tired, both fractions propose that we confine ourselves to hearing two speakers only, one from each fraction. The speakers nominated are Comrades Matushev and Ryskulov. These comrades will be allowed ten minutes each, and we shall then take the vote. Please translate. (*Translation*)

I call upon Comrade Matushev.

MATUSHEV *(Communist)*: Comrades, my time is very limited, so I request your cooperation as regards silence and attention. The picture of the national and colonial question as it stands today has been drawn for you so far as its general features are concerned. It is fitting to add to the image portrayed by the comrade who gave the report a few words about national-colonial policy, looking at the question in motion, so to speak, from a fixed vantage point.

Comrades, we have to approach this serious question in a realistic way. It is not a question that is raised merely for effect, but an extremely vital one, and on its correct solution depends the entire fate of the revolution. In the short time at my disposal, I will try to give you a brief account of the actual, objective situation.

What is the East? The division between East and West has its own history, but, in the last analysis, we mean by the East today the countries of Asia and of the north coast of Africa, mainly Egypt. In particular, by the Muslim East we mean: Turkey, Persia, Baluchistan, Afghanistan, Bukhara, Khiva and all the regions of Turkestan, India, and part of China. That is what is meant by the Muslim East. Naturally, in such an extensive territory as this there is tremendous heterogeneity, an enormous exotic bouquet of nationalities, speaking a variety of languages, but they are all united by common features in their culture—by Islam.

It is, of course, impossible in ten minutes to embrace this ocean of concepts called the East. Accordingly, in speaking about national-colonial politics, we shall examine this question within the limits of our program.

Comrades, taking stock of an objective situation means assessing reality in practical terms and as accurately as possible. It means looking to see how property is distributed, what the means of production are, and what are the production relations. It also means taking into account the colossal ideological accumulation of spiritual culture that has been conditioned by the given economic basis. That is, strictly speaking, what is meant by taking stock of an objective situation, and I unfortunately lack the time to do that.

By developing revolutionary tactics the Soviet government, which heads and inspires the revolutionary movement in the East, gives guidance to this movement and brings to the East the totality of its proletarian Soviet culture. Is there such a culture, is there a proletarian culture, and, if so, what is it? I take it as my task to show to you that, in the situation that has come about, the only way out for the peoples of the East is through a very close alliance with Soviet Russia, through living contact with it, as the leader of the revolutionary movement on a world scale.

Let us note first of all what exists in the areas concerned, before we proceed to what is entering the East. In the East we have masses of peasants while, with rare exceptions, the factory proletariat is almost completely absent. We ask ourselves: Where is the center, where is that main point around which the social revolution in the East has to be accomplished? The answer is: the peasant masses, agrarian relations, the barbarous despotism of the local rulers, and the imperialism of the West. And we understand the revolutionary movement in the East as meaning organization of the peasantry against the feudal survivals with which the sad life of the East is so filled, and overthrow of the shameless, predatory imperialism of the West.

Just as in past times the movement of the peoples from East to West was agrarian, concerned with land, so also now, in the twentieth century, the movement of the revolution from West to East will be basically a movement concerned with land. We bring to the East emancipation of the land and of the working peasantry.

Let us look at Turkey, which plays so big a role throughout the East. It provides a striking picture, at which we have only to glance in order to feel the social ghastliness of rural life as led by the Turkish peasantry. Twelve years of unbroken rule in Turkey by the party of "Disunion and Regress," [12] crowning the previous nightmare history of the sultans' absolutism, has brought the Anatolian peasants to a state of pauperism.

Here is the picture. Far off on the horizon we see a Turkish aul. In the foreground a gray-haired old Turk is plowing the land: he has harnessed to the plow, along with his one and only ox, his own daughter. The enormous social significance of this picture is clear. All the young men have been taken away from productive work to fight in wars, and almost all the draft animals have been killed.

This is the economic dead end into which Turkish absolutism has led the Turkish peasantry, with the benevolent cooperation of Western imperialism. This is the fulcrum upon which the lever of the revolution must accomplish social revolution in Turkey. There is, however, a spark of proletarian organization in Turkey; there are Communist cells that carry on propaganda, both legal and illegal. Mustafa Kemal's movement is a national liberation movement. We support it, but as soon as the struggle against imperialism is concluded we are sure that this movement will advance to a social revolution.

Let us proceed to Persia. The dreadful situation of unheard-of poverty in which the Persian peasants live has lasted for many years. It is enough to look round in the streets of Baku and you will see a mass of people, the so-called ambali [laborers], dragging out a most miserable existence—products of an inhuman capitalist economy. These are human beings deprived of the elementary meaning of life, who spend the whole day carrying out the heaviest labor merely so as not to die of hunger that same night. When you look at them, you realize that there is a "surplus population of workers" in Persia; the soil exists there for social revolution.

It is not hard to appreciate what goes on farther off, in Afghanistan, Baluchistan, and India, under the "paternal" care of British imperialism. From India the European brigands extort countless treasures, while the legitimate owners of these treasures—the workers and peasants of India—die like flies from hunger and epidemics.

Everyone understands, I believe, that the whole essence of our work at this congress is to explain that Soviet power and the dictatorship of the proletariat, unification of the entire world proletariat, awareness of the common interests and tasks of the whole of toiling mankind, is the sine qua non for the victory of labor over capital and the emancipation of the oppressed masses of mankind from the yoke of imperialism.

What cultural assets does the proletariat possess, and what does it bring to the East? The scientific basis of communism is furnished by the works of Marx, Engels, and many other learned men. This trend in social science is called Marxism, historical materialism. Thus, in working out their proletarian conception of the world, the toilers possess a scientific asset to which the bourgeoisie has no equal.

It must be added that the proletariat sees itself as a class that cannot free itself from the yoke of capital without also freeing all the other classes of society. From this it is clear that the proletariat is the only class that strives to realize a culture truly common to all mankind. It brings to the East not disunity but the unity of all the working people of the human race, and with this aim it has created great cultural assets in the shape of the trade unions and cooperatives. This is the outstanding strength of the proletariat, expressed in the mutual solidarity it has established—mutual confidence and firm determination to go forward together to the final, life-and-death battle with capital.

Moreover, the proletariat has created an unprecedented form of governmental organization—Soviet power. This is a very great achievement by the proletariat in the political field: very simple in structure, brilliant in concept. These are the cultural assets that the proletariat brings to the East in the name of the emancipation and liberation of the oppressed masses.

Of course, every human movement has its shortcomings; here too, matters do not proceed without unevenness. And so it is necessary to say a few words about the peculiar features of proletarian culture, so that you may realize that shortcomings are inevitable, that it is pointless to talk about some of them, and that, finally, there are and will be shortcomings about which it is dishonest to remain silent.

The famous Christian theologian Thomas Aquinas distinguished between the church militant, fighting for its place in the world arena, and the church triumphant in victory. The former is romantic, the latter classical. But it is not only the church that experiences this fate—the same is true of art and culture. Every culture is at first a militant culture, a culture fighting for the right to exist. Proletarian culture is a culture of struggle, of quest for the true roads by which mankind must advance; it is a romantic and not yet a classical culture. In it there is no triumphant tranquillity; it is all passion and fervor—and that is why it includes both mistakes and shortcomings.

Do not forget, either, that the class struggle, the social revolution, is a life-and-death battle between two irreconcilable camps. From this battle either labor or capital will emerge victorious—or else they will both perish. The salvation of the East lies in the victory of the proletariat, and so our only road is that of contact with Soviet Russia. Under its leadership and instruction, along with it, we must go forward against the common enemy—world capital.

I have spoken to you briefly about what exists in the East and what is coming to the East. The policy of the proletariat on the national and colonial question is expressed in the resolutions of the Eighth Congress of the Russian Communist Party,[13] the main burden of which is as follows: unity of the proletariat and semiproletariat of all countries and all nations, that is, what we see before us in the shape of the Third International; and abolition of the privileges and domination of one nation over another, with federation as the transitional form of the union of all the working people—

CHAIRMAN: The time allowed for the speech is up. (*Voices: "Please continue."*) The comrade has spoken for twenty minutes. That is more than ten minutes, but, if the congress is willing, he can, of course, be allowed to finish his speech. (*Voices: "Yes, yes."*) Will those in favor of Comrade Matushev finishing his speech please raise their hands? Who is against? The majority is in favor. The congress then wants

Comrade Matushev to go on with his speech. Comrade Matushev, please continue.

MATUSHEV: (*Applause*) Comrades, I was interrupted and I don't remember what I was saying at that moment. Although I have been permitted to continue, it is not possible to enlarge very much owing to the lack of time.

My only wish is that you may take away from this congress one simple idea, one firm consciousness. That is, either we will perish together with Soviet Russia or we, together with Soviet Russia, will live a bright new life based on communist principles. There are two centers on our planet: the center of bourgeois domination, Versailles, and the center of proletarian struggle, Red Moscow.

Comrades, I would like to remind you that our ancestors once advanced from the East to the West as predatory conquerors. While there is distrust among the oppressed peoples of the East toward the oppressor countries of the West, there is also the same distrust, as a survival from the past, in the countries of the West toward the peoples of the East. The days of Tamerlane and Genghis Khan have not been forgotten. The working masses of the East and the West must not permit such mutual distrust to continue, for they have a common foe—world capital and imperialism.

Let me remind you of some lines from the verses of the great Lermontov: "'The East shall not affright my ease,' Kazbek made answer fair; 'Already nine long centuries the race of men sleeps there.'"[14] Today we can say with pride that the East is awakening from its centuries-long sleep and coming out onto the common human road of social construction in fraternal unity and contact with the proletariat of the West, embodied in Red Russia.

I should like to convey to you one sharp image to portray in your imaginations the "culture and civilization" that Western imperialism is bringing to the East, to the colonies. In his poem "Coffee," published in the Baku workers' paper *Voyenmor* (Fighting navy), the poet Gorodetsky expressed the whole power of poetic protest against this "culture." On the island of Java a native woman with a dark-red skin is picking coffee. On the quay a Britisher, whip in hand, is supervising the packing of the coffee, and when the work slackens however slightly he urges the slave woman on with cruel blows of his "civilized knout." And on the island of Java, wounds and groans poison life for the dark-red native woman. The poem continues. The coffee has been picked and sent off to Europe and America. In taverns in Paris, London, or Chicago, the bourgeois, accompanied by prostitutes, guzzles on profit extracted from the sweat and blood of the proletariat. And he drinks the coffee that the Britisher got from Java. Inspired by all the power of his poet's heart, the poet writes:

"That is why, when the black coffee bubbles with a golden glint in the porcelain cup, there rises to the brain a wave of desire for violent actions, and the heart suddenly yearns for catastrophe. Blow up Europe! Sweep away with fierce will the evil of buying and selling! No whip is needed for the flowers of the magnolia, no guard for the sun that shines on the ocean." (*Applause*)

CHAIRMAN: Please take your seats. I call upon Comrade Ryskulov. (*Applause*)

RYSKULOV: The colonial and national questions, which we are discussing today, are of very great importance for us. These questions are also very important for the capitalist system.

The last half-century of the existence of the capitalist system has been based chiefly on this colonial, national policy. If we follow the activity of the capitalist powers during the last half-century, we see that this most recent stage is a completely new form of the capitalist system. Comrade Lenin has called this monopoly capitalism, that is, the stage of capitalism in which large markets have been concentrated in the hands of separate alliances of capitalists—trusts—and in which competition proceeds between these separate alliances and groups.

As a result of this policy, this competition, we see the frenzied grabbing of colonies and of particular markets, and the forcible transformation of the inhabitants of these colonies into slaves subject to inhuman exploitation.

We see that the territories of the black continent of Africa and of Asia have been more and more completely divided up between the different large states. As a result of this colonial policy, the world powers that lead in carrying it out clashed in their interests, formed two coalitions, and brought about the five-year-long war that we have experienced. This resulted in the social revolution that has taken place in Europe and has begun in the East.

At the present time it is quite pointless to dwell upon the different features of particular forms of colonial exploitation, for we have left this period behind us.

When the Second International existed, colonial policy was discussed, but only on paper, in words. In reality, the Second International endorsed the striving of the great powers for conquest. Today the Eastern question presents itself in quite a different way.

With the establishment of the dictatorship of the proletariat in Russia, with the victory of the Communist Party, we see that light has been thrown upon the colonial question from a different angle. Gone is the fear entertained by the leaders of the Second International that the peoples of the East would destroy the culture of Europe. For the leaders of the Second International did fear this. They feared to offend the feelings of their bourgeois rulers. But there is nothing of this, nothing at all, in the Communist Party, in the Third International.

The slogan of unity of the Western proletariat with the revolutionary current in the East, with the peasants' and toilers' movement in the East, has been firmly advanced.

Despite the fact that the Communist tendency is growing stronger in all countries, despite the fact that the Third International is a mighty force shaking the foundations of capitalism, despite the achievement of the victory of socialism, nevertheless the colonial question, along with the agrarian question, is of paramount importance for our policy.

Solving these questions correctly is of enormous importance, and we can promote the solution of our tasks by presenting these questions correctly.

Conditions today in the East are completely favorable for the introduction of a revolutionary movement, for drawing the mass of the working people into the socialist movement. A precondition for this is the situation of the peasants brought about by the colonial activity of the great powers. A precondition for this is the legacy of the five-year-long war, which has created a mass of poverty, oppression, and ruin in the colonies. As a result, the working people of the colonies are prepared for revolt, prepared for a revolutionary offensive against imperialism.

But while in the West the socialist movement takes a Communist form, we certainly cannot count on a purely Communist movement in the East. There the movement assumes a petty-bourgeois character, that of a movement for national self-determination, for the unification of the East. But it will undoubtedly develop into a social movement, an agrarian movement. (*Applause*)

To some degree, the working class of the West still lies under the influence of the opportunists, of the compromisers. The Communist International has the task of wresting it away from their influence and training conscious advocates of communism. At the same time, its most important task is that of uniting the scattered revolutionary movement in the East with the movement in the West. This is the most important task facing the Third International.

It is for this question that we have assembled here, and this is the question we will solve here. Or rather, we will show the way to achieve its solution; we will show how to bring about as quickly and soundly as possible the unity of the West with the East for the final smashing of the foundations of capitalism.

In relation to the East, the Third International is proving not only on paper—in appeals, in words—but in practice, in deeds, that fifty million of the peoples of the East have joined the Soviet power. We see that Soviet republics have been created from the former colonies in Turkestan, the Caucasus, and other countries with a Muslim population, and these Soviet republics are entering Soviet Russia as federated units. These Soviet republics, inhabited by oppressed toilers, are now developing culturally, raising their cultural level. Now liberated, they are building their social life.

Truly, the Communist International has performed a great deed here. The break experienced by these borderlands, these republics—what has happened there—must serve as an example to the entire East. Let all the working people not just listen to our appeals, to our ideas. Let them look at these republics, which serve them as examples. In these borderlands the Communist Party has shown that its program is applicable not only for the Western proletariat but also in the East.

However much the supporters of the Second International and the compromisers may have argued that the colonies of the East are inhabited by slaves who can never come up to the level of Europe, who are so backward that no labor, no effort can make them progress; nevertheless we see that this East, held in such low esteem by bourgeois Europe, has shown that it can join forces with communism. This is what we see in the republics of the borderlands, where it is precisely among these backward Muslim peoples that communism and Soviet power have struck roots.

The forms of state structure and the methods of reforming economic life in the borderlands will undoubtedly serve as a graphic example for countries of the East that have not yet freed themselves and that must be freed.

In countries of the East where revolutionary organizations are weak, where the organizations of the working people are weak, the movement, of course, assumes at this time a bourgeois-national character. This movement is headed by those who favor a petty-bourgeois revolution, who favor democracy, but who do not favor Soviet communism. The movement, which is more united and more powerful at its inception, is of course rendering us a great service. For this force acts against the Entente, against world capital, and that helps us greatly.

The Third International, the Communist Party, must of course support this movement, but at the same time we have to say that this is not the movement that will finally liberate the toiling masses. Liberation of the toiling masses can be effected only through social revolution. Therefore, although the petty-bourgeois revolutionaries in the East oppose capitalism, they have nothing in common with communism. Always they want to set up their own independent national republics, republics that will exist as such only on paper and will never be really independent. For they must join either the camp of the bourgeoisie, of the capitalists, or that of the world proletariat—there is no middle way between these two options.

This is proved by the facts. The examples of such states as Armenia, Finland, and Poland are all too eloquent. These states are not distinct entities. They were deliberately set up by the Allies with a purpose: they are quite simply different organized gangs fighting against Soviet Russia on special assignment from world capital. Let us suppose that somewhere in the East, say in Turkey or elsewhere, supporters of the revolutionary movement who simultaneously oppose communism try to set up such independent states. These states would not survive. They would fall under the influence of the imperialists, of world capital, and would turn their weapons against the proletariat, against the working people of the East.

The situation is therefore clear. It is clear that the working people of the East have only one choice: to organize themselves as quickly as possible under the slogan and banner of the Communist International, to carry through the agrarian revolution, to take the land and power into their own hands. This is the only solution, the only way, the only means of achieving real self-determination of the peoples, real emancipation from the yoke of world capital. (*Applause*)

In his theses at the Second Congress on the colonial and national questions, Comrade Lenin defined the tasks of the Communist Party, the tasks of the Third International in the East quite exactly and realistically. Although he has not been in the East, in his theses he registers everything as though taken from life. These theses point, first and foremost, to the need for liberation from the yoke of world capital and for a call for not only the Communist but also the bourgeois-national currents to struggle against it. While appealing to the bourgeois-national currents for an alliance, the theses also show concretely that these currents do not bring the final emancipation of the toilers. This movement cannot bring liberation. Furthermore, the theses indicate the social bases for this liberation, pointing out that this revolution finds its main buttress in the agrarian question.

For all the toiling classes the moment has unquestionably arrived when they, now organized, must go forward together with the Western proletariat, go forward resolutely against world capital. And the precondition for this is that the oppressed peoples of the East, crushed for centuries by capitalism, must rise up. The very East that once gave light to Europe was crushed by that same Europe. In the depths of the East are hidden mighty forces, a tremendous power, now rising up in one mighty stream. Uniting with the stream of the Communist movement, it will finally smash the rule of world capital.

The basis for this is the fact that many Communist parties have been formed and have been joined by the leaders of the working people of the East. Many Soviet republics have been formed in former colonies. For us, a precondition for this is the fact that a Congress of the Peoples of the East, of the toilers of the peoples of the East, is now in session. We are on the threshold of a powerful, tremendous movement that will begin in the near future. United in a mighty Eastern International and together with the Western proletariat, this movement will strike a final blow at the very heart of world capitalism.

Long live the Communist International, leader of the world proletariat and of all the world's toilers!

Long live the leaders of the Third International!

Long live the toilers of the East, who are now rising up, powerful and united, against capital! (*Applause*)

VOICES: Gajiyeva! Come and translate into Uzbek. Gajiyeva!

CHAIRMAN *(ringing his bell)*: There will now be a translation. (*An interpreter translates into Turkic.*)

CHAIRMAN: There will be a five-minute break. (*Translation into Turkic*)

CHAIRMAN: The discussion of the colonial question is concluded. The Presiding Committee is not proposing a special resolution on this question, assuming that the congress identifies itself with the relevant resolution of the Second Congress of the Communist International.

The following written statements have been received:
1. A declaration on Palestine by the Central Bureau of the Jewish Sections of the Russian Communist Party.
2. A declaration by the Jewish Communist Party (Poale Zion) on the national and colonial questions.
3. A declaration by representatives of the working masses of Armenia.
4. A declaration by the Mountain Jews.
5. An address by the Muslims of the southwest Caucasus to the Congress of the Peoples of the East.[15] (*Translation*)

CHAIRMAN: A translation into Turkic is also needed.

VOICE: And a translation into Azerbaijani. Please! (*Translation*)

CHAIRMAN: All these documents are very important but they are also very long, and it is unfortunately not possible to read them out and translate them. The Presiding Committee proposes that they be appended to the report of the congress as documents. (*Translation*)

Comrades, with this we now close the congress. The next session will be tomorrow at 5:00 p.m.

(*The session ended at 10:05 p.m.*)

SESSION 6
SEPTEMBER 6, 1920

Soviets in the East; agrarian question

(*The session opened at 7:10 p.m. Comrade Zinoviev took the chair.*)

CHAIRMAN: I declare the sixth session of the Congress of the Peoples of the East open. Today we have on the agenda the question of Soviet construction in the East. Translation, please. (*Translation*)

Accordingly, we shall proceed to hear the report on this question. I call on Comrade Béla Kun. (*Applause*)

BÉLA KUN: Comrades, the Presiding Committee has discussed the theses in detail and now unanimously places them before you. I would like to say the following in support of them.

Mighty tsarist Russia, an immediate neighbor of the peoples of the East, fell beneath the blows of the workers and the poorest peasants. This revolution did not stop halfway. It did not leave state power in the hands of the classes that harbored more or less of a dislike for the tsarist regime while basing their whole existence on oppression of the working people. This revolution did not leave the former structure of government intact but smashed it, in order to build upon its ruins the authority of the workers and the poorest peasants. Using this authority, it strived to carry the struggle forward until no possibility was left of any sort of oppression.

In another sense, too, this revolution did not stop halfway. It was not checked at the frontiers of the state but spread both westward and eastward like a devouring flame. The revolution's extension to West and East threatens to bring about the final downfall of the system that, not content with exploiting the working people of its own countries, came to flower in imperialist colonial policy and bore fruit in world war. A revolution in the West and in the East must inevitably follow upon the social revolution of the workers and poorest peasants of Russia. These two revolutions are organically linked not only because they are directed against a common foe, world imperialism, but also because the necessary premise of their victory is common, concerted struggle.

In order to subjugate the colonial peoples, the imperialist exploiters have mobilized the European workers, trying to win them over by means of bribes—crumbs from the superprofits extorted from the colonial peoples. This happened in both Britain and Germany. In this way it was hoped to deflect the workers from their revolutionary vocation. On the other hand, the imperialist bourgeoisie have given much thought, especially in recent times, to using colonial troops they have recruited against the European workers' movements, exploiting the lack of consciousness of these soldiers in order to defend their shaken state power against the working class.

Comrades, I have had the opportunity to witness personally this sort of policy on the part of the imperialist bourgeoisie. When we, the workers and poorest peasants of Hungary, seized power, the French bourgeoisie at once attempted to strangle our revolution, making use of Muslim colonial troops. However, despite our difficulty in communicating with these soldiers owing to the difference of language, we nevertheless managed to find a way to their minds and hearts, and they threw down their arms when they were called upon to drown our revolution in blood.

The imperialist bourgeoisie usually succeeds in finding a stratum of the indigenous population in the colonial countries—or, in the semicolonial countries, a ruling class—whose aid it can utilize. This aid makes its exploiting policy less difficult and less expensive—and also less costly in blood—than it would otherwise be. Once their own resistance has been broken, the sultans and emirs—and the ruling strata associated with them in the Eastern countries—have always readily agreed to become collectors of tribute for the imperialist oppressors. Thus, the shah of Persia agreed to collect tribute for both Russian imperialism and British imperialism in turn. The Young Turks fleeced the Turkish peasants on behalf of the German imperialists, and now the Anglophiles headed by the sultan are depriving the Turkish peasant of his last cow in the interests of the Anglo-French imperialist bloc. The emir Faisal, who is on the payroll of the French bankers, has agreed to break up the unity of the Turkish people and to reduce the Turkish peasantry to the position of beasts of burden to the French imperialists.

The imperialist bourgeoisie found allies in the colonial and semicolonial countries of the East sooner than did the revolutionary proletariat. It helped these allies not only by giving them miserable crumbs from what it had plundered from the toiling poor of these countries, but also by training them in the methods by which it had deceived and stupefied its own working class.

Capitalism succeeded in holding the rebellious worker masses of Europe in submission only by persuading them that they too shared in state power, even though this power remained in fact merely an instrument used by the ruling class to oppress working people. Similar to this was the parliamentary constitution in Turkey, drafted in accordance with the European pattern. Although it appeared to give rights to the working people, in reality everything remained as before—domination by the pashas, tyranny of the officials, and no hindrance to the activity of the usurers who brought ruin upon the people.

The revolution of the European and American proletariat and poorest peasantry is directed precisely against the lies that aim to keep exploitation and oppression in being behind a screen of democracy, freedom, and equality. The revolution of the Russian workers and poorest peasants created a form of government that puts power into the hands of the working masses not merely in words but in deeds. This form is the soviets of workers and peasants. Until the Russian workers and peasants took power through their soviets the land remained in the hands of the landlords, and the factories and mines in those of the capitalists. "Freedom" merely gave the bourgeoisie freedom to squeeze sweat out of their workers and to deny the non-Russian nationalities the right to decide for themselves whether they wanted to remain within the Russian state or to be independent of it. The communist revolution and the victory of the Soviet order at once transferred to the working people the land, factories, and mines and, in place of the inequality between exploiters and exploited, established the equality of all working people.

Putting an end to exploitation also ended all interest in enslaving and exploiting other peoples. One of the first steps taken by the Soviet republic was recognition of the right to self-determination for all peoples and liberation of Russia's colonies. Just as the tsarist regime had secured alliances with the shahs and emirs, that is, with the ruling strata of the oppressed countries, so Soviet Russia immediately proposed an alliance to the toilers whom the old Russia, both tsarist and democratic, had kept in a colonial situation.

Only the Soviet system made it possible to transfer power to those whose concern it was that the instruments of production should not serve the interests of a tiny handful of persons but should belong to all the working people.

As fighting organs of the workers and peasants, organs of their authority and government, the soviets represent a new form of state. The workers and poorest peasants, having disarmed the enemies of the people, organize themselves in soviets, take up arms, and themselves promulgate laws, determining the norms of the social order. Either directly or through their representatives, the toiling masses themselves pass the laws.

No parasites or exploiters boss the workers about, no usurers lord it over the poor. All these elements have been deprived of all rights. Soviet power stands in sharp contrast to what prevails in the East today. It means rule by the toilers and the poor peasants, in place of rule by the rich and the parasites. I am sure that there is no delegate present here who is not convinced that oppression and exploitation can be ended only by introducing this form of state power. So long as our beys, khans, usurers, and tribute collectors possessed political rights and were able to distort the truth through tricks and deceptions of all kinds, to interpret the law in accordance with their own interests, and to resort to force of arms whenever their cunning did not help them—so long as this held true, it was clearly quite futile to talk of putting an end to oppression and exploitation.

The theses I am laying before you set down in brief outline the essential features of Soviet power. The system of Soviet power is not incapable of adaptation to the special conditions of a particular people or a particular region. In places where industrial workers predominate, where exploitation is carried on by factory owners and bankers, the Soviet structure will be quite different from its form in places where the main part of the population is engaged in agriculture, and exploitation takes the form of usury. In Western states it is above all the factory owners, bankers, and big landowners who must be removed from power and stripped of rights, while Soviet power in the Eastern countries must be directed, first and foremost, against usurers, kulaks, khans, beys, foreign exploiters, and officials. The Eastern soviets must of course be soviets of the peasant poor. Just as a method has been found in Dagestan and Azerbaijan for determining at what number of cattle the exploitation of others' labor begins, so it will be possible in all tribal communities to fix rules ensuring that soviets will really be organs of the toiling poor.

In the West, Soviet power is the expression of the dictatorship of the proletariat. In the East, however, in countries where there is no industrial working class, it will express the dictatorship of the poorest peasantry. It is self-evident that where a factory exists, where there are some better-educated and experienced industrial workers, even if only in small numbers, these workers will be the leaders of the rural poor. They will not, of course, be leaders of the same sort as the previous rulers, who, concerned with their own well-being, led the poor peasants into exploitation and want. They will rather be leaders who are themselves concerned to end all forms of oppression and exploitation and will therefore act in the interests of the general good of the people.

The hangers-on of the bourgeoisie know how to spread all manner of dreadful stories about the Soviet order. Those in the East with a stake in keeping the toilers of the East in slavery, either along with the Western capitalists or independently of them, have quickly learned to do this.

Very briefly, I want to speak against the time-hardened view that peoples who have not passed through a phase of capitalist development, and thus through bourgeois democracy, have to experience all this before they can go over to the Soviet system. This idea is maintained for the sole purpose of prolonging the power of the emirs, pashas, beys, and foreign colonialists over the poorest peasantry of the East.

Another objection advanced against the formation of soviets in the East holds that the dictatorship of the proletariat is impossible without an industrial proletariat, and in the East the industrial proletariat is infinitesimal in size. To this we reply that although Soviet power in the West is indeed the form and expression of the dictatorship of the proletariat, in the East, where the exploited element is not the industrial workers but the poorest peasants, these peasants must also be the leading element in the soviets.

There is yet another objection: "The peoples of the East are not yet mature enough to decide their fate for themselves; they need to pass through the phase of bourgeois democracy in order to acquire the capacity for self-government." Only imperialist colonialists argue like this.

In the language of the people this means: "Wait, Muslim poor peasants, until the pashas, beys, speculators, and usurers deign to teach you how to take the land and power away from them."

I am sure that all delegates take this for a lie. The Muslim poor have lived for many centuries under the rule of the sultans, pashas, and the like. And then came the colonialist merchants, those oppressors. Not only did they teach the people nothing, but they strived to keep them in ignorance. If the people are to wait, they will wait for centuries, until these hangmen have not only plundered them but have made them quite incapable of taking power for themselves. The ability to rule, like the ability to use a weapon, demands that you make a start and get in some practice: those who never handle a rifle will never learn to shoot.

In conclusion, I want to remind you of the changes that will be brought about in the pattern of everyday life, for the peoples of both East and West, by the common victory of their revolution. Economic intercourse between West and East will certainly not cease with the victory of the revolution. On the contrary, these ties will be very much closer than before, but they will be of quite a different kind from what they are today.

Today the East is united with the West by bonds of oppression and the coercion exercised by colonial troops. For the means of colonial rule have always been alcohol, syphilis, and weapons. It is not only with their eyes that officers of the British and French imperialist armies have undressed the womenfolk of the oppressed Muslims. The natural resources of the fertile Eastern lands have flowed away to the West—not into the hands of the Western workers, however, but into the coffers of the Western bankers, factory owners, and landlords.

These bankers and factory owners, the oppressors of the Western workers, have always found allies in the East. The usurer who gathers the fruits of Eastern fields, the state ruler and his entourage who have obtained loans from Western capitalists and ruthlessly collect the interest on these loans from working people—these have always served as tools of colonial policy.

Above: Opening rally of congress, held jointly with Baku soviet and Azerbaijan trade unions in Baku opera house, August 31, 1920. Seated behind Presiding Committee table, from left, unidentified, Thomas Quelch, Ramón Merino Gracia, John Reed, Béla Kun, Gregory Zinoviev, Karl Radek.

Left: V.I. Lenin addressing Second Congress of Communist International.

EXCEPT AS NOTED, PHOTOS ARE FROM THE JULES HUMBERT-DROZ ARCHIVES, CITY LIBRARY, LA CHAUX-DE-FONDS, SWITZERLAND.
DRAWING OF LENIN: G. VEREYSKY.

ТЕАТР
НАРОДА
Кто знает, тот побеждает.

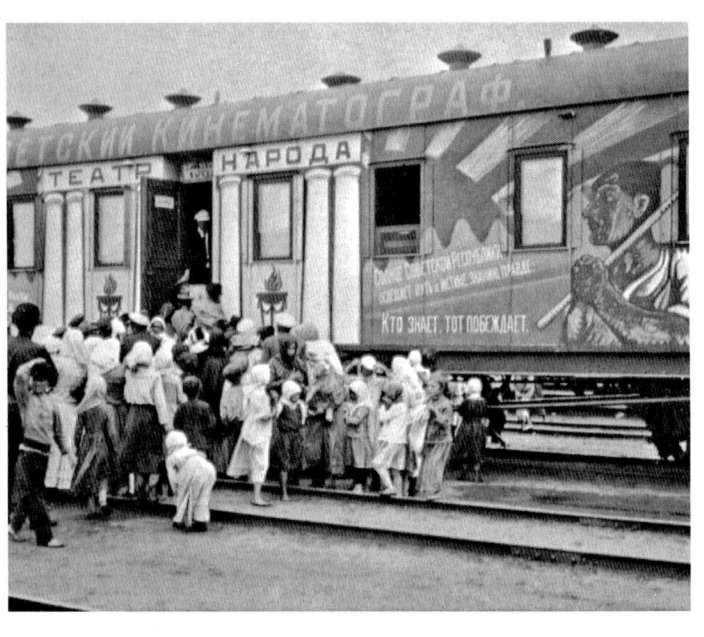

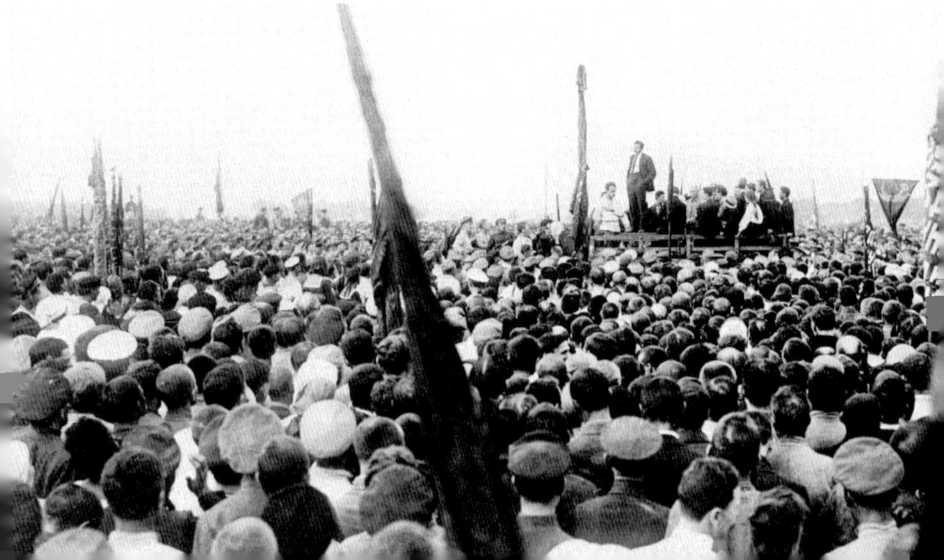

Above: On the road to Baku: Zinoviev speaks to workers and soldiers during a stopover. Beside him, with pipe, Radek.

Facing page

Top: Film showing in the People's Theater, part of the "V.I. Lenin" propaganda train, which campaigned to build participation in the Baku congress. Inscriptions: "The sun of the Soviet republic lights the way to knowledge and truth; those who have knowledge will be victorious."

Bottom: Béla Kun speaks at congress-building rally in Rostov.

Above: On the road to Baku: welcoming the delegates' train at the Azerbaijan border.

Facing page

Top: Returning from Baku: repairing the tracks near Naurskaya after White Guard sabotage.

Bottom, left: The uncoupled locomotive of the delegates' train leaves to inspect the damage. John Reed, not seen here, was aboard.

Bottom, right: A Red Army armored train.

Above: Congress delegates; Bibinur at left, beside her, Quelch. Seated, bottom right, with arm upraised, John Reed.

Facing page:
On the road to Baku: oil derricks in the Caucasus.

Overleaf:
The congress in session.

Above: Presiding Committee table. In white coat and tie, Nariman Narimanov. Right of him, Zinoviev, Radek.

PHOTO: AZERBAIJAN STATE ARCHIVES.

Facing page, clockwise from top left: Turar Ryskulov, Narimanov, Mikhail Pavlovich, V.G. Yegorov, Quelch, DadashBuniatzadeh.

PHOTOS OF RYSKULOV, NARIMANOV, YEGOROV, BUNIATZADEH: AZERBAIJAN STATE ARCHIVES. DRAWING OF QUELCH: ISAAC BRODSKY.

Above: Najiye Hanum proposes a program for the liberation of women in the East.

Facing page

Top: Delegates eating at the Red Army Club.

Bottom: Delegates of the Sarts, a town-dwelling, trading people of Central Asia, at the Red Army Club.

Left: Demonstration of Baku Women's Union, August 22, 1920. On banner at right, Azerbaijani text reads, "Long live the world revolution"; Russian text links "liberation of women" with "liberation of the world's toilers." At left, red flag with Islamic crescent. In center, emblem of Azerbaijan Soviet republic.

Above: From left, Bibinur and Khaver Shabanova on stage with Presiding Committee. In background, between them, Pavlovich.

Overleaf

Top: Dedication of monument to Karl Marx, September 3, 1920. Inscription: "The proletarians have nothing to lose but their chains. They have a world to win."

Bottom: Congress delegates.

The revolution of the proletariat and the poorest peasantry will deprive the capitalists, landlords, factory owners, and bankers of all power; it will send to the devil their stooges—generals, officials, and priests. Power will pass to the soviets, which represent the masses of the working people. And when this happens, these new workers' and peasants' states will not, of course, pursue any aggressive aims in the East. They will not seek their allies among the sultans and emirs, among the pashas and beys, and will not allow usurers to act as intermediaries in the economic dealings between the West and the peasantry of the East.

The workers of the West and the peasants of the East can regulate their economic relations only directly, through their Soviet states. The Soviet state of the workers can sell the fruits of its labor only directly to the peasants of the East. Never will it consent, never can it consent to receive goods produced by the stubborn labor of Eastern peasants through the mediation of usurers who rob them. Soviet states cannot follow the example of the capitalist system, which is based entirely upon buying and selling. Fraternal aid one to another, a just distribution of the fruits of common labor—that is what can serve as the fundamental principle in the economic relations linking West and East after the victory of the revolution.

And when the Soviet system triumphs in the West and the East, the difference that has existed—and exists today—between colonial and metropolitan countries will disappear. Entry into an international federation, into a world union of Soviet states, will equalize, so to speak, the East with the West, organically ruling out any possibility of exploitation of the Eastern peoples.

Anyone who grasps that the liberating revolution of the peoples of the East, like the social revolution, will lead on to socialism can have no view on the state system for the East other than advocacy of Soviet power. In the days when bourgeois revolutions and the bourgeois order were flourishing, it was quite comprehensible that the ruling strata of the East would strive to establish a parliamentary system for the East as well, fully corresponding to capitalism and bourgeois democracy. At that time, establishing a parliamentary system meant trying to raise the East to the level of the West and to give economic forces the opportunity to develop freely. Strictly speaking, the idea was that the working people would bear on their shoulders, instead of the foreign exploiters and oppressors, the native variety of the same breed.

At the present stage of development of the international revolution, the point at issue is no longer who will be the oppressors, among whom and in what way the wealth created by the toiling people is to be divided up. The Soviet system means an end to all forms of exploitation. The point is that the fruits of the toilers' labor are to be enjoyed by the toilers alone. "Whoever does not work shall not eat."

Naturally, anyone who seeks the complete emancipation of the toilers of the East cannot be for a system that tries, by means of its organs of power, to maintain exploitation. Anyone who wants the peoples of the East to be freed from all forms of exploitation and oppression, anyone who wants to be liberated from foreign colonialists and from the native agents of foreign imperialists, anyone who wants to replace the rule of the pashas, khans, beys, usurers, and other bloodsuckers by the rule of the working masses, can take no road but that of Soviet power. Anyone who wants the poor peasants to be subject no longer to the tyranny of the rich and their hangers-on, anyone who wants the poor to be able to settle their affairs for themselves, will, on his return from the congress to his aul, to his village, fight tirelessly for the peasant agrarian revolution that is being realized in the East by Soviet power and will lead the East out of its present condition of oppression.

We are sure that at the Second Congress of the Peoples of the East, representatives of the federation of Soviet states of the East will report on how the poor of the East took power, how they are building their Soviet organs, and how they are marching onward along the road that leads to the abolition of all exploitation—to communism. I propose the adoption of the following theses.

THESES ON SOVIET POWER IN THE EAST

1. The revolution of the peoples of the East against external and internal oppression, against the foreign imperialists and the local exploiters, puts on the agenda the question of the state system in all the countries of the East. Using all sorts of machinations, the European bourgeoisie has succeeded for a long time in concealing from the propertyless and those with little property—the proletarian and semiproletarian elements—the essential nature of state power as an instrument of oppression. In contrast to this, in the states of the East the coercive nature of the ruling power is quite obvious.

As for the poor, who are totally without political rights, their lives and all the products of their labor are objects to be bought and sold by various sultans, shahs, emirs, and tribal leaders, and by the rich and the bureaucratic cliques associated with them. This situation prepared the way for the imperialist exploiters. In the colonial countries and in those reduced to a semicolonial condition, they always concluded their deals with the help of the heads of government, commanding officers, and officials—at the expense of the poor.

2. As in Western states, the rich, exploiting strata of the population in the Near Eastern countries have tried to give their rule an appearance of democracy. Turkey and Persia have been parliamentarized. Georgia (under the leadership of the Mensheviks), Armenia (under the leadership of the Dashnaks), and Azerbaijan (under the leadership of the Musavatists) have been transformed into democratic republics. All this has taken place under the slogans of freedom and equality. These policies, however, all proved incapable of creating even a facade of democracy. Unheard-of poverty of the masses persists side by side with the prosperity of the agents of the foreign imperialists. The land remains under the control of its previous owners; the old tribute system continues, bringing immeasurable harm to the working people; and usury is not only tolerated but is backed by the state power, to the detriment of the poor. All this has revealed the falsity of the slogans about equality put forward by the Turkish, Persian, and Azerbaijani national-democratic parties and also by the Menshevik and Dashnak parties, which operate under cover of socialist slogans.

3. Even after the rule of the foreign imperialists has been eliminated, the revolution of the toiling masses of the East will not come to a halt. It will not stop with a system that seeks—using the false slogan of democracy, under cover of slogans of equality—to maintain the power of the sultans, shahs, emirs, pashas, and beys; to maintain the oppression of the working people and inequality between the haves and the have-nots, the oppressors and the oppressed, rich and poor, those who pay tribute and those who live on this tribute. The revolution will not halt at the boundaries, declared to be sacred, of the landlords' estates. The Eastern peasantry, like the Russian, will develop their revolution to the dimensions of a huge

agrarian peasant revolution, as a result of which the land must pass over to the working people, and all exploitation must disappear.

The Russian peasantry carried through their agrarian revolution with the support of the industrial workers under the leadership of the Communist Party. Welded together in soviets, these peasants are now defending the land they took from the landlords and the power they took from the exploiters. In the same way the oppressed peasantry of the East will count in their revolutionary struggle upon the support of the revolutionary workers of the West, the Communist International, and the present and future Soviet states.

4. Soviet power and Soviet organization are not only the instrument of power and the organizational form of the industrial proletariat. They also constitute the only system that permits the working masses themselves—after excluding from power the privileged, and consequently hostile, elements (landlords, speculators, higher officials, officers)—to shape their own destiny. Only Soviet power gives authority exclusively to the toiling poor. Unity of the soviets, and their federation, is the only way to secure peaceful cooperation between the toilers of different peoples in the East, who have slaughtered each other in the past. It will help them to join forces to destroy the power of their oppressors, both foreign and native, and repel their attempts to restore the old order.

5. So-called democratic self-government, putting the administration exclusively into the hands of the privileged strata (khans, beys, and so on) prevents the toiling masses from managing their own affairs. It deprives them of the possibility of learning to govern and stops them from acquiring the knowledge they need for this purpose. In contrast to this, experience among the peas-

ants of Soviet Russia, Siberia, the Bashkir-Kirghiz republic, and Turkestan has shown that the peasants of the Eastern countries are capable of managing their own affairs.

6. The victory of the Communist Party in the West will put an end to the exploitation of the Eastern peoples. But such a victory in the West will not mean that East and West can then get on without mutual economic links. On the contrary, the victory of the revolution in the East and in the West will mean that relations between different countries will be based not on exploitation but on reciprocal support and aid. After the victory of the communist revolution, economic intercourse will take place between states. Thus the economic relations of Eastern states that have not adopted the Soviet system would serve the interests only of a small group of capitalists. Securing grain and raw materials, these capitalists would carry on trade with the Western Soviet states in exactly the same way as they now do with the imperialist states—exploiting for this purpose the toiling masses of the East.

Complete liberation from imperialist exploitation, transfer of the land to the toilers, and emancipation from the power of speculator-exploiters requires the removal from power of the nonworking element, all foreign colonialist elements (generals, officials, and so on), and all privileged persons. It also requires organization of the rule of the poor on Soviet principles. And all the other interests of the working people demonstrate to the East that it is imperative to establish Soviet power.

(*Translation*)
CHAIRMAN: Comrades, we now come to the vote on Comrade Béla Kun's theses, which were unanimously approved by the Presiding Committee. Will those in favor please

raise their hands. Who is against? No one. The theses are adopted. (*Applause*)

Let us proceed to the next question. Comrade Skachko will give the report on the agrarian question.

(*Translation*)

SKACHKO: Comrades, all the Eastern countries are peasant countries. The inhabitants have been kept in an oppressed state by the Western European capitalists, who have denied them the possibility of independent development. This is chief among the reasons why these countries have not developed their own industry and are still to this day engaged exclusively in agricultural labor. In the Eastern countries the great mass of the population as a whole consists of peasants. Emancipation of the peoples of the East means emancipation of the peasants. In the Western countries the productive class consists mainly of industrial workers, and the industrial proletariat can be called the king of the West. In the Eastern countries, however, the sole producers of material values are the peasants. Thus only they can be called the kings of the East, and the Eastern countries should belong to them alone.

Let us look, comrades, at how these kings of the East live, these men and women whose labor sustains not only all the peoples of the East but also a good part of those of the West. They live in the same wretched, pitiful, downtrodden, and oppressed conditions that the peasantry of Western Europe lived in many centuries ago. Creating everything, they themselves enjoy nothing. They bear the burden of unlimited oppression both by foreign capitalist conquerors and by their own privileged classes and despots. Various sultans, shahs, khans, and beys, the masters of Eastern countries and lands, wallow in fabulous Eastern luxury while the peasants whose labor created all this are dying of hunger and want. Peasants are forced to leave their own very rich and fertile countries for alien lands, in search of the crust of bread they cannot obtain at home.

The Muslim religion is rooted in principles of religious communism, by which no man may be slave to another, not a single piece of land may be privately owned, and all religious institutions must make it their principal concern to care for the orphaned and indigent. Nevertheless, these religious principles have not saved the peasants from being reduced to serfdom or preserved the land from seizure by landlords and despots. Gradually, these principles have been modified to the advantage of the ruling classes. The land, free and belonging only to God, was first declared to belong to the ruling sultans and shahs, and then became the property of feudalists and capitalists.

The waqf lands, which were given to the mosques and the clergy so that their income might support charitable institutions of value to the people, gradually lost their original function and became lands belonging to the clergy and to private persons. Instead of being used for the benefit of the poor, the income from them was taken by the secular and ecclesiastical rulers—parasites who used these lands merely in order to exploit the poor peasants.

The peasant, a free man according to the shariat, was gradually reduced to conditions of slavery, either by direct coercion on the part of the khans and beys or by economic compulsion based on the seizure of the land by the landlords.

The situation of the peasantry among the Eastern peoples has not improved but constantly deteriorated. Finally it has now become so impossible and unbearable that no way out is left to the peasants other than to die a slow death from hunger or to break their servile chains and make a new life for themselves through social revolution.

Indeed, how is life possible in the conditions in which the Eastern peasant is living? Can we really call the existence dragged out by the wretched Persian rayat [peasant] a human life? He is not a human being, he is only the beast of burden of his landlord, the molkdar. This landlord has power to dispose of his life and property, to execute him or to punish him with strokes of the cane, or to take the peasant's wives and daughters for his harem. Comrades, all this is going on a few hundred versts from Baku, over which flies the red flag of the workers' and peasants' socialist republic.

A few hundred versts from this place, where the peasants have taken power into their hands, we find other peasants living in a state of utter slavery. The Persian peasant cannot call a single fragment of land his own. He can even be easily evicted from his farmhouse by his landlord, to die of hunger in the barren steppe. For the right to work his land, for the right to grow grain, he has to hand over to the landlord four-fifths of the crop, four-fifths of what he has produced by the labor of his hands. Of what he wrests from the soil by his own toil he is allowed to keep only miserable leavings, while the main part is devoured by the various parasites who perch on his shoulders, making his life a sheer unbearable torment of grim slavery.

That is the state of affairs in Persia. But in the other countries of the East the position of the peasants is no better. Even in Turkey, the most advanced of the Muslim countries, the peasant is poverty-stricken. Although serfdom has been abolished in Turkey, nevertheless even there economic conditions are reducing the peasant to a servile situation. The despotic government of Turkey, which always looked upon those subject to its rule as conquered peoples, pursued in its administration one constant aim and one alone: to extract from the population as much income as possible, taking no account at all of what it cost the population to produce this income and what frightful want was created by this barbarous, ruthless extortion. For centuries the despotic government of Turkey and its minions enforced such a frightful system of taxation and such a barbarous system of levying taxes through tax farming that the peasantry was completely ruined and rendered quite incapable of cultivating their holdings.

In Turkey huge tracts of land, located in the most fertile vilayets [provinces], lie uncultivated and in utter desolation: the peasants have left the country in search of a bite to eat. This has happened because the peasants are unable to work the abandoned land, since they have neither oxen, nor money, nor seed—none of the things they need in order to cultivate the land. In the southern part of Asia Minor, which also has huge uncultivated tracts, there are more than 100,000 so-called marabas [shepherd boys]—nomadic farm laborers without land, farmsteads, or shelter—wandering in hordes all over the country, looking for miserably paid seasonal work on the landlords' estates. Even peasants who still have a holding of their own cultivate it not for themselves but for all manner of usurers, to whom their indebtedness obliges them to hand over four-fifths of their crop.

The extent of the exploitation and impoverishment of the Turkish peasants can be shown statistically. The figures reveal that even in peacetime, out of all the grain he produces, the Turkish peasant never has left more than six poods per year per head, or three-quarters of a pound a day. Today the Russian proletariat—ruined by many years of war, and receiving, in the big centers that are worst stricken with famine, only one and a half pounds of bread a day—is better supplied with bread than the Turkish peasant living in a fertile country abounding in free land!

In Turkey as in Persia the position of the peasant is absolutely unbearable. It is a position of utter want, chronic hunger, endless indebtedness, and work for the tribute collectors and usurers, with no security regarding his title to the land and no hope whatsoever of any improvement in his wretched situation.

The peasants of other Eastern countries find themselves in the same desperate, oppressive situation. Not to speak of the Armenians, driven off their lands and into the barren mountains, deprived of their homes and livelihoods, and stripped of all they possess by the Kurdish landlords, the aghas. Even if not driven from their land, the peasants of all the other nationalities have lives of little joy, for they work not for themselves but for their oppressors. In Khiva, Bukhara, and Afghanistan, where agriculture is possible only on irrigated land, all such land has been grabbed by the landlords, the beys, and khans, and the peasants are able to work it only as wage laborers subject to dreadful exploitation.

In India the British rulers have taken nearly all the land. Seeking to squeeze the maximum revenue from this unfortunate country, they have leased it out to big capitalists, so that the peasant can gain access to the land only as a subtenant or wage laborer. Out of what he produces from the land, the Indian peasant has to hand over the lion's share to the British rulers and another share to the capitalist farmer. The share he keeps for himself enables the peasant only to die of hunger amid the flowering valleys of his fertile homeland, his wondrous country with its countless riches.

Everywhere, in all the countries of the East, the peasants, who alone create all the material values that sustain their people and others as well, drag out the wretched existence of downtrodden, starving slaves. Everywhere in the countries of the East the peasant, the king and creator of riches, is starving to death and groaning beneath the whips of his own and foreign oppressors. "Starving to death"—comrades, that is no mere phrase. The peasants of the East are actually starving—it has been proved statistically. In order to escape from his miserable situation, to escape from want, poverty, and hunger, the peasant of the Eastern countries must throw off the centuries-old oppression both of the foreign capitalist exploiters and of his own oppressors—the sultans, khans, shahs, and beys. (*Applause*)

Long enough the peasantry of the East have starved, serving their various oppressors. Now they must free themselves and become the actual owners of their land and the absolute masters of their fate. The many-millioned masses of peasants of the East must now rise up in all their colossal might and throw off all their oppressors. They must take power into their own hands (*Applause*) by forming their own peasant Soviet government, by forming revolutionary peasant soviets. All the sources of the oppression of the peasants must be destroyed—first and foremost, the system of landlordship, which enslaves the peasant. Whoever does not work shall not eat; whoever does not till the land shall not possess it! (*Applause*)

All the land belonging to the landlords and feudalists, shahs and khans must be taken from them and given to the peasants, without any payment, without any compensation to the former owners. Together with the land, all the animals and farm implements belonging to the estates of the feudalists and landlords must be taken, for the peasant must receive not only land but also the possibility of working it. For this purpose he must seize all the instruments of production and all the wealth that his landlord oppressors possessed.

In addition to the landlords' land, there are in the East huge tracts of state-owned land used by various secular and ecclesiastical institutions, officials, and clergy. This land too must be taken from the ruling privileged classes and turned over to the peasants. Comrades, the fact that some of this land belongs to the clergy is no cause for concern. Of course the clergy, who have concentrated huge tracts of land in their hands and exploit peasant labor on this land, declare that it belongs to God. It is therefore inviolable, they say, and the peasant dare not reach out to take it. But this is all lies and fraud, comrades!

Even according to the shariat, the land can belong only to those who till it—and not to the clergy who have grabbed it, like the mujtahids in Persia, who were the first to violate the fundamental law of the Muslim religion. They are not defenders of this religion but perverters of it. Just like the feudal landlords, they are parasites and oppressors—except that they are also hypocrites who disguise their character as oppressors behind the white turban and the Holy Koran. This mask of sanctity must be torn from them, comrades, and the land they own must likewise be wrested from them and given to the working peasantry. (*Applause*)

The confused and complicated legislation of the countries of the East disguises private ownership with various masks and restricts the right of the possessor of a holding to use it as he pleases—preventing the peasant from cultivating his land as he wishes. All this must be swept away. Every peasant must have the right to utilize his land as he chooses, ignoring all such prohibitions and restrictions. (*Applause*) Instead of the complicated and confused land laws that serve to enslave the peasant, it is necessary to establish just one land law, consisting of a single article: all land belongs to the state, and the right to use it belongs only to whoever works it with his own labor. (*Applause*) That must be the only land law, giving the land to the toilers, to the peasants, and casting out from the land all parasites, exploiters, and slave owners. (*Loud applause*)

Now, comrades, we must turn to a scourge of the peasants of all the countries of the East—one that beats sweat and blood out of them and devastates their holdings: the fearful burden of taxes borne by the peasantry of Turkey, Persia, and India for hundreds of years. There is no need to tell you what these taxes have meant, what a fearful burden they have laid upon the peasants, how these taxes, imposed by a venal, corrupt administration, have taken the peasants' skin, their blood, their very lives. You know how the tithe provided for in the shariat has been turned into three-quarters and four-fifths of the peasant's crop, and how these taxes have reduced the peasantry of the Eastern countries to utter poverty. The scourge of taxation and the tyranny of officials and administrators associated with it must be destroyed; all taxes must be canceled. The peasants must be freed from exploitation not only by the landlords but also by the state. (*Applause*)

No human organization, however, can exist without incurring certain expenses. The newly formed peasants' Soviet government will therefore need to have a certain amount of revenue at its disposal. The peasants will thus have to give their government a certain portion of what they produce, which will be needed to support the urban workers, the state machine, and the Red Army, which defends the peasants' freedom. However, this levy, its amount, and the way it is to be actually collected will be decided and put into effect not by venal, bloodsucking officials but by the peasants' soviets. (*Applause*)

The peasantry must be relieved not only of taxes but of debts. You know, comrades, how burdened the Eastern peasant is with debt. You know that he is always in debt to a neighboring landlord, or to some kulak, trader, or usurer. You know that without contracting loans the Eastern peasant cannot carry on cultivation of his exhausted holding. Therefore he is always up to his ears in debt. This indebtedness of the peasants makes them serfs to the usurers, obliging them to work their whole lives through for the latter's enrichment. If the land were taken over, but the peasants were left in the grip of the old debts, the peasants would have escaped from the claws of the landlords merely to fall into those of the usurers. The heavy yoke of debt that harnesses the peasantry to the old world of slavery must be left behind in that old world. One of the first steps taken by the revolutionary peasantry as it rises up must be a complete and categorical cancellation of all peasant debts whatsoever—to the state, to land banks, to landlords, to traders, to usurers. All the debt liabilities of the peasants must be declared invalid. The new revolutionary world must tell the old world of the usurers that the peasants of the Eastern countries no longer owe anyone so much as a kopeck. (*Applause*)

I have mentioned these, comrades, as the first steps to be taken by the revolutionary peasants in the countries of the East. I have indicated the measures the peasants will need to take at once. When you return home you will advise the peasants what they must do. They must eliminate their feudalists and landlords; overthrow the power of the despots who rule them; take power into the hands of peasant soviets; take possession of all landlords', state-owned, and waqf land, along with all the livestock and implements belonging to those lands; share them out among the peasant poor; stop paying taxes; cancel debts; and thereby free the peasantry from all exploitation from any and every quarter.

When the peasants of the East have succeeded in casting off the yoke of the foreign capitalists and the local oppressors and in forming Soviet republics, closely linked with the Soviet republics of the West, it will then be necessary, with the aid of the fraternal republics of the industrial proletariat, to organize on a wide scale the supply to the peasants of all the means and instruments of production needed for agriculture. In this way, agriculture will flourish in the Eastern countries; the land in these countries—rich and abundant, and once the cradle of all mankind—will bloom again with splendid flowers and bring forth again all the wealth of former times, and even more. The furnishing of these supplies will be the concern of the governments of the Eastern Soviet republics and of the proletariat of the Soviet republics of the West.

As well as supplying the peasants with means of production, with machines of tremendous power such as the East has not yet seen, it will be necessary to teach the peasants how to use them collectively. For these machines, which are extremely productive, easing the peasants' labor tenfold, are not suitable for work on small holdings. They are adapted only to large areas and entail the need for joint cultivation of the peasants' land, the need to merge scattered labor into joint, collective labor, properly organized and shared. Only such joint, collective labor, properly organized, can transform the convict labor of the cultivator into labor that is sufficiently easy and pleasant.

And it is for you, comrades, to use every means to show the peasantry the need to go over from scattered labor to joint labor. It is for you to show that a way of life based on separate little economic cells, separate households, has always led the peasants—and will lead them in the future—to disintegration, making possible their enslavement and oppression. For the peasants to become a mighty force, they must merge into a close, organized unity such as that achieved by the proletariat of the industrial countries of the West. To achieve this unification it will be necessary to bring the peasants together into tens and hundreds of organizations of all kinds, agricultural and handicraft producers' cooperatives as well as consumers' cooperatives of every sort, supplying the peasants with all the products of urban industry that they need. All these organizations will free the peasantry from commercial middlemen and enable them to exchange their products directly for the products of factory industry. All middlemen, all parasites will be swept away, and the toilers will not hand over to them the slightest share of what they produce.

To achieve such a complete liberation from all the oppressors and parasites who feed at their expense, the peasantry will have to wage a protracted struggle against not only the foreign capitalist conquerors but also their own sultans and shahs, their own landlords and feudalists, their own bourgeoisie.

Today in many Eastern countries, in Turkey, Persia, and India, the peasantry is marching arm in arm with its bourgeoisie in the fight to win independence for their countries from the foreign imperialist enslavers. This path is the right one. At present, all the efforts of the Eastern peasantry must be directed to throwing off the yoke of the foreign imperialists that weighs upon them, freeing their countries from the yoke of the Western European bourgeoisie, the capitalists of Britain and France. But the peasantry of the Eastern countries must remember that achieving this liberation will not end their task. If they stop there, if they rest content with expelling the foreign oppressors, they will not be liberated at all.

A political independence in which the capitalist system is retained will in no way guarantee liberation for the peasantry. If the government of Mustafa Kemal in Turkey or liberal-national governments in Persia and India were to expel the British and then make peace with Britain on the basis of political independence of the Eastern countries, while retaining the capitalist system in these countries, all the politically independent Eastern countries would remain dependent economically. Political independence would not save them from penetration by industrial capital. And given this penetration, or the formation of native industrial capital and the development of native industry on the basis of private ownership of the means of production, the peasants would be obliged to undergo an agonizing period of primitive capitalist accumulation, in which they would finally be ruined, driven from their land, and turned—all of them—into wage laborers with no holdings of their own. And this peasantry transformed into workers would be driven by the bourgeoisie, either native or foreign, into its plantations, factories, and mines and made to work there, at miserable wages, for the enrichment of the capitalists. These peasants would find themselves in even worse enslavement to capital than what they experience today.

The peasantry of the Eastern countries must firmly keep in mind that liberation from the yoke of the foreign conquerors alone will not bring them real freedom. They also need to liberate themselves from their own oppressors, their own despotic rulers, their own landlords, and their own bourgeoisie. After setting up their own peasants' Soviet power, they need to fight in alliance with the Soviet republics of Europe against the bourgeoisie of the entire world for the overthrow of capitalism in all countries, both East and West. So long as somewhere the capitalist system has escaped destruction, so long as the entire world has not been transformed into a great federation of free workers' and peasants' Soviet republics, in which there will be no place for exploitation or oppression, the peasantry of the East will be unable to attain real liberation and will not have ensured for themselves a free, human existence.

Only with the final victory of the social revolution, only with the final establishment of the communist order throughout the world, will the peasantry of the Eastern countries secure genuine freedom, both political and economic. Then they will become able to work for themselves on their own land, enjoying all the produce of their labor and giving nothing to oppressors and exploiters.

The only road for the peasantry of the East is therefore to go forward together with the revolutionary workers of the West, in close alliance with the Soviet republics the latter have created, into struggle against both the foreign capitalist conquerors and their own despots, landlords, bourgeois, and other oppressors. This fight must be waged to the end, not retreating, until the complete victory of the social revolution is won—the establishment of a communist order, which alone can bring real liberation to all the peoples of both West and East and can destroy all forms of oppression of one people by another and all forms of exploitation of man by man. (*Applause*)

Comrades, all that I have said is summed up in the brief theses that the congress Presiding Committee has adopted. They explain how our congress sees the situation of the peasants in the East, and the roads to their liberation that it advocates.

THESES ON THE AGRARIAN QUESTION

1. The peasantry of the countries of the East, which is the sole productive class and sustains by its labor not only

the landlords but also the entire bourgeoisie and bureaucracy, is crushed beneath a burden of survivals of feudalism, relations of bondage, landlords' extortions, and state taxes. The peasants find themselves in an absolutely unbearable situation of utter ruin, chronic hunger, and endless indebtedness, obliged to work for landlords, tribute collectors, and usurers.

The oppression and exploitation of the peasants of the Eastern countries by governmental authorities, foreign capitalists, and their own landlords has reached such a degree that not only development but even human existence has become impossible for the peasants. They have been degraded into the position of downtrodden and perpetually hungry beasts of burden.

2. The sources of the oppression and exploitation of the peasants are:

a) The retention of feudal relations, which place the peasants in both personal and economic dependence upon the landlords.

b) The seizure of the land by the landlords, which enables them, owing to the shortage of sufficient free land, to reduce the peasants to bondage and turn them, though legally free, into de facto serfs.

c) The seizure of the land by the governmental authority, which leases out considerable tracts to the privileged classes and the capitalists, thus giving them a monopoly of land ownership and obliging the peasants to become subtenants and laborers under very burdensome conditions.

d) The unbearable burden of taxes and the predatory way these are levied by the irresponsible bureaucratic organs of the despotic ruling power.

e) The lack of personal security, anarchy, and the systematic brigandage by half-savage nomad tribes, backed in their attacks on the peasants by the governmental authority.

f) Together, these conditions ruin the peasants utterly, resulting in their complete impoverishment and monstrous indebtedness. They fall into absolute economic dependence on usurers, and they work solely in order to repay loans—principle and interest—to various banks, landlords, kulaks, and usurers.

g) Because of this ruin, peasants totally lack means and instruments of production—money, agricultural machinery, draft animals, seed grain, etc. It thus becomes impossible for the peasants to work for themselves on their own land, even when free and accessible land is available to them.

3. To bring about liberation from the unbearable burden of oppression, exploitation, and ruin and to create the conditions necessary for them to work for themselves so as to satisfy all their needs and make further development possible, the peasants of the Eastern countries must:

a) Remove the prime source of all their oppression and exploitation: the power of the foreign capitalist conquerors and their own despotic tyrants—the sultans, shahs, khans, and beys, with their entire parasitic train of bureaucrats and spongers. The peasants must take into their own hands power—in all its administrative, economic, and financial forms—by forming local and central peasants' soviets and setting up peasant Soviet republics of the East, linked in one indissoluble federation with the Soviet republics of the countries of the West.

b) Refuse to fulfill any obligations toward the feudal landlords; overthrow their power; abolish all personal and economic dependence upon them; abolish large-scale land ownership (under whatever legal form it may be concealed); take the land from the landlords without any payment or compensation; and divide it among the peasants, tenants, and laborers who till it.

Along with the land, the peasants must take the herds of livestock belonging to the landlords and divide them, first of all among the laborers who possess no animals at all, and then among the tenants and poor peasant cultivators. Implements found on the landlords' estates must be turned over to collective ownership by the peasants who have occupied the land. The peasants should unite in groups, concentrating the implements made available to them for use in collective cultivation of the land, which ensures the best results and the most rapid development of the peasants' farms and of their well-being.

c) Take over all lands belonging to the state and to its various institutions, both secular and spiritual (including waqf lands), and divide them among the peasants and tenants, subtenants and laborers who work these lands. The rights of the big tenant farmers who act as intermediaries between the state and the peasants must be completely abolished. All livestock and all implements belonging to these tenant farmers must be confiscated for the benefit of the peasants.

d) Cancel all existing land legislation and all restrictions on the right to use the land and to make changes on the surface of the holdings.

Proclaim that all land, regardless of its origin and independently of the rights of any owners or occupiers, belongs to the state and can be utilized free of charge by anyone who works it with his own labor.

Establish by means of a single land law the rule that whoever works a plot of land with his own labor is the possessor of that land and the owner of what it produces.

In addition, small-scale holdings of peasants who do not use others' labor must be declared inviolable; no one has the right to encroach upon them for any purpose whatsoever.

e) Regulate the utilization of local irrigation water supplies and irrigated land, giving this responsibility to the peasant soviets, both local and central.

f) Secure the interests of the nomadic tribes, assigning for their use areas of pasture sufficient to meet their needs, while also taking all measures required to ease the transition of the nomads to a settled way of life.

g) Cancel all existing taxes, including the tithe, replacing them with a single assessed levy of a proportion of all the peasants' produce, which is necessary to maintain urban workers and the army. The amount of this levy, its assessment, and also the actual process of collection will be determined and implemented by the peasant soviets. Everything taken from the peasants through this levy will be compensated by an assessed payment to them of all the goods produced by urban industry that they need.

h) Cancel peasants' debts, of every kind, to the state and its various secular and spiritual institutions, to banks, landlords, and traders, and declare invalid all manner of peasants' debt liabilities.

i) After organizing peasant soviets and peasant Soviet republics in the East and with the help and support of the Soviet republics of the industrial West, undertake to supply to the peasants, on an extensive scale, the agricultural machinery, tools, draft animals, and other means of production needed for carrying on agriculture, arranging for their joint use by all the peasants.

Undertake the organizing of agronomic aid to the peasants; of collective working of the land, without any compulsion of individual cultivators to participate in this; and of peasant producers' cooperatives, both for agriculture and for handicrafts, with extensive state support and gradual statization.

Set about organizing consumers' cooperatives among the peasants, with extensive state support and gradual statization, and arrange through them to supply the peasants with all the products of urban industry that they need.

j) In step with supplying the peasants with all the means of production needed for agriculture, organize communist Soviet farms on free, uncultivated land, to be run under state supervision by agricultural workers organized in production associations. Endeavor to develop these communist Soviet farms on as wide a scale as possible, with a view to using their surplus produce for exchange with needed products of urban industry from the industrial countries of Europe.

4. The establishment of mere political independence of Eastern countries—such as Turkey, Persia, Afghanistan—and the proclamation of mere political independence of colonial countries—India, Egypt, Mesopotamia, Arabia, etc.—cannot liberate the peasants of the East from oppression, exploitation, and ruin. If the capitalist system is retained in Europe and Asia, the industrially more backward countries of the East that win freedom from political dependence on the imperialist countries of the West will inevitably remain in complete economic dependence upon them. They will continue, as before, to serve as outlets for investment of finance capital of the European industrial countries, which brings with it capitalist exploitation of the peasants and workers.

Even if the countries and colonies of the East win complete political independence, the maintenance of the capitalist system compels the peasants of these countries to pass through an agonizing period of primitive capitalist accumulation. That process will bring about their final ruin, eviction from the land, proletarianization, and transformation into wage-earning factory hands or agricultural laborers, deprived of their own holdings and compelled to sell their labor power.

The peasants of the East, now marching arm in arm with their democratic bourgeoisie to win independence for their countries from the Western European imperialist powers, must remember that they have their own special tasks to perform. Their liberation will not be achieved merely by winning political independence, and therefore they cannot halt and rest content when that is won. The peasantry of the East must go forward even after the achievement of their countries' independence, continuing to fight against their dependence on their landlords and their bourgeoisie. When independence is won, the local landlords and bourgeoisie will certainly try to take the place of the Western European capitalists in the exploitation of these peasants.

For complete and real liberation of the peasantry of the East from all forms of oppression, dependence, and exploitation, it is also necessary to overthrow the rule of their landlords and bourgeoisie and to establish the Soviet power of the workers and peasants in the countries of the East. Only the complete abolition of the capitalist system, in West and East alike, will enable the peasants of the East not to lose but instead to retain and develop their holdings. Avoiding the necessity of passing through an agonizing phase of primitive capitalist accumulation, they will then be able, with the help of the working class of the more advanced countries, to advance through a certain period of development and on to a communist order, which will ensure for every peasant full freedom and full use of all the products of his labor.

Only the complete triumph of the social revolution and the establishment of a worldwide communist economy can free the peasantry of the Eastern countries from ruin, want, poverty, famine, oppression, and exploitation. And so for the peasants of the East, in their struggle for emancipation, there is no other road than that of struggle—together with the advanced revolutionary workers of the West and in close alliance with the Soviet republics they have formed—against both foreign capitalist conquerors and the local despots: landlords, bourgeois, and other oppressors. This struggle must be carried on without retreating until complete victory has been won over the world bourgeoisie, until the complete victory of the social revolution, until the final establishment of the communist order. Only this social order can bring true liberation to all the peoples of West and East alike, abolishing all oppression of one people by another and every kind of exploitation of man by man.

(*Translation*)

CHAIRMAN: I request the comrades to come over here so that we can take the vote. Comrades, we are going to vote on the resolution on Comrade Skachko's report. You have heard his report and his clear theses, which have been approved by the Presiding Committee.

All in favor of the theses, please raise your hands. Anyone against? No one. Adopted unanimously. (*Loud applause. Shouts of "Bravo."*)

Please give me your attention. Tomorrow at 10:00 a.m. a meeting will be held here of the nonparty fraction. I request the nonparty delegates to be present in as large numbers as possible. Comrade Zinoviev will also be present.

SECRETARY: Comrades, the Communist fraction will meet tomorrow at 9:00 a.m. in the Red Army Club. Everyone is to attend. Important questions will be decided.

CHAIRMAN: Comrades, tomorrow at 5:00 p.m. we shall hold the last session of our congress. It is understood that absolutely every delegate must be present at this last session.

(*The session ended at 9:28 p.m.*)

SESSION 7
SEPTEMBER 7, 1920

Council for Propaganda and Action; women of the East; concluding remarks

(*The session opened at 7:30 p.m. Comrade Zinoviev took the chair. Before the session began, the orchestra played the "Internationale."*)

CHAIRMAN: I declare the seventh session of the Congress of the Peoples of the East open. Today we have to deal with one of the most important, perhaps the most important matter before our congress, namely, setting up a permanent executive organ of the Congress of the Peoples of the East. When the congress disperses, we want to leave behind a body that can continue the work so splendidly begun by our historic congress.

We are sure that this congress will be not the last but only the first of its kind, and that we will convene congresses of the peoples of the East no less frequently than once a year. In order to continue the work of revolutionary propaganda, agitation, and struggle for the liberation of the East in the intervals between congresses, we propose that the First Congress of the Peoples of the East set up a permanent Council for Propaganda and Action of the Peoples of the East. Both of the fractions and the Presiding Committee have discussed this question, and we propose adoption of the following resolution.

RESOLUTION ON COUNCIL FOR PROPAGANDA AND ACTION

The First Congress of the Peoples of the East resolves to form, under the aegis of the Executive Committee of the Communist International, a permanent body uniting the peoples of the East. It will be called the Council for Propaganda of the Peoples of the East. The council will be made up as follows (the secretary will read the list of members separately).[1] The outcome is that forty-seven persons will be elected to it. In addition, Eastern peoples not represented at the First Congress are entitled to send delegates to the council.

The Council for Propaganda and Action will organize propaganda throughout the East; publish a journal, to be called *Narody Vostoka* [Peoples of the East], in three languages; organize the publication of pamphlets, leaflets, etc.; support and unify the liberation movement throughout the East; organize a university of the social sciences for activists in the East; and so on. The seat of the Council for Propaganda and Action of the Peoples of the East will be in Baku until the next congress of the peoples of the East, to be held not later than one year from now.

Plenary meetings of the Council for Propaganda and Action taking up all relevant matters will be held in Baku at least once every three months. Between plenary meetings of the Council for Propaganda and Action, all questions will be dealt with by a presidium of seven, elected by the council. The council will organize branches in Tashkent and in other places where there is need.

All the council's work will be carried on under the guidance and supervision of the Executive Committee of the Communist International. It will appoint two of the seven members of the council's Presiding Committee, and these two will have the right of veto.

CHAIRMAN: Particular groups may not have been given adequate representation in this list. And as always happens at large congresses, there are a few minor complaints and claims that small groups have not been represented or that not all those nominated have been chosen.

This is inevitable at a large congress. But altogether we have spent more than one session working on this list, and both fractions are convinced that the maximum possible fairness has been achieved, and that with this composition we can form a committee able to carry out the task entrusted to it.

We are giving the council a colossal task to perform, and I am sure that the organization we are about to set up has a great future before it. Today it is still an insufficiently centralized organization. But tomorrow, and the day after tomorrow, and every day in the course of the development of the liberation movement in the East, the Council for Propaganda and Action that we are forming today will become a genuine "great power" of the peoples of the East.

(*The "Internationale." Translation.*)

CHAIRMAN: Comrades, we will read the list a little later, so that a few changes that are now needed can be made. I ask the congress to confirm the proposal to set up a Council for Propaganda and Action in the form that has been outlined. Who is in favor of this proposal? Anyone against? Adopted.

Comrades, during the last two days in which our congress has been meeting, events of major importance have taken place in Bukhara. Two Bukharan comrades will now be called upon to give the Congress of the Peoples of the East a brief account of these events. First, Comrade Rojabov.

ROJABOV (*speaking in Turkic*): Comrades, very important events have taken place in Bukhara. "Bukhara the Magnificent," that wellspring of learning, was named the Magnificent and regarded as a center of learning a few centuries ago, but for some years now it has been transformed into a mere wretched kishlak [village]. This has happened because a despotic form of government has existed in Bukhara.

Such has been the rule of the emir of Bukhara that out of the 25 million inhabitants, only 5 million have in recent times been left under his yoke. The remaining 20 million have been split up and conquered by the imperialists and the Russian imperial government. Imperialism has seized purely Bukharan dominions. Until now the Bukharans have not led a human existence. Oppressed, they have wept night and day, unable to live like people in other countries.

Now things have changed. After the October revolution the emir of Bukhara sought his happiness under the wing of the British imperialists, sent presents to British officers, and so on, but nevertheless the people's oppression continued. The workers made their preparations, and now they have done what needed to be done, and we see the revolution already on the march in Bukhara.[2] Bukhara, Karshi, Chardzhou, Khatyrchi, and Kerki have been captured by the Red troops. The red flag is flying from the towers of these five towns, hoisted there by the Soviet and workers' forces.

Comrades, the workers and peasants of the Red Army greet you on this day! The peoples of Bukhara have been freed at last—and so too, very soon, will the other peoples! (*The "Internationale"*)

CHAIRMAN: The other representative of Bukhara, Comrade Jabarzadeh, will now speak.

JABARZADEH: (*Speaks in Uzbek.*)

KIZIZADEH (*interpreter*): I will just say that Comrade Jabarzadeh confined himself to greeting us. The rest of his speech was concerned only with the events now under way in Bukhara, which we know about from what the previous speaker said. So I think there is no need for a translation.

CHAIRMAN: The Presiding Committee has decided also to call upon a representative of the women, Comrade Najiye. (*Applause*)

NAJIYE: (*Speaks in Turkish. Her speech is interrupted by applause.*)

CHAIRMAN: I call upon Comrade Shabanova to translate.

SHABANOVA: Comrades, Comrade Najiye said: The women's movement beginning in the East must be looked at not from the standpoint of those frivolous feminists who are content to see woman's place in social life as that of a delicate plant or an elegant doll. This movement must be seen as a vital and necessary consequence of the revolutionary movement taking place throughout the world. The women of the East are not fighting merely for the right to walk in the street without wearing the chador, as many people suppose. For the women of the East, with their high moral ideals, the question of the chador, it can be said, comes last in priority. If the women, who form half of every community, are set up against the men and do not enjoy the same rights, obviously it is impossible for society to progress; the backwardness of Eastern societies is irrefutable proof of this.

Comrades, you can be sure that all your efforts and labors to realize new forms of social life, however sincere and however vigorous your endeavors may be, will be fruitless unless you summon the women to become real helpers in your work.

In Turkey, owing to the conditions caused by the war, women have been obliged to quit the home and the household and take on the performance of a variety of social duties. Women have had to take over the responsibilities of the men who have been called up for military service. What is more, in roadless localities of Anatolia that are inaccessible even to pack animals, women have been dragging artillery equipment for the troops. This fact cannot, of course, be called a step forward in the conquest of equal rights for women. People who view the fact that women are making up with their labor for the shortage of beasts of burden as a contribution to the cause of equal rights for women are unworthy of our attention.

We do not deny that at the beginning of the 1908 revolution some measures were introduced for women's benefit. In view, however, of the ineffectiveness and inadequacy of these measures, we do not regard them as highly significant.

The opening of one or two schools of elementary and higher education for women in the capital and in the provinces, and even the opening of a university for women, does not accomplish a thousandth of what still needs to be done. Of course, more fundamental or serious measures on behalf of women held in bondage cannot be expected from the Turkish government, whose actions are based on the oppression and exploitation of the weaker by the stronger.

But we also know that the position of our sisters in Persia, Bukhara, Khiva, Turkestan, India, and other Muslim countries is even worse. The injustice done to us and to our sisters, however, has not remained unpunished. Proof of this is to be seen in the backwardness and decline of all the countries of the East. Comrades, you must know that the evil done to women has never gone and will never go without retribution.

Because this conference of the Congress of the Peoples of the East is drawing to a close, lack of time obliges us to refrain from discussing the position of women in the various countries of the East. However, the comrade delegates are entrusted with the great mission of taking back to their homelands the noble principles of the revolution. Let them not forget that all the efforts they devote to winning happiness for the peoples will remain fruitless unless there is real help from the women.

In order to deliver us from all calamities, the Communists consider it necessary to create a classless society, and to this end they declare relentless war against all the bourgeois and privileged layers. The women Communists of the East have an even harder battle to wage because, in addition, they have to fight against the despotism of their menfolk. If you, men of the East, continue now as in the past to be indifferent to the fate of women, you can be sure that our countries will perish, and you and we together with them. The alternative is for us, together with all the oppressed, to begin a bloody life-and-death struggle to win our rights by force.

I will briefly set forth the women's demands. If you want to bring about your own emancipation, listen to our demands and render us real help and cooperation.
1. Complete equality of rights.
2. Ensuring to women unconditional access to educational and vocational institutions established for men.

3. Equality of rights of both parties to marriage. Unconditional abolition of polygamy.
4. Unconditional admission of women to employment in legislative and administrative institutions.
5. Establishment of committees for the rights and protection of women everywhere, in cities, towns, and villages.

There is no doubt that we are entitled to raise these demands. In recognizing that we have equal rights, the Communists have reached out their hand to us, and we women will prove their most loyal comrades. True, we may stumble in pathless darkness, we may stand on the brink of yawning chasms, but we are not afraid, because we know that in order to see the dawn one has to pass through the dark night.

CHAIRMAN: Comrades, Comrade Bibinur will also speak, on behalf of the women of Turkestan. (*Loud applause*)

BIBINUR (*in Turkic*): I bring you greetings, dear comrades, from the working women, both Russian and Muslim, of the town of Aulie Ata [Dzhambul].

Dear comrades, you have gathered here in the Congress of the Peoples of the East to take decisions about the tremendous tasks that confront you. You represent the very best forces of the toiling and oppressed masses. All the oppressed nationalities of the East, who have been ruthlessly exploited by tsarism and imperialism for hundreds of years, look to you, their deputies, with hope.

We, the women of the East, are exploited ten times worse than the men, and are more closely affected by the ugly sides of the secluded life led by the Muslim women of the East.

But now at last, dear comrades, a bright sun has reached us, warming and comforting us like little children in their cradles—the first we have known. It is the power of the soviets of workers', peasants', and dehkhans' deputies. Soviet power is our mother and we are its children. The soul of this Soviet power, the liberator and vanguard of working people around the world, is the Russian Communist Party and the valiant Red Army, which has won justice for the oppressed with the fraternal workers' blood.

We too must fight tirelessly, working for the emancipation of all the oppressed peoples of the East. We women have awakened from our nightmare of oppression and every day are strengthening your ranks with our best forces. We look forward to your fruitful work.

Long live the Congress of Peoples of the Red East!
Long live all the oppressed peoples of the East!
Long live the Third International!
Long live the women's section of the town of Aulie Ata and of all Turkestan!

CHAIRMAN: We will now proceed to approve the list of members of the Council for Propaganda and Action of the Peoples of the East. I call on Comrade Ostrovsky.

OSTROVSKY: Here is the list of members of the Council for Action and Propaganda in the East. I will read first the members of the Communist fraction, and then those of the nonparty members.

1) Ismail Hakki and (2) Suleiman Nuri, (*both from Turkey*)
3) Haydar Khan and (4) Sultanzadeh, (*both from Persia*)
5) Agazadeh (*Afghanistan*)
6) Narimanov and (7) Guseinov, (*both from Azerbaijan*)
8) Rakhmanov (*Khiva*)
9) Abdur Rashidov (*Uzbek, from Fergana region*)
10) Jurabayev (*Tajik, from Samarkand region*)

11) Ryskulov (*Kirghiz, from Syr Darya and Semirechiye regions*)
12) Karpov (*Turkmen, from Transcaspian region*)
13) Acharya (*India*)
14) Makharadze (*Georgia*)
15) Avis (*Armenia*)
16) Jabarzadeh (*Bukhara*)
17) Krimazov and (18) Gobiyev (*both from Dagestan*)
19) Mansurov (*Dagestan*)
20) Khamzatov (*Chechenia*)
21) Cherkas (*Kuban*)
22) Amur-Sanan (*Kalmyk republic*)
23) Genikoy (*Tatar republic*)
24) Ibrahimov (*Bashkiria*)
25) Januzakov (*Kara-Kirghizia*)
26) Ostrovsky (*Eastern Jews*)
27) *Kirghiz republic*
28) Mamedov (*Crimea*)
29) Shabanova (*Muslim women*)
30) Pavlovich (*Communist International*)
31) Kirov (*Communist International*)
32) Ordzhonikidze (*Communist International*)
33) Stasova (*Communist International*)
34) Yeleyeva (*Communist International*)
35) Skachko (*Communist International*)

From the nonparty fraction:
36) Baha [Bahaeddin] Shakir (*Turkey*)
37) Narbutabekov and (38) Mahmudov (*Turkestan*)
39) Musayev and (40) Yelchiyev (*Azerbaijan*)
41) Kari Tajiyev (*Afghanistan*)
42) Abdulayev (*Khiva*)
43) Nazir Sidiq (*India*)

44) Abas Haji (*Bukhara*)
45) Khemzatov (*Terek*)
46) Wang (*China*)
47) Khajan Kuliyev (*Turkmen*)
48) Kubse Osman (*Kirghizia*)

CHAIRMAN: Please be so good as to hand in to the Presiding Committee any necessary amendments. I will take a vote on the list as a whole. All in favor of the list as a whole? Anyone against?

VOICES FROM THE BALCONY: In the case of Persia it is irregular.

CHAIRMAN: Please stop all this noise immediately at this moment when the Congress of the Peoples of the East is electing its first council. Comrades, in an assembly of two thousand people there will always be two or three to shout: "Irregular!" The council has been properly elected. Long live the Council for Propaganda and Action! (*Applause. The "Internationale."*) Comrades, it has been proposed that we send greetings to the Red Army. I call upon Comrade Tajiyev.

TAJIYEV (*in Turkic*): The First Congress of the Peoples of the East sends greetings to the valiant Red Army of the Russian Soviet Federated Socialist Republic. The peoples of the East, tormented for so long by the armies of the European powers, greet the Red Army as their deliverer. The congress asks every Red warrior, on whatever front he is fighting, to bear in mind that millions of people in the East are following his struggle with bated breath, looking forward to the moment when the military situation will permit the Red Army to turn its weapons to the task of their liberation. The Red Army of the workers and peasants is today the only bulwark of these peoples against international imperialism, and it is the first priority and responsibility of all the peoples of the East to strengthen this bulwark.

Honor and glory to every Red soldier and every Red commander! The sons of the East, oppressed but thirsting for freedom, await you!

BÉLA KUN: Long live the Red Army!

(*Shouts of "Hurrah!" Applause.*)

TAJIYEV: If this gathering approves the text of the telegram, the Presiding Committee intends to send it to the Red Army. (*Voices: "Yes, yes." "Hurrah."*)

CHAIRMAN: Permit me to consider the telegram adopted.

VOICE: Send greetings to Comrade Lenin.

VOICE: Send greetings to the leader of the Red Army, Comrade Trotsky.

CHAIRMAN: Permit me to consider that proposal as adopted. I now call on Comrade Yegorov to make an unscheduled statement on behalf of the Baku Soviet of Workers' and Red Army Men's Deputies.

YEGOROV: Dear comrades, a short time ago, at the beginning of this historic session, you took a decision clearly stating that you chose the city of Baku as the seat of the Council for Action and Propaganda in the East, which you had elected. Allow me, comrades, on behalf of the Baku soviet, to express our profound Communist gratitude for the confidence in the proletariat of Baku you have shown by taking this decision. (*Applause*)

We, comrades, the Baku workers, are proud that the First Congress of the Peoples of the East has met in our Red capital, and that it was here, in our Red Baku, that the foundation was laid for the future liberation of the entire oppressed East. (*Applause*) We are proud that for the seat of your council, the center of its revolutionary struggle, the residence of the general staff of this struggle, you have chosen—Baku.

The Baku proletariat has made no few sacrifices and efforts for the cause of its own emancipation, for the emancipation of the Azerbaijani and Turkish people. And now it will contribute no few sacrifices and efforts for the emancipation of the East from the capitalist yoke.

The Baku workers will consider the sacred banner of bloody war handed over to them here at the congress as a call summoning them to this holy war. I can assure you, comrades, that this banner will not fall from the grasp of the Baku workers, who have already proved by revolutionary struggle in the past how firmly they uphold this banner.

Dear comrades, to commemorate this historic moment I propose on behalf of the Baku Executive Committee that the building we are now in, and where we have planned our joint actions against the common enemy, be named the "Palace of the Peoples of the East." (*Applause*)

Previously, comrades, the bourgeoisie delighted their ears in this place, listening to all sorts of love songs. But now we will meet here to learn how to overthrow the bourgeoisie, how to free ourselves from their rule, how to build palaces like this in places where at present our comrades are rotting in shanties, unable not merely to confer together as we are doing today but even to live like human beings.

In addition, facing the Boulevard stands the best building in Baku, the house of Isa-Bek Gajinsky, formerly the biggest exploiter in Baku; the house that he thought he would enjoy for life. I propose to name this building "House of the Peoples of the East." This house will be the place where your general staff will establish itself, where you can gather to obtain advice and instructions. (*Applause*)

Furthermore, comrades, Stanislavsky Street is a place where, previously, national and chauvinist passions reigned, and Armenians and Muslims could not look upon each other calmly.[3] I propose that it be renamed "Street of the Peoples of the East."

Today we are showing the workers of Baku that there are no more barriers between nations, but only one house of free working people, for whose liberation we are now fighting and whom we summon to unified struggle on behalf of all the oppressed masses of the East.

Comrades, long live the East, enslaved today but already awakening to the bloody struggle! Long live the Council for Action and Propaganda that has been formed here! Long live the proletariat of Baku!

CHAIRMAN: I call upon Comrade Narimanov.

NARIMANOV: Comrades, I addressed you in a cheerful spirit at the opening of the congress, but now I have to speak to you about a matter of sadness for all of us, namely, the funeral of twenty-six of our dear comrades.

In 1918, when Soviet power prevailed here for a few months, the Dashnak and Menshevik traitors handed over power, or at least contributed to surrendering Soviet power in Baku into the hands of the British. Until September 14 our dear comrades proudly, bravely, and honorably remained at their posts down to the last moment. Then, as the Turks drew near, the Menshevik and Dashnak traitors allowed our comrades to leave for Astrakhan. While they were on their way, these same traitors arrested them and changed the ship's course to Krasnovodsk. Our comrades fell into the hands of the British scoundrels and were shot by them there, between Ashkhabad and Kizyl-Arvat.

When Soviet power was restored in Turkestan, our comrades' bodies were removed to Astrakhan. And now the Azerbaijan Soviet Republic has brought the bodies of these dear comrades to Baku, and they will be buried here tomorrow. The Azerbaijan republic considers that the presence here of the tombs of these dear comrades will have educational significance for the young generations. Our children, seeing the monument to these dear comrades, will know how Soviet power in Azerbaijan, and Soviet power generally, values honorable and brave comrades.

We invite you to come tomorrow to Parapet, until ten o'clock, and then to Petrovsky Square. There together, with sorrow in our hearts, we will commit the bodies of our dear comrades to the ground.

CHAIRMAN: I propose that the congress honor the memory of the fallen comrades by standing. (*All rise. The orchestra plays the "Revolutionary Funeral March."*)

NARBUTABEKOV: Comrades, the work of the congress is concluded. The chairman of the First Congress of the Peoples of the East, Comrade Zinoviev, will make summary remarks before our congress is closed. (*Loud applause. The "Internationale."*)

CHAIRMAN: And so, comrades, the Congress of the Peoples of the East, convened by the Executive Committee of the Communist International, has not only been held but has successfully concluded its work, and crowned it by setting up a permanent center for the revolutionary struggle of the peoples of the East. (*Applause*)

Comrades, in my many years of revolutionary activity it has been my lot to take part in more than one major congress. But in all conscience I must say that none of us has ever had to organize or take part in a congress that was more significant, fraught with greater revolutionary consequences, or as enormously important as this one. For the congress we have just held has dealt with something quite new and unprecedented. It went down in the history of mankind from the moment when it began and when the enslaved, oppressed, exploited peoples of the East assembled here. The first tinkle of the chairman's bell on this platform was the funeral knell of the world bourgeoisie.

Comrades, we do not always have the time to appreciate what a great historical event we are taking part in.

Just think what has happened, what has gone on in this hall. Peoples who until now have been looked upon by the whole bourgeois world as draft animals whose task was to draw their water, as peoples of inferior blood, as peoples who seemed specially destined to haul water for the bourgeoisie, peoples about whom the bourgeoisie always felt complacent (no danger of fire there, they said)—these peoples are now rising in revolt.

During the last few years, the bourgeoisie has been afraid that the workers in the West would revolt. But as regards the peoples of the East, until very recently it has been quite complacent. And then, just as it was sleeping sweetly on a soft pillow, certain that no danger was to be expected from that quarter, at that very moment a congress of the oppressed peoples of the East assembles, gets organized, and goes onto the attack with unprecedented, amazing, heart-lifting unanimity. (*Loud applause*) That is the most important aspect of our congress.

Just think. Peoples who for decades were at daggers drawn with each other, who did not associate with each other, who were baited against one another—delegates from these peoples have felt from the first moment like members of one family, despite their not understanding each other's languages. At once, a fraternal unanimity arose, so that it has seemed obvious that we were one family, a fraternal, friendly family. This is the greatness of our congress.

This is a simple, elementary fact, but it is precisely for that reason that it is great. And we have the right to say that a congress such as that witnessed by the walls of this building in Baku, at the beginning of September 1920, is without precedent in the world. This congress means that the old, bourgeois, oppressors' world has come to its end. It means that the main reserves of toiling mankind have awakened to create a completely new order, a wholly unprecedented way of life on earth.

Comrades, our congress has been heterogeneous, many-colored, in its composition. Represented at it have been peoples who have already won Soviet power, who are sister republics of our Russian Soviet Republic. Also represented here, on the other hand, have been peoples among whom the struggle is still on the boil, where it is still only just flaring up. This heterogeneity has resulted in some misunderstandings. When we discussed the question of our executive body, some comrades felt they were at a congress of soviets of the peoples of the East. That does not yet exist. Look at India, which has only a handful of representatives here—a huge country oppressed by British capital, where there is still no Soviet republic, where the struggle has only begun to flare up. We have countries like Turkey, where an overt civil war is in progress, where several governments are in conflict, and the struggle between them has not yet ceased. We see a similar scene in Persia, where there are two governments and where the struggle burns more fiercely with every passing day.[4] And we also have here bourgeois-democratic republics like Armenia.

We have frequently spoken here about Armenia. There is not just one Armenia. First there is workers' and peasants' Armenia, to which we extend a fraternal hand; and then, the accursed, bourgeois Armenia of the Dashnak hangmen. (*Loud applause*)

And the same situation exists in Georgia. Today the Georgian workers and the Georgian peasants are oppressed as nowhere else. Because Social Democrats are in power there, the best veteran fighters of Georgia have been put in prison. And the present leaders of Georgia, such as Zhordania, have descended to such a level of shamelessness that their own old teacher, such an old revolutionary as

Comrade Mikha Tskhakaya, was held in prison by these gentlemen. There is not one Georgia; there is the Georgia of Messrs. Chkheidze, Gegechkori, and company, who scurry around in the anterooms of bourgeois ministers in Europe, and there is the Georgia of the honest workers and peasants, our brothers, with whom we march arm in arm and shoulder to shoulder. (*Applause*)

It is all the more remarkable that a congress so mixed in composition should have been united on all fundamental questions.

Comrades, I want to touch upon one question that is rather painful for the Soviet republics, above all for Turkestan and others. These republics are our sisters. The struggle there was very hard; the workers and peasants there achieved the Soviet form of government only with great difficulty. They are loyal to their fraternal alliance with Soviet Russia. Alongside gigantic work to establish workers' and peasants' rule, along with tremendous changes and overturns, a phenomenon has been observed there that we have to admit is extremely undesirable and regrettable. We are intentionally raising it in this very great, triumphant, and historic assembly.

Yes, the Soviet government in Russia, the Council of People's Commissars, and the Communist International know that in Turkestan and in the other fraternal Soviet republics in the East, certain elements who have attached themselves to the Communist Party act in a way that brings shame on the title of Communist. They incite one section of the population against another, offend the indigenous peasantry, and take their land from them. Certain scions of the old bourgeois Russia who have settled there and have wormed their way into our ranks, carrying on the accursed tradition of the bourgeoisie and of tsarism, continue to look upon the local population as an inferior race. And this gives rise to the most legitimate and justified indignation.

We address ourselves in this assembly to the Russian Communist comrades, to the Red Army men, to all the activists whose task it is to carry out the line of the Soviet government in the East. We turn to them, saying: Remember that you are at a post of threefold responsibility. Every mistake you make, even a very small one (not to speak of straightforward abuses) will cost us very dear. We address ourselves to the activists from Russia who are called upon to work in Turkestan and other Soviet republics of the East. We point out that our party and the Communist International require that they fulfill completely the requirements of the honored title of Communist. That means they must never forget that the indigenous working population are our brothers. They must break once and for all with the accursed old heritage left to use by the bourgeoisie and tsarism. They must not dare to insult the toilers, the local inhabitants. They must rather cut off their hand than commit an injustice. (*Loud applause*)

There was a time, a dark, sad time, when Russian officers and a Russian army of serfs led by these officers were sent by the tsar to suppress popular revolts and destroy the best section of the Polish people of those days. And at that time one of Russia's best writers, A.I. Herzen, exclaimed: "When I see what my kinsmen are doing, what the Russian army and Russian officers are doing, I am ashamed to be a Russian." So spoke Herzen. We do not live in such a time as that; none of us need be ashamed to be Russian, for Russia has been the first country to raise the red flag and to help other peoples to emancipate themselves. But it is a matter for shame that persons have wormed their way into our ranks, through misunderstanding or self-interest, who are behaving in our sister republics in a way that compels us to blush and to remember the harsh words of A.I. Herzen.

Comrades, at this assembly we give a solemn undertaking to those present that our party and the Communist International are doing everything in their power to clear the weeds out of our garden, (*Loud applause*) to purge our ranks, and to ensure that every one of us who is called upon to carry out Soviet policy in the awakening East understands that this is a holy place, that this work needs to be approached with clean hands and a clear head.

A distrust has been implanted in the peoples of the East by decades of experience—a justified distrust of Europeans, who always have merely deceived and swindled them, merely mocked them. Today this distrust is sometimes involuntarily, semiconsciously transferred to the new, workers' Europe and, in the first place, to our Soviet power, to Soviet Russia. As people of labor, as serious revolutionaries, we have to understand where the roots of this distrust lie. And by our work and our fraternal support in these, the most difficult years, we must create the feeling that we are one fraternal family, all members of which look with the same horror on the old, accursed past, and all as one fight against those who divide us.

I hope, indeed I am sure, that this congress, and the fact that we have heard what you have told us here, will bring us so close together and bind our fraternal family so firmly that no mistakes made by individuals, or even crimes committed by particular groups, will divide us from you, now and forever. We are one single, fraternal family, facing the same enemies, wanting the same friends, and recognizing only the same ideals. (*Loud applause*)

Comrades, the 1905 revolution in Russia, which was essentially only a dress rehearsal for the great revolution that we are experiencing today, was soon crushed. Nevertheless, as you recall, it spread at once to the East, evoking echoes in Turkey, Persia, and other Eastern countries.

Just as the 1905 revolution was mere child's play in comparison with the great revolution of October 1917, so the response our revolution is meeting with in the East is a million times greater today than in 1905.

Yes, comrades, across thousands of versts, despite distance and differences of language, a great revolution in a great country will inevitably kindle the hearts of the toilers of other countries. And the greatest pride for a Russian revolutionary must be the knowledge that the sparks of our revolution have spread to the powder keg of the East, and that the effect of this is being borne back to us here in explosion after explosion. In this lies the great significance of our revolution. Not only has it set fire to the West, but the East too is in conflagration before our eyes. Our congress has stepped forward in the role of the greatest organizer and collective incendiary of the East, for it is kindling the greatest revolt on earth—against the bourgeoisie, against the serf owners and capitalists. (*Applause*)

We have discussed only a few questions, but we have discussed them very seriously and have adopted resolutions in full unanimity. We have had to translate everything said into many languages, comrades, but it has not been necessary to translate the word *soviets*, for it is known throughout the world, in West and East alike. The East will be Soviet! (*Applause*)

Comrades, we have set up a council of action. At the moment this is still a young organization, only just born. But no one sitting in this hall will say that I am a great optimist if I express the view that this council of action in the East is already stronger than the bourgeois cabinet in Britain, or than any other cabinet. (*Applause*) The cabinets of Britain and France will decline in power, will wane with every passing day, will perish before the eyes of mankind—they are living out their last days like dogs.

But the peoples of the East are the rising star. We and you, comrades, will become a greater power with every day that passes. Paraphrasing Marx's words, we can say that today the British and French imperialists are all unable to take a single step without first asking themselves: How will the peoples of the East react? Won't they do something against us, against the imperialists?

We did not argue here as to whether soviets are necessary or not—that is clear to us. We did not argue whether we needed to unite—that also is clear. But look at how united the bourgeoisie are. In every language, they say, "Entente, Entente." What does this word mean? An entente is a heartfelt agreement. But we say that in this agreement it is not so much the heart as the purse that is operative. (*Applause*) Look and see how this Entente is breaking up before our eyes. It cannot decide a single question. The partners are tripping each other up, quarrelling, and traveling around all the spas of Europe discussing the "Russian question." They discuss the Russian question more than any other. It is a hard nut for them, which they cannot crack and never will. (*Loud applause*)

Comrades, after our congress we are perfectly justified in saying that the brigands, the British and French imperialists, will never solve the so-called Russian question that is such a curse to them. But we and you and the Communist International will within a few years solve the European question completely. (*Loud applause*)

Comrades, the first two days of our congress were spent in discussing what our attitude should be toward the Entente, toward imperialism. And for us that moment after the first report, when the assembled representatives of the peoples of the East swore to begin a holy war, that moment will be preserved in our hearts as a sacred experience. That was the basis for everything else, that is what unites us all. *Yes, a holy war against the plunderers and capitalists!*

And, as practical people, all of you will translate that oath into the language of facts. When you return home you will tell the peasants, both men and women—you will tell all the working people what we have decided, the oath we took, the line we marked out. And with every hour we will feel our unity growing, our forces strengthening. We will climb still higher, drawing near to the last barrier, and this last barrier we will take. We will end the civil war, stretch out a fraternal hand to the West—to Europe and America—and unite in one family, so as, together, to build a new life! (*Applause*)

Seventy years ago, Karl Marx, the teacher of us all, issued the call, "Workers of all countries, unite!" As Karl Marx's pupils, the continuators of his work, we can expand this formulation, supplementing and broadening it, and say: "Workers of all lands *and oppressed peoples of the whole world*, unite!" (*Loud applause. The "Internationale."*)

Comrades, we cannot bring to the Communist International and to the workers around the world any news more joyful than the fact that, after the unification of the workers of the West and of America, the toilers of the entire East have united. Let us remember only what unites us. Let us tear out of our hearts whatever can disunite us. Let us remember that we have one enemy—British and French imperialism. Let each of us devote his life—even dozens of lives, if we had them—to the cause of liberating the peoples of the East and of the world as a whole! (*Loud applause. The "Internationale."*)

Comrades, the Presiding Committee congratulates you on the successful conclusion of the congress and declares the First Congress of the Peoples of the East closed.

Long live the Third International!

(*Loud applause. Shouts of "Hurrah!" The "Internationale."*)

(*The session ended at 10:40 p.m.*)

MANIFESTO

Manifesto to the peoples of the East

On September 1, 1920, in the city of Baku, the capital of Azerbaijan, a congress of representatives of the peoples of the East was held.[1] Our congress was attended by 1,891 delegates from the following countries: Turkey, Persia, Egypt, India, Afghanistan, Baluchistan, Kashgaria, China, Japan, Korea, Arabia, Syria, Palestine, Bukhara, Khiva, Dagestan, Northern Caucasia, Azerbaijan, Armenia, Georgia, Turkestan, Fergana, the Kalmyk autonomous region, the Bashkir republic, the Tatar republic, and the Far Eastern district.

The Congress of the Peoples of the East was convened by the Communist International. Every peasant, every toiler needs to know what the Communist International is. It is a union of workers and peasants, of Communists around the world, that has set itself the aim of smashing the power of the rich and bringing about the complete equality of all.

At the Second World Congress of the Communist International, held in Moscow in August 1920, the following countries were represented: America, Britain, France, Austria, Italy, Spain, Poland, Bohemia, Yugoslavia, Hungary, Switzerland, Belgium, Holland, Denmark, Sweden, Norway, Finland, Estonia, Latvia, Lithuania, Romania, Bulgaria, Turkey, Persia, India, China, Japan, Korea, Indochina, Georgia, Azerbaijan, Armenia, Khiva, Bukhara, Afghanistan, Argentina, Russia, Ukraine.

The Communist International wants to put an end not only to the power of the rich over the poor but also to the power of some peoples over others. For this purpose the workers of Europe and America must unite with the peoples of the East.

The congress of representatives of the peoples of the East calls on these peoples to bring about this unity, which is needed for the liberation of all the oppressed and all the exploited.

Peoples of the East! Six years ago a colossal, monstrous slaughter—a world war—broke out in Europe. Thirty-five million human beings were killed; hundreds of cities and thousands of other settlements were devastated. The war ruined the countries of Europe, subjecting all the peoples to the torment of unheard-of want and unprecedented starvation.

This colossal conflict has so far been carried on mainly in Europe, affecting Asia and Africa only partially. The war was fought between European peoples, with the peoples of the East participating in it only to a relatively small extent. Some hundreds of thousands of Turkish peasants took part, deceived by their rulers, who were under the German imperialists' thumb. Two or three million Indians and Negroes, bought like slaves by the British and French capitalists, were, like slaves, hurled to their deaths on fields of France far distant and strange to them, serving interests alien and unintelligible to them—those of the British and French bankers and industrialists.

But although the peoples of the East held aloof from this gigantic conflict, playing only an insignificant part in it, nevertheless this war was fought not for the countries of Europe, not for the countries and peoples of the West, but for the countries and peoples of the East. It was fought for the partition of the world, and chiefly for the partition of Asia, of the East. It was fought to decide who was to rule the countries of Asia and whose slaves the peoples of the East would be. It was fought to decide whether the British or the German capitalists would skin the peasants and workers of Turkey, Persia, Egypt, and India.

The monstrous four-year carnage ended in victory for France and Britain. The German capitalists were shattered, and along with them the German people were crushed, destroyed, and doomed to starvation. In victorious France, almost all the adult population was wiped out by the war, and all the industrial areas were devastated. Bled white by the struggle, France was left quite powerless after its victory. As a result of the colossal, barbarous slaughter, imperialist Britain emerged as the sole and omnipotent master of Europe and Asia. In all Europe, Britain alone was still able to muster sufficient strength, for it had waged the war with other peoples' hands, those of the enslaved peoples, the Indians and Negroes. It had waged the war at the expense of the colonies it oppressed.

As victor and omnipotent master of half the world, the British government proceeded to carry out the objectives for which it had waged the war—to consolidate its hold on all the countries of Asia and to enslave, fully and finally, all the peoples of the East.

Hindered by no one, fearing no one, and casting aside all shame, the handful of greedy banker-capitalists at the head of the British state have openly and brazenly set about reducing to slavery the peasants and workers of the Eastern countries.

Peoples of the East! You know what Britain has done in India, you know how it has turned the many-millioned masses of the Indian peasants and workers into dumb beasts of burden without any rights.

The Indian peasant has to hand over to the British government a proportion of his crop so large that what remains is not enough to sustain him for even a few months. The Indian worker has to work in the British capitalist's factory for such a miserable pittance that he cannot even buy the daily handful of rice he needs for subsistence. Every year millions of Indians die of hunger. Every year millions perish in the jungles and swamps from the heavy labor launched by the British capitalists for their own enrichment.

Millions of Indians, unable to find a crust of bread in their very rich and fertile homeland, are obliged to join the British armed forces. Leaving their homeland, they spend their whole lives enduring the hard lot of the soldier. They fight endless wars in all corners of the world, against all the peoples of the world, upholding everywhere the ruthless dominion of Britain. They pay with their lives and blood for the unceasing expansion of the wealth of the British capitalists, securing for them monstrous profits, luxury, and prosperity. But the Indians themselves enjoy no human rights. The British officers who rule over them—insolent sons of a British bourgeoisie grown fat on Indian corpses—do not regard them as human.

An Indian dare not sit at the same table with a Britisher, lodge in the same quarters, enter the same railway carriage, or attend the same school. In the eyes of the British bourgeois every Indian is a pariah, a slave, a beast of burden, an animal that dare not have human feelings or put forward demands. Every uprising by Indian peasants and workers, driven to extremities, is met by the British with ruthless mass shootings. In Indian villages that have revolted the streets are covered with hundreds of corpses of those shot down, and British officers, for their amusement, force the survivors to crawl on their bellies and lick the boots of their enslavers.

Peoples of the East! Do you know what Britain has done in Turkey? Britain offered Turkey a peace by which three-quarters of Asia Minor, a land inhabited exclusively by Ottoman Turks that includes all the country's industrial cities, was to pass into the possession of Britain, France, Italy, and Greece. What remained of Turkish territory was to be burdened with such payments that the Ottomans would become permanent undischarged debtors of Britain.

When the Turkish people refused to accept such a peace, which would have destroyed them, the British occupied Constantinople, a holy place to Muslims, and dispersed the Turkish parliament. They arrested all the people's leaders, shot the best of them, and exiled hundreds of others to the island of Malta, where they were shut up in the dark and damp dungeons of an ancient fortress. Now the British rule the roost in Constantinople. They have taken from the Turks everything that could be taken: money, banks, factories, railways, and ships. They have closed all the points of entry into Asia Minor. In Asia Minor today there is not one piece of cloth, not one fragment of metal. The Turkish peasant must go about without a shirt and till the soil with a wooden plow.

The British used the Greek army to occupy the vilayet of Smyrna, the French army to take Adana, and colonial troops to take Brussa [Bursa] and Izmid. They have besieged the Turks on all sides and are steadily pushing into Turkish territory, trying to reduce to complete exhaustion the Turkish people, who have already been as tormented and ruined as they can be by decades of continuous war.

In the already occupied parts of Turkey, the British—true to their custom—scoff and jeer intolerably at the Turkish people. In Constantinople the British have taken all the schools and universities for use as barracks, stopped all Turkish educational activity, closed down all Turkish newspapers, broken up all workers' organizations, and filled the prisons with Turkish patriots. They have placed the entire population under the uncontrolled authority of British police, who consider themselves authorized—without any excuse and in broad daylight in the streets of Constantinople—to club the head of anyone wearing a fez. As the British see it, anyone who wears the fez and is a Turk is a creature of an inferior species, a pariah, a slave, a beast of burden, who can be treated like a dog.

In occupied regions of Turkey, the British truly treat the Turks like dogs, subjecting them to forced labor and punishing them with blows. The British are endeavoring through tricks, base methods, and violence of every kind to turn Turkey into a conquered country, forcing the Turkish people to work for their enrichment.

Peoples of the East! What has Britain done to Persia? The British capitalists crushed a peasants' revolt against the shah and the landlords, shooting or hanging thousands of Persian peasants. They restored the rule of the shah and the landlords that the people had overthrown. They took back from the peasants the land they seized from the landlords and thrust the peasants back into serfdom, making them once again rayats, slaves of the molkdars without any rights.

Then, bribing the shah's venal government, the British capitalists used a base, traitorous treaty to acquire all Persia and the entire Persian people as their absolute property. They have laid hands on all the wealth of Persia. In every city of Persia they have installed their garrisons of deceived Indian sepoys, bought into slavery. They have begun to behave in Persia as though in a conquered country, treating the Persian population—nominally independent—as an enslaved people.

Peoples of the East! What has Britain done to Mesopotamia and Arabia? Without any ado, it has proclaimed these independent Muslim countries to be its colonies. It has driven from the land Arabs who have owned it for centuries, taking from them the best, most fertile valleys of the Tigris and the Euphrates. It has taken the best pastureland, which the people need in order to survive. It has taken the very rich oil fields of Mosul and Basra. Stripping the Arabs of all means of livelihood, it is trying to force them through hunger to become its slaves.

What has Britain done to Palestine? First, acting for the benefit of Anglo-Jewish capitalists, it drove Arabs from the land and gave it to Jewish settlers. Then, trying to appease the discontent of the Arabs, it incited them against these same Jewish settlers, sowing discord, enmity, and hatred between the communities and weakening both to reinforce its own rule and command.

What has Britain done to Egypt? There for eight decades the entire indigenous population has groaned beneath the heavy yoke of the British capitalists, a yoke even heavier and more ruinous for the people than was that of the Egyptian pharaohs who built their huge pyramids with slave labor.

What has Britain done to China? Together with its partner, imperialist Japan, Britain turned that enormous country into a colony, exploiting its 300 million people and poisoning them with opium.[2] With its own and Japanese troops, Britain is putting down with unheard-of cruelty the revolutionary ferment that has begun there. Restoring old despots that the people had overthrown, it strives with all its strength to keep the many-millioned Chinese people under its yoke of despotism, oppressed and impoverished, so as the better to be able to exploit them.

What has Britain done to Korea, a flourishing land with a thousand-year-old culture? It has handed Korea over to the Japanese imperialists for them to tear to pieces. With fire and sword they are now making the Korean people submit to the British and Japanese capitalists.

What is Britain doing to Afghanistan? By bribing the emir's government it has kept the people in subjugation, poverty, and ignorance, trying to reduce this country to a desert, in order that this desert may guard India, which Britain oppresses, from any contact with the outside world.

What is Britain doing with Armenia and Georgia? Britain uses its gold to keep the peasant and worker masses there under the yoke of the hated mercenary Dashnak and Menshevik governments. These governments terrorize and oppress their peoples and drive them to fight against the peoples of Azerbaijan and Russia who have freed themselves from the bourgeois yoke.

Imperialist Britain penetrates even into Turkestan, Khiva, Bukhara, Azerbaijan, Dagestan, and the North Caucasus. Everywhere its agents dart about, generously scattering bribes—British gold extorted from the blood and sweat of the oppressed peoples. Everywhere these agents seek to uphold the tyrants and despots, the khans and landlords, to combat the incipient revolutionary movements, and to keep all the peoples, at any cost, in a state of oppression and ruin, in want and ignorance.

Oppression and ruin, want and ignorance among the Eastern peoples serve as sources of enrichment for imperialist Britain.

Peoples of the East! To you belong the richest, most fertile, and most extensive lands in the whole world. Once the cradle of all humanity, these lands could feed not only their inhabitants but the population of the entire world. Yet now, every year, ten million Turkish, Persian, and Indian peasants and workers are unable to find a crust of bread or any employment in their wide and fertile homelands and are obliged to go abroad and seek a livelihood in alien lands. They have to do this because in their homelands everything—land, money, banks, factories, workshops—belongs to British capitalists. They are not masters in their own homelands; they dare not give orders there. On the contrary, they themselves are ordered about by foreigners, the British capitalists.

That is how it has been up to now. That is how it was before the war, when imperialist Britain still had rivals in the shape of the German, French, and Russian imperialist predators. Then Britain still hesitated to stretch out its paw over all the countries of the East, for fear of receiving a blow on this paw from some rival beast of prey. But now imperialist Britain has beaten all its rivals, rendering them powerless. Now it has achieved omnipotent mastery of Europe and Asia. The capitalists who rule Britain are now giving their wolfish appetites free rein. Without restraint or shame, they are sinking voracious teeth and claws into the bleeding body of the peoples of the East.

British capital feels cramped in Europe. It has grown and cannot find places for investment. Besides, the European workers, enlightened by revolutionary consciousness, have become bad slaves. Unwilling to work for nothing, they want good wages. In order for capital to have elbowroom, in order for it to bring in a good profit, in order for European workers to be thrown a sop so as to hold back the growth of their revolutionary mood, in order for the possibility to exist of bribing the leading strata of the worker masses, British capital needs fresh land and fresh workers—slaves with no voice and no rights.

And the British capitalists think they have found these fresh lands in the Eastern countries, and these rightless and voiceless slave laborers in the peoples of the East.

The British capitalists are trying to grab Turkey and Persia, Mesopotamia and Arabia, Afghanistan and Egypt. They aim to buy from the ruined and indebted peasants all their holdings for trivial sums, driving all these peasants from the land. They aim to merge these holdings into huge estates and plantations, on which the Eastern peasants, reduced to landlessness, will then be driven to work as slave laborers. In Turkey, Persia, and Mesopotamia, they want to use the cheap labor of the hungry Turkish, Persian, and Arab laborers to build factories, lay railways, and work mines. They want to use the cheap goods produced by factory industry to destroy the handicrafts of the millions of local craftsmen who fill the cities of the East, and throw them into the street without income. By setting up huge trading firms, they want to ruin the local petty merchants, throwing them too into the street, into the ranks of the proletariat, which has only its labor power to sell.

The British capitalists want to proletarianize completely the peoples of the East, to ruin economically all the peasants, craftsmen, and merchants, forcing them to work as hungry slaves on their plantations and in their factories and mines. And then, through unbearable labor and starvation wages, they will squeeze sweat and blood out of the enslaved peoples of the East. And they mean to turn the workers' sweat, the peasants' blood, into surplus value, into profit, into pure, ringing gold! This is the future which imperialist Britain is preparing for the peoples of the East.

Britain is a country of barely 40 million people, among whom the oppressors and exploiters make up only one-fortieth, while the remaining 39 million are oppressed and exploited workers and farmers. Yet Britain wants to rule half the world and to hold in slavery the 800 million toilers that live in the East. A single British bourgeois capitalist, who already forces 39 British workers to work for him, now wants to force an additional 2,000 workers and peasants in Persia, Turkey, Mesopotamia, and Egypt to work for him. Thus, 2,040 hungry and tortured people, enjoying none of the good things of life, are to work all their lives long for one idle parasite, a British capitalist. One million such exploiters, British bankers and industrialists, want to reduce 800 million of the peoples of the East to slavery. And it must be said that they know how to achieve their aim. They have neither shame, nor conscience, nor fear—only savage greed and unlimited thirst for gain. The ruin, hunger, blood, suffering, and groans of 800 million people mean nothing to them. All that matters is profit, all that counts is gain.

And in pursuit of this profit and gain, the British imperialists have taken a tenacious grip on the throat of the peoples of the East and are preparing for them a dark future—a future without rights, one of utter ruin, permanent slavery, oppression, and unlimited exploitation. That is what awaits the peoples of the East if the present British government remains in power, if imperialist Britain keeps its strength and stabilizes its rule over the Eastern countries. A miserable handful of British bankers will devour hundreds of millions of peasants and workers in the East.

But this shall not be!

Against the British capitalists, the rulers of imperialist Britain, the organized might of the peasants and workers of the East is rising up. They stand united under the red banner of the Communist International, under the red banner of the union of revolutionary workers, who have made it their aim to liberate the whole world and all humanity from every form of exploitation and oppression.

The first congress of representatives of the peoples of the East loudly proclaims to the whole world, to the capitalist rulers of Britain: This shall not be! You dogs will not devour the peoples of the East. You, a wretched handful of oppressors, will not reduce to everlasting serfdom hundreds of millions of Eastern workers and peasants. You have bitten off too big a piece, more than you can chew, and it will choke you!

The peoples of the East have long stagnated in the darkness of ignorance under the despotic yoke of their own tyrant rulers and of foreign capitalist conquerors. But they have been awakened by the roar of the World War and the thunder of the Russian workers' revolution, which has released the people of Russia, an Eastern people, from the century-old chains of capitalist slavery. Today, aroused from their sleep of centuries, they are rising to their feet.

They are waking up and are hearing the call to a holy war, to a ghazavat. That is our call! It is the call of the first congress of representatives of the peoples of the East, united with the revolutionary proletariat of the West under the banner of the Communist International.

We are representatives of the toiling masses of all the peoples of the East: India, Turkey, Persia, Egypt, Afghanistan, Baluchistan, Kashgaria, China, Indochina, Japan, Korea, Georgia, Armenia, Azerbaijan, Dagestan, Northern Caucasia, Arabia, Mesopotamia, Syria, Palestine, Khiva, Bukhara, Turkestan, Fergana, Tatarstan, Bashkiria, Kirghizia, and more. We are united in unbreakable union among ourselves and with the revolutionary workers of the West. We summon our peoples to a holy war. We say:

Peoples of the East! Often you heard a call from your governments to holy war, and you marched under the green banner of the Prophet. But all those holy wars were fraudulent, serving only the interests of your self-seeking rulers. After these wars, you, the peasants and workers, remained in slavery and want. You conquered the good things of life for others, but you yourselves never enjoyed any of them.

Now we summon you to the first genuine holy war, under the red banner of the Communist International. We summon you to a holy war for your own well-being, for your freedom, for your life.

Britain, the last powerful imperialist predator left in Europe, has spread its dark wings over the Eastern Muslim countries. It is trying to make the peoples of the East its slaves, its booty. Slavery! Frightful slavery, ruin, oppression, and exploitation—that is what Britain brings to the peoples of the East. Save yourselves, peoples of the East!

Arise and fight against this beast of prey! Go forward as one man in a *holy war* against the British conquerors!

Stand up, Indian exhausted by hunger and unbearable slave labor!

Stand up, Anatolian peasant crushed by taxes and usury!

Stand up, Persian rayat strangled by the molkdars!

Stand up, Armenian toiler driven out into the barren hills!

Stand up, Arabs and Afghans, lost in sandy deserts and cut off by the British from all the rest of the world!

Stand up and fight against the common enemy, imperialist Britain!

Wave high the banner of the holy war!

This is a holy war for the liberation of the peoples of the East, for the ending of the division of humanity into oppressor peoples and oppressed peoples, for complete equality of all peoples and races, whatever language they may speak, whatever the color of their skin, and whatever the religion they profess.

Wage holy war to end the division of countries into advanced and backward, dependent and independent, metropolitan and colonial!

Wage holy war for the liberation of all humanity from the yoke of capitalist and imperialist slavery, for the ending of all forms of oppression of one people by another and of all forms of exploitation of man by man!

Wage holy war against the last citadel of capitalism and imperialism in Europe, against the nest of pirates and bandits by sea and land, against the age-old oppressor of all the peoples of the East, against imperialist Britain!

Wage holy war for freedom, independence, and happiness for all the peoples of the East, all the East's millions of peasants and workers enslaved by Britain!

Peoples of the East! In this holy war all the revolutionary workers and all the oppressed peasants of the East will stand with you. They will help you, they will fight and die along with you.

It is the first congress of representatives of the peoples of the East that tells you this.

Long live the unity of all the peasants and workers of the East and of the West, the unity of all the toilers, all the oppressed and exploited!

Long live the battle headquarters of this united movement—the Communist International!

May the holy war of the peoples of the East and of the toilers of the entire world against imperialist Britain burn with unquenchable fire!

HONORARY MEMBERS OF THE PRESIDING COMMITTEE
Radek (Russia)
Béla Kun (Hungary)
Rosmer (France)
Quelch (Britain)
Reed (America)
Steinhardt-Gruber (Austria)
Jansen (Holland)
Shablin (Balkan Federation)
Yoshiharo (Japan)

CHAIRMAN OF THE CONGRESS
Zinoviev

MEMBERS OF THE PRESIDING COMMITTEE
Ryskulov, Abdur Rashidov, Kariyev (Turkestan)
Mustafa Subhi (Turkey)
Wang (China)
Karid (India)
Bekkhan Rakhmanov (Khiva)
Muhamedov (Bukhara)
Korkmasov (Dagestan)
Digurov (Terek region)
Aliyev (Northern Caucasia)
Kostanyan (Armenia)
Narimanov (Azerbaijan)
Yenikeyev (Tatar republic)
Amur Sanan (Kalmyk republic)
Makharadze (Georgia)
Haydar Khan (Persia)
Agazadeh (Afghanistan)
Narbutabekov (Tashkent)
Mahmudov (Fergana)
Takhsim Baari, Haavis Mahomed (Anatolia)

Kuleyev (Transcaspia)
Niyas Kuli (Turkmenia)
Kari Tajiyev (Samarkand)
Nazir Sidiq (India)
Sidajedin Kardash Ogly (Dagestan)
Yelchiyev, Musayev (Azerbaijan)
Azim (Afghanistan)
Abdulayev (Khiva)

SECRETARY TO THE CONGRESS
Ostrovsky

APPEAL

Appeal to the workers of Europe, America, and Japan

Workers of Britain, America, France, Italy, Japan, Germany, and other countries![1] Hear the representatives of millions of toilers of the East. Listen to the voice of sorrow, speaking to you from the enslaved countries of Asia and Africa, from Turkey, Persia, China, Egypt, Afghanistan, Bukhara, and Khiva.

For many years, for many decades we have been silent. You did not hear our voice. No one told you of us, of how we live, how we suffer under the rule of those who are your masters too.

Your masters, the European and American factory owners, merchants, generals, and officials, broke into the peace of our villages and towns, plundered us for centuries, took from us what our work in the past had created, and sent all this off to Europe to embellish their lives, their homes, with the labor of our hands and of our ancient culture. They turned us into slaves.

Where previously we had to pay tribute to our own rich men, to the landlords, slave owners, sultans, emirs, khans, and maharajas, now the whip of the European slave owners was also laid across our backs. We were forced to labor on the plantations of the European capitalists. Sweat poured from our brow so that they might obtain rice, tea, sugar, tobacco, and rubber at a cheap rate. Our children were born and died in bondage. If it suited the interests of your bosses and ours, they parted child from mother, wife from husband, and drove them from one country to another.

To you they said that they were bringing European knowledge and science to our countries. But what they brought in fact was opium and vodka, so that when sorrow welled up in the heart of the Asian and African slaves, they would more easily forget their intolerable life and would not dare to lift their chained hands against their enslaver.

Your bosses, the European capitalists, supported our own enslavers, making them their guard dogs to watch over us. But when the whip of the local ruler was not enough, they sent in white soldiers, they sent in cannon. They destroyed the independence of our countries, subjecting us to their laws and their governors and making slaves of us in the full sense of the word. The aim of their colonial rule, they told us, was to train us for future independence. But they fought with every means against the spread of knowledge among us toilers of the East. Prisons and barracks for us they had in number, but they did not build schools where the children of Asia might learn what the white men had discovered that was great and good. They looked on us as an inferior race; they forbade us to sit in the same railway carriage that white men traveled in; they forbade us to live in the same neighborhood as white people or to eat at the same table with them.

You did not see our wounds; you did not hear our songs of sorrow; you believed your own oppressors when they said we were not people but cattle. You, who are servants to the capitalists, saw us as your own servants. In America you protested when Chinese and Japanese peasants, evicted by your capitalists from their villages, came to your country in search of a crust of bread. You did not approach us in a fraternal way in order to teach us how to fight along with you for the common cause of emancipation. Instead, you denounced us for our ignorance, you shut us out of your lives, you excluded us from your unions.[2]

We heard that you had founded Socialist parties, that you had formed an international workers' association. But for us these parties and this International had only words. We did not see its representatives come among us when the British shot us down in the streets of Indian cities, when the united forces of the European capitalists shot at us in Peking, when in the Philippines our demand for bread was answered by the American capitalists with the voice of their rifles. And those of us whose hearts were athirst for the unity of the working people around the world stood on the threshold of your International, looking through the grille, and saw that although in words you accepted us as equals, in fact we were for you people of inferior race.

Six years ago the great slaughter began. The capitalists around the world quarrelled among themselves as to which of them should have the most slaves, which of them should grab the most land in Asia and Africa. You, the workers of Europe and America, saw this war of robbers and murderers as your own war, a war for the independence of your countries, even though you did not own the tiniest scrap of these countries, even though the land you soaked with your sweat belonged not to you but to your exploiters, your bosses.

You helped your factory owners and bankers force us to take part in this war, a war against you and against us. The bayonets of European soldiers forced Moroccan and Algerian peasants to die of bullets, cold, and disease on the battlefields of Flanders, Normandy, and Champagne. They forced the peasants of India to die in the sands of Mesopotamia and Arabia, and the fellahin to carry out hard labor in the wilderness for the British expeditionary force fighting against the Turks. They made Indian peasants into pack camels carrying shells on their backs for the white soldiers in Mesopotamia. For the gold of the European capitalists, Chinese and Annamite [Vietnamese] workers were sold to Russia and France, to dig under a hurricane of fire the trenches in which you were to die, and to toil to the point of exhaustion in arms factories, making the shells that killed you.

Our blood and sweat merged with yours in a single stream. But even on the field of battle, dying in the dead of night, yearning for his homeland, the colored man was not seen as your brother but regarded as a savage slave, whose death caused no one to sigh or shed a tear. But in our homes beyond the seas, women wept for their fallen husbands, and children wept for their fallen fathers, the breadwinners.

The war is over. Now your masters and ours, who waged this war under the banner of justice and democracy, the banner of emancipation for the oppressed peoples, have thrown off the mask. The cities of India are ruled by the bayonet, the saber, and the machine gun. In Amritsar the British General Dyer shot down peaceful Indian citizens with machine guns and jeeringly ordered them to crawl on their bellies. But in the British Parliament not one workers' MP got up to demand that this murderer be sent to the gallows.

In Mesopotamia the British capitalists keep eight thousand Indian soldiers, brothers of the victims of Amritsar, in order to tighten their grip on the oil of Mosul. In Smyrna Greek soldiers hired by the British capitalists slaughter the Turks. For £2 million Persia's freedom has been sold to the British government, so as to make that country a stronghold of British capital against the Persian and Russian working people. In Algeria, Tunisia,[3] and Annam the absolute power of French generals prevails, just as before the war. In northern China and in Korea, Japanese gendarmes and officers are in charge, shooting and hanging anyone who dares even think of freedom. From the blood of the Asian and African workers and peasants shed in this war has grown not a tree of liberty but a gallows for those who fight for it.

But through the creaking of the gallows, through the groans of those suffering under the whip, we hear new cries. We hear the voice of the workers risen arms in hand against their enslavers. We hear the roar of the cannon of the Russian workers' and peasants' Red Army, created by workers and peasants of Russia who have risen in revolt. We hear that they have overcome the Russian capitalists and landlords, and in our hearts grows a great joy, a confidence that the humiliated and insulted working people will be able to summon up sufficient strength to put an end to the rule of bondage and establish the reign of labor and freedom.

Through the roar of the guns in the just war waged by the Russian workers and peasants, we hear your voice, the voice of the workers of Germany, Austria, and Hungary. We hear that you too have taken up arms, that you too have raised your hands against your enslavers. And although we are aware that you have not yet vanquished your foe, we are confident that victory will be yours.

From the cities of Italy we hear the voice of hundreds of thousands of workers who are confronting the bayonets of the Italian capitalist bandits. We hear the voices of French workers from behind the bars of the prisons where they have been thrown by the government of the French rich, who fear their great wrath and tremble at the flame burning in their hearts. We have heard the sound of the rising sea of the British workers, a sea whose waves beat against the cliffs on which stands the stronghold of British capitalism, strangler of the peoples, robber of the world, destroyer of peaceful lives.

With profound joy, with profound inspiration we listen to these sounds, and the belief grows within us that the day is close when our torments will cease, when our struggle will be united with yours. We believe that you will not fight for your victory, your liberation, alone. We believe that you will not cast off the chains from your hands and feet while leaving them on ours. We believe that you will discard like a dirty shirt all the contempt toward the toilers of the East instilled in you by our masters, who are striving to set the white workers against the colored ones and to get the white workers' aid in the business of their oppression.

Only a common victory of the workers of Europe and America and the toiling masses of Asia and Africa will bring liberation to all who have until now toiled for the happiness of the wealthy few. If you were to free yourselves alone, leaving us in slavery and bondage, you yourselves would fall the next day into the same bondage. For in order to keep us in chains and in prison, you would have to form packs of prison bloodhounds to guard us in the East and in the South. You would have to raise armies to keep us under an iron heel. You would have to give power over us to your generals and governors. And once they had tasted the sweetness of the idle life lived at the expense of our labor and learned how to hold generations of colored toilers in bondage, they would soon turn their bayonets against you—and the wealth accumulated in Asia and Africa would be used to thrust you back into your previous slavery.

If you were to forget us now, you would pay dearly for that mistake; you would have cause to remember our chains when you felt chains on your own hands. You cannot free yourselves unless you help us in our struggle for liberation. The wealth of our countries is, in the hands of the capitalists, a means of enslaving you. So long as the British capitalist can freely exploit Indian, Egyptian, and Turkish peasants, so long as he can rob them, so long as he can force them to serve in the British army, he will always have wealth enough and executioners enough to subdue the British workers. Without our revolt there can be no victory for the British workers over the British capitalists, for the world proletariat over world capital.

And just as you cannot wrest power from the hands of the capitalists without unity with us, so you are not in a position to maintain power without this unity. The capitalist countries of Europe do not produce enough grain and raw materials to provide food, clothing, and footwear for their workers. Our countries, the countries of the East and of Africa, are rich in grain and raw materials. Without these supplies, the workers of Europe would die of starvation after their victory. They will be able to obtain these supplies by uniting with the toilers of Africa and Asia, by helping the toiling masses of Africa and Asia and thus inspiring them with confidence and love.

Such unity between ourselves and you will bring invincible strength. We will be able to feed and clothe each other; we will be able to help each other with armies of warriors fired with the single idea of common liberation.

We have been summoned to this common struggle by the Third, Communist International. It has broken with the rotten past of the Second International, which is stained with your blood and ours and disgraced by its servility to imperialism, its betrayal of the interests of the toiling masses around the world. The Communist International gave us the slogan of a common holy war against the capitalists. What is more, it summoned us to a congress in Baku, where workers from Russia, Turkey, and Persia, and Tatar workers labored for many decades for the capitalists while at the same time learning how to struggle together against their oppressors.

Here in Baku, on the borders between Europe and Asia, we representatives of tens of millions of peasants and workers of Asia and Africa in revolt showed the world our wounds, showed the world the marks of the whip on our backs and the traces left by chains on our feet and hands. And we raised our daggers, revolvers, and swords and swore before the world that we would use these weapons not to fight each other but to fight the capitalists.

Deeply convinced that you, the workers of Europe and Asia, will unite with us under the banner of the Communist International for common struggle, for a common victory, for a new life together based on fraternal aid between all toilers, we have formed here a Council for Propaganda and Action. Under the guidance of the Communist International, a union of our elder brothers in revolutionary struggle, this council sets the goal of rousing the working masses of all colors, organizing them, and leading them to the attack against the fortress of slavery.

Workers of Britain, America, France, Italy, Japan, Germany, and other countries! Listen to the representatives of the millions of the peoples of the East in revolt, who have taken an oath to rise up and help you in your fight, and who look for fraternal aid from you in their fight. Disregarding centuries of bondage and enslavement, we turn to you with faith in your fraternal feelings, with confidence that your victory will mean the liberation of mankind, without distinction of color, religion, or nationality. May confidence be awakened in you as well that ours is a struggle for a new and better life, for the development of the peoples of the East on the same foundations of labor and fraternity on which you want to build your life. May you hear the thunder with which tens and hundreds of millions of working people in Asia and Africa respond to our oath. And may this crashing be answered by the thunderclaps of your fight for the common liberation of all the toilers!

Long live the unity of the workers of all countries with the laboring masses of Asia and Africa! Long live the world revolution of all the oppressed!

Long live victory over the world of oppression, exploitation, and violence! Long live the Communist International!

*G. Zinoviev,
Chairman of the Congress*

*Ostrovsky,
Secretary*

COMPOSITION OF THE CONGRESS

235	Turks	10	Ajars
192	Persians and Farsis	9	Kabardians
157	Armenians	8	Chinese
104	Russians	8	Kurds
100	Georgians	7	Avars
82	Chechens	5	Poles
61	Tajiks	3	Hungarians
47	Kirghizians	3	Germans
41	Jews	3	Kalmyks
35	Turkmens	3	Koreans
33	Kumyks	3	Arabs
25	Lezgins	2	Teke
17	Ossetians	2	Abkhazians
15	Uzbeks	1	Bashkiris
14	Indians	1	Ukrainians
13	Ingushes	1	Croats
12	Jamshidis	1	Czechs
11	Hazaras	1	Latvians
10	Sarts		
		1,275	Total

1,891	Total number attending the congress
1,273	Of whom, Communists
266	No nationality stated
more than 100	Did not complete above questionnaire
55	Total number of women delegates

Editor's note: The above list is taken from the Russian edition of the congress proceedings. Reports of the congress in the Baku press indicate that the figure of 1,891 delegates reflects attendance when the congress began; the final total was greater. A list of delegates found among archival records of the congress includes 2,050 participants.[1]

The archival list includes 336 Azerbaijanis, a category omitted from the list in the congress proceedings. This category appears to include only Azerbaijani delegates from the Azerbaijan Soviet Republic, and not those from Iran.

The archival breakdown also gives the following totals for other nationalities: Turks, 273; Lezgins (probably including all the nationalities of Dagestan), 218; Persians, 204; Armenians, 160; Georgians, 110; Russians, 109; Uzbeks, 90; Chechens, 85; Kirghizians, 77; Tatars, 70. The figure given for women delegates is 53.

The archival source identifies the party affiliation of 1,926 of the delegates as follows: Communists, 1,071; Communist Party sympathizers, 334; Young Communists, 31; nonparty, 467; Communist Bundists, 11; Persian revolutionaries, 9; Socialist Revolutionaries, 1; Left Socialist Revolutionaries, 1; Anarchists, 1.

A social breakdown of all 2,050 delegates gives: workers, 576; peasants, 495; professionals and educated workers, 437; no occupation stated, 542.

A breakdown of the delegates by country of origin gives: Azerbaijan, 469; Caucasian Mountain republic, 461; Turkestan, 322; Persia, 202; Georgia, 137; Armenia, 131; Turkey, 105; Kirghizia, 85; Afghanistan, 40; Tatar republic, 20; India, 14; Bukhara, 14; Khiva, 14; Bashkiria, 13; Crimea, 8; Kalmyk republic, 8; China, 7.

In the list of nationalities taken from the congress proceedings, "Persians and Farsis" probably refers to inhabitants of Iran, both of Farsi (Persian) and of non-Farsi nationality.

Kumyks, Lezgins, and Avars are peoples of Dagestan. Chechens, Ingushes, and Kabardians live west of Dagestan on the north side of the Caucasus Mountains, along with many Ossetians. Another part of the Ossetian people live south of the mountains, in Georgia.

Other Caucasian peoples south of the mountains (in the Transcaucasus) include Ajars, from southwest Georgia; Abkhazians, from northwest Georgia; and Kurds, mainly from Armenia and Nakhichevan. A larger Kurdish population lives in Iran, Turkey, and Iraq.

Indigenous Asian Jewish communities of the Mountain country and of several localities in Turkestan were represented among the congress delegates.

The Jamshidis and Hazaras are two of the peoples of Afghanistan.

In Soviet Central Asia, where boundaries were redrawn along ethnic lines in 1924, most Uzbeks in 1920 lived in Khiva or western Bukhara. Most Turkmens (including the Teke, one of their largest tribes) inhabited the Transcaspian region of Turkestan. Tajiks lived in eastern Bukhara and along the Afghanistan frontier. The Sarts were an urban people of Central Asia who traditionally engaged in trade.

First congress of the peoples of the East

Appendixes

APPENDIX 1
NOVEMBER 15, 1917

Declaration of Soviet government on rights of peoples of Russia

The October revolution of the workers and peasants began under the general banner of emancipation.[1]

Peasants are now freed from the power of the landowners, since ownership of the land by big landowners is no more—it has been abolished. Soldiers and sailors are now emancipated from the power of despotic generals, for generals from now on are elected by vote and subject to recall. Workers are now freed from the whims and arbitrary caprice of capitalists, since from now on workers' control is established over factories and plants. Everything living and viable is being released from hateful shackles.

There remain only the peoples of Russia, the past and present victims of oppression and tyranny. Their emancipation must be undertaken immediately; their liberation must be achieved decisively and irrevocably.

Under tsarism, the peoples of Russia were systematically incited against each other. The results of this policy are notorious: massacres and pogroms on the one hand, enslavement of the peoples on the other.

There can be no return to this shameful policy. From now on, it must be replaced by a policy of voluntary and honest union of the peoples of Russia.

In the imperialist period following the February revolution, when power fell into the hands of the bourgeois Constitutional Democrats, there was a transition from an undisguised policy of incitement to one of cowardly distrust of the peoples of Russia, one of backhanded chicanery and provocations, glossed over by verbal declarations on "freedom" and "equality" of the peoples. The results of this policy are equally notorious: intensification of national hatred and undermining of mutual trust.

We must put an end to this unworthy policy of lies and distrust, of chicanery and provocation. From now on, it must be replaced by an open and honest policy leading to complete mutual trust among the peoples of Russia.

Only on the basis of such confidence can we build an honest and lasting union of the peoples of Russia.

Only on the basis of such a union can we weld the workers and peasants of the peoples of Russia into a single revolutionary force capable of withstanding every thrust by the annexationist imperialist bourgeoisie.

Last July the Congress of Soviets proclaimed the right of the peoples of Russia to self-determination.

In October the Second Congress of Soviets decisively and definitively confirmed this inalienable right of the peoples of Russia.

Pursuant to the will of these congresses, the Council of People's Commissars has decided to base its activities on the nationality question in Russia on the following principles:

1. Equality and sovereignty of the peoples of Russia.
2. The right of the peoples of Russia to free self-determination up to and including the right to secede and form an independent state.
3. Abolition of any and all privileges and constraints based on nationality or religion.
4. Unhampered development of national minorities and of ethnographic groups inhabiting Russian territory.

The specific decrees relevant to these matters will be worked out immediately, once a commission on nationalities questions has been formed.

*Joseph Dzhugashvili (Stalin),
Commissar of Nationalities*

*V. Ulyanov (Lenin),
Chairman of the Council of
People's Commissars*

APPENDIX 2
DECEMBER 7, 1917

Appeal to all toiling Muslims of Russia and the East

Comrades! Brothers![1]

Great events are taking place in Russia. An end is drawing near to the bloody war for the division of foreign lands. The supremacy of the plunderers, who have enslaved the peoples of the world, is tottering. The old edifice of servitude and slavery is ready to collapse under the blows of the Russian revolution. The world of tyranny and oppression is living its last days. A new world is being born, a world of the toilers and those fighting for liberation. At the head of this revolution stands the workers' and peasants' government of Russia, the Council of People's Commissars.

The whole of Russia is dotted with revolutionary soviets of workers', soldiers', and peasants' deputies. Power in the country is in the people's hands. The working people of Russia burn with the single desire to achieve an honorable peace and to assist the oppressed peoples of the world in winning their freedom.

Russia is not alone in this sacred cause. The Russian revolution's great call to liberation is being taken up by working people East and West. Exhausted by war, yearning for peace, the peoples of Europe are already reaching out to us. Already the workers and soldiers of the West are gathering under the banner of socialism, assaulting the strongholds of imperialism. Even far-off India, oppressed for centuries by the "enlightened" predators of Europe, has raised the banner of rebellion by organizing its councils of deputies, throwing off its hated servitude, and summoning the peoples of the East to the struggle and to liberation.

The kingdom of capitalist plunder and violence is falling in ruins. The ground is slipping from under the feet of the imperialist robbers.

In the face of these great events we turn to you, the toiling and disinherited Muslims of Russia and the East.

Muslims of Russia, Tatars of the Volga and of Crimea, Kirghizians and Sarts of Siberia and Turkestan, Turks and Tatars of Transcaucasia, Chechens and Mountaineers of the Caucasus! All you whose mosques and shrines have been destroyed, whose beliefs and customs have been trampled on by the tsars and the Russian oppressors!

Henceforth your beliefs and customs, your national and cultural institutions are declared free and inviolable. Build your national life freely and without hindrance. It is your right. Know that your rights—like those of all the peoples of Russia—are defended by the full force of the revolution and its organs, the soviets of workers', soldiers', and peasants' deputies.

Support this revolution and its authorized government.

Muslims of the East! Persians, Turks, Arabs, and Indians! All you whose lives and property, whose freedom and homelands were for centuries merchandise for trade by rapacious European plunderers! All you whose countries the robbers who began the war now want to divide among themselves!

The tsar's secret treaties for the seizure of Constantinople, confirmed by the deposed Kerensky government, are now declared null and void. The Russian republic and its government, the Council of People's Commissars, oppose the seizure of foreign territory. Constantinople must remain in the hands of the Muslims.

We declare the treaty providing for the partition of Persia null and void. Once military activities cease, troops [of Russia] will be withdrawn from Persia and the Persians assured the right to determine freely their own destiny.

We declare null and void the treaty providing for the division of Turkey, which was to despoil it of Armenia. Once military activities cease, Armenians will be assured the right to determine freely their own political destiny.

Do not expect enslavement from Russia and its revolutionary government; expect it rather from the European imperialist robbers who have plundered and fleeced your homelands and transformed them into their "colonies."

Overthrow these robbers and enslavers of your countries! Today, when war and ruin are demolishing the pillars of the old order, when the entire world burns with indignation against the imperialist annexationists, when the least spark of discontent bursts out in the mighty flame of revolution, when even the Indian Muslims, cowed and tormented by the foreign yoke, are rising up against their slave drivers—today, one must not remain silent.

Lose no time in throwing off the ancient oppressors of your homelands. Permit them no longer to plunder your native lands. You yourselves must be the masters in your own land. You yourselves must build your life as you see fit. You have this right, because your fate is in your own hands.

Comrades! Brothers!

Firmly and resolutely we are advancing toward an honest, democratic peace.

We inscribe the liberation of the oppressed peoples of the world on our banners.

Muslims of Russia! Muslims of the East!

In this task of regenerating the world we look to you for sympathy and support.

Council of People's Commissars

APPENDIX 3
NOVEMBER 22, 1919

Address to the Second All-Russia Congress of Communist Organizations of the Peoples of the East

by V.I. Lenin

Comrades, I am very glad of the opportunity to greet this congress of Communist comrades representing Muslim organizations of the East and to say a few words about the present situation in Russia and throughout the world.[1] The subject of my address is current affairs, and it seems to me that the most essential aspects of this question at present are the attitude of the peoples of the East to imperialism and the revolutionary movement among those peoples.

It is self-evident that this revolutionary movement of the peoples of the East can now develop effectively, can reach a successful outcome, only in direct association with the revolutionary struggle of our Soviet republic against international imperialism. Owing to a number of circumstances, among them the backwardness of Russia and her vast area, and the fact that she constitutes a frontier between Europe and Asia, between the West and the East, we had to bear the whole brunt—and we regard that as a great honor—of being the pioneers of the world struggle against imperialism. Consequently, the whole course of development in the immediate future presages a still broader and more strenuous struggle against international imperialism, and will inevitably be linked with the struggle of the Soviet republic against the forces of united imperialism—of Germany, France, Britain, and America.

As regards the military aspect of the matter, you know how favorable our situation now is on all the fronts. I shall not dwell in detail on this question. I shall say only that the civil war forced upon us by international imperialism has in two years inflicted incalculable hardship upon the Russian Socialist Federated Soviet Republic, imposing upon the peasants and workers a burden so intolerable that it often seemed they would not be able to endure it.

But at the same time, because of its brute violence, because of the ruthlessly brutal onslaught of our so-called allies, turned wild beasts, who robbed us even before the socialist revolution, this war has performed a miracle. It has turned people weary of fighting and seemingly incapable of bearing another war into warriors who not only have withstood the war for two years but also are bringing it to a victorious end.

The victories we are now gaining over Kolchak, Yudenich, and Denikin signify the advent of a new phase in the history of the struggle of world imperialism against the countries and nations which have risen up to fight for their emancipation. In this respect, the two years of our civil war have fully confirmed what has long been known to history—that the character of a war and its success depend chiefly upon the internal regime of the country that goes to war, that war is a reflection of the internal policy conducted by the given country before the war. All this is inevitably reflected in the prosecution of the war.

Which class waged the war, and is continuing to wage it, is a very important question. Our civil war is being waged by workers and peasants who have emancipated themselves. It is a continuation of the political struggle for the emancipation of the working people from the capitalists of their country and of the whole world. Only thanks to this were people to be found in such a backward country as Russia, worn out as she was by four years of imperialist war, who were strong-willed enough to carry on that war during two years of incredible and unparalleled hardship and difficulty.

This was very strikingly illustrated in the history of the civil war by the case of Kolchak. Kolchak was an enemy who had the assistance of all the world's strongest powers. He had a railway protected by some hundred thousand foreign troops, including the finest troops of the world imperialists, such as the Japanese, for example, who had been trained for the imperialist war, but took practically no part in it and therefore suffered little. Kolchak had the backing of the Siberian peasants, who were the most prosperous and had never known serfdom, and therefore, naturally, were furthest of all from communism. It seemed that Kolchak was an invincible force, because his troops were the advance guard of international imperialism. To this day, Japanese and Czechoslovak troops and the troops of a number of other imperialist nations are operating in Siberia.

Kolchak's rule over Siberia and her vast natural resources was at first supported by the Socialist parties of the Second International, by the Mensheviks and the Socialist Revolutionaries, who set up the Constituent Assembly Committee front. Therefore, under these conditions, from the standpoint of the man in the street and of the ordinary course of history, his rule appeared to be firm and invincible. Nevertheless, more than a year's experience of this rule actually revealed the following. The farther Kolchak advanced into the heart of Russia, the more he wore himself out, and in the end we witnessed Soviet Russia's complete triumph over Kolchak.

Here we undoubtedly have practical proof that the united forces of workers and peasants emancipated from the capitalist yoke can perform real miracles. Here we have practical proof that when a revolutionary war really does attract and interest the working and oppressed people—when it makes them conscious that they are fighting the exploiters—such a revolutionary war engenders the strength and ability to perform miracles.

I think that what the Red Army has accomplished, its struggle, and the history of its victory, will be of colossal, epochal significance for all the peoples of the East. It will show them that, weak as they may be, and invincible as may seem the power of the European oppressors, who employ in the struggle all the marvels of technology and of the military art—nevertheless, a revolutionary war waged by oppressed peoples, if it really succeeds in arousing the millions of working and exploited people, harbors such potentialities, such miracles, that the emancipation of the peoples of the East is now quite practicable. This holds true from the standpoint not only of the prospects of the international revolution but also of the direct military experience acquired in Asia, in Siberia—the experience of the Soviet republic, which has suffered the armed invasion of all the powerful imperialist countries.

Furthermore, the experience of the civil war in Russia has shown us and the Communists of all countries that, in the crucible of civil war, the development of revolutionary enthusiasm is accompanied by a powerful inner consolidation. War tests all the economic and organizational forces of a nation. In the final analysis, infinitely hard as the war has been for the workers and peasants, who suffer famine and cold, it may be said on the basis of these two years' experience that we are winning and will continue to win, because we have a home front, and a strong one. Despite famine and cold, the peasants and workers stand together, have grown strong, and answer every heavy blow with a greater cohesion of their forces and increased economic might. And it is this alone that has made possible the victories over Kolchak, Yudenich, and their allies, the strongest powers in the world.

The past two years have shown how a revolutionary war can be developed, and, in addition, that the Soviet system is growing stronger under the heavy blows of a foreign invasion which aims to destroy quickly the revolutionary center, the republic of workers and peasants who have dared to declare war on international imperialism. But instead of destroying the workers and peasants of Russia, these heavy blows have served to harden them.

That is the chief lesson, the chief content of the present period. We are on the eve of decisive victories over Denikin, the last enemy left on our soil. We feel strong; we may reiterate a thousand times over that we are not mistaken when we say that internally the republic has become consolidated, and that we shall emerge from the war against Denikin very much stronger and better prepared for the task of erecting the socialist edifice. To this task we have been able to devote all too little time and energy during the civil war. But now that we are setting foot on an open road, we shall undoubtedly be able to devote ourselves to it entirely.

In Western Europe we see the decay of imperialism. You know that a year ago it seemed even to the German Socialists, and to the vast majority of Socialists—who did not understand the true state of affairs—that what was in progress was a struggle of two world imperialist groups. They believed that this struggle constituted the whole of history, that there was no force capable of producing anything else. It seemed to them that even Socialists had no alternative but to join sides with one of the groups of powerful world predators. That is how it seemed at the end of October 1918. But we find that in the year that has since elapsed, world history has witnessed unparalleled events, profound and far-reaching events, which have opened the eyes of many Socialists who during the imperialist war were patriots and justified their conduct on the plea that the enemy was at hand. They justified their alliance with the British and French imperialists on the grounds that these were supposedly bringing deliverance from German imperialism.

See how many illusions were shattered by that war! We are witnessing the decay of German imperialism, which has led not only to a republican, but even to a socialist revolution. You know that in Germany today the class struggle has become still more acute and that civil war is drawing nearer and nearer—a war of the German proletariat against the German imperialists, who have adopted republican colors but remain imperialists.

Everyone knows that the social revolution is maturing in Western Europe by leaps and bounds. The same thing is happening in America and in Britain, the countries ostensibly representing culture and civilization, victors over the Huns, the German imperialists. Yet when it came to the Treaty of Versailles, everyone saw that it was a hundred times more rapacious than the Treaty of Brest which the German robbers forced upon us. It was the heaviest blow the capitalists and imperialists of those luckless victor countries could possibly have struck at themselves.

The Treaty of Versailles opened the eyes of the people of the victor nations. It showed that Britain and France, even though democratic states, stand before us not as representatives of culture and civilization, but as countries ruled by imperialist predators. The internal struggle among these predators is developing so swiftly that we may rejoice in the knowledge that the Treaty of Versailles is only a seeming victory for the jubilant imperialists. In reality it signifies the bankruptcy of the entire imperialist world and the resolute abandonment by the working people of those Socialists who during the war allied themselves with the representatives of decaying imperialism and defended one of the groups of belligerent predators. The eyes of the working people have been opened because the Treaty of Versailles was a rapacious peace, which showed that France and Britain had actually fought Germany in order to strengthen their rule over the colonies and to enhance their imperialist might.

That internal struggle grows broader as time goes on. Today I saw a radio message from London dated November 21, in which American journalists—people who cannot be suspected of sympathizing with revolutionaries—say that in France an unprecedented outburst of hatred towards the Americans is to be observed, because the Americans refuse to ratify the Treaty of Versailles.

Britain and France are victors, but they are up to their ears in debt to America. And America has decided that however much the French and the British may consider themselves victors, she is going to skim the cream and exact usurious interest for her assistance during the war. The guarantee of this is to be the American navy which is now being built and is overtaking the British navy in size. And the crudeness of the Americans' rapacious imperialism may be seen from the fact that American agents are buying white slaves, women and girls, and shipping them to America for the development of prostitution. Just think, free, cultured America supplying white slaves for brothels.

Conflicts with American agents are occurring in Poland and Belgium. That is a tiny illustration of what is taking place on a vast scale in every little country that received assistance from the Entente. Take Poland, for instance. You find American agents and profiteers going there and buying up all the wealth of Poland, who boasts that she is now an independent power. Poland is being bought up by American agents. There is not a factory or branch of industry which is not in the pockets of the Americans.

The Americans have become so brazen that they are beginning to enslave that "great and free victor," France. Formerly a country of usurers, France is now deep in debt to America, because she has lost her economic strength, has not enough grain or coal of her own, and cannot develop her material resources on a large scale, while America insists that the tribute be paid unreservedly and in full. It is thus becoming increasingly apparent that France, Britain, and other powerful countries are economically bankrupt.

In the French elections the Clericals have gained the upper hand. The French people, who were deceived into devoting all their strength supposedly to the defense of freedom and democracy against Germany, have now been rewarded with an interminable debt, with the sneers of the rapacious American imperialists and, on top of it, with a Clerical majority consisting of representatives of the most savage reaction.

The situation all over the world has become immeasurably more complicated. Our victory over Kolchak and Yudenich—those lackeys of international capital—is a big one, but far bigger, though not so evident, is the victory we are gaining on an international scale. That victory consists in the internal decay of imperialism, which is unable to send its troops against us. The Entente tried it, but to no avail, because its troops become demoralized when they contact our troops and acquaint themselves with our Russian Soviet constitution, translated into their languages.

Despite the influence of the leaders of rotten Socialism, our constitution will always win the sympathy of working people. The word *soviet* is now understood by everybody, and the Soviet constitution has been translated into all languages and is known to every worker. He knows that it is the constitution of working people, the political system of working people who are calling for victory over international capital, that it is a triumph we have achieved over the international imperialists. This victory of ours has had its repercussions in all imperialist countries, since we have deprived them of their own troops, won them over, deprived them of the possibility of using those troops against Soviet Russia.

They tried to wage war with the troops of other countries—Finland, Poland, and Latvia—but nothing came of it. British minister Churchill, speaking in the House of Commons several weeks ago, boasted—and it was cabled all over the world—that a campaign of fourteen nations against Soviet Russia had been organized, which would bring victory over Russia by the New Year. And it is true that many nations participated in it—Finland, Ukraine, Poland, Georgia, as well as the Czechoslovaks, the Japanese, the French, the British, and the Germans. But we know what came of it! We know that the Estonians left Yudenich's forces in the lurch, and now a fierce controversy is going on in the press because the Estonians do not want to help him. And Finland, much as her bourgeoisie wanted it, has not assisted Yudenich either. Thus the second attempt to attack us has likewise failed.

The first stage was the dispatch by the Entente of its own troops, equipped according to all the rules of military technique, so that it seemed they would defeat the Soviet republic. They have already withdrawn from the Caucasus, Archangel, and the Crimea; they still remain in Murmansk, as the Czechoslovaks do in Siberia, but only as isolated groups. The first attempt of the Entente to defeat us with its own forces ended in victory for us.

The second attempt consisted in launching against us nations which are our neighbors, and which are entirely dependent financially on the Entente, and in trying to force them to crush us, as a nest of socialism. But that attempt, too, ended in failure: it turned out that not one of these little countries is capable of waging such a war. What is more, hatred of the Entente has taken firm root in every little country. If Finland did not set out to capture Petrograd when Yudenich had already captured Krasnoye Selo, it was because she hesitated, realizing that she could live independently side by side with Soviet Russia, but could not live in peace with the Entente. All little nations have felt that. It is felt in Finland, Lithuania, Estonia, and Poland, where chauvinism is rampant, but where there is hatred of the Entente, which is expanding its exploitation in those countries.

And now, accurately assessing the course of developments, we may say without exaggeration that not only the first, but also the second stage of the international war against the Soviet republic has failed. All that remains for us to do now is to defeat Denikin's forces, and they are already half-defeated.

Such is the present Russian and international situation, which I have summarized briefly in my address. Permit me, in conclusion, to say something about the situation that is developing regarding the nationalities of the East.

You are representatives of the Communist organizations and Communist parties of various Eastern peoples. I must say that the Russian Bolsheviks have succeeded in forcing a breach in the old imperialism, in undertaking the exceedingly difficult, but also exceedingly noble task of blazing new paths of revolution. But you, as representatives of the working people of the East, have before you a task that is still greater and newer.

It is becoming quite clear that the socialist revolution which is impending for the whole world will not be merely the victory of the proletariat of each country over its bourgeoisie. That would be possible if revolutions came easily and swiftly. We know that the imperialists will not allow this. All countries are armed against their domestic Bolshevism, and their one thought is how to defeat Bolshevism at home. That is why in every country a civil war is brewing in which the old Socialist compromisers are enlisted on the side of the bourgeoisie.

Hence the socialist revolution will not be solely, or chiefly, a struggle of the revolutionary proletarians in each country against their bourgeoisie. No, it will be a struggle of all the colonies and countries oppressed by imperialism, of all dependent countries, against international imperialism. Characterizing the approaching world social revolution in the party program we adopted last March, we said that the civil war of the working people against the imperialists and exploiters in all the advanced countries is beginning to be combined with national wars against international imperialism.[2] That is confirmed by the course of the revolution, and will be more and more confirmed as time goes on. It will be the same in the East.

We know that the masses in the East will rise as independent participants, as builders of a new life, because hundreds of millions of the people belong to dependent, underprivileged nations which until now have been the objects of international imperialist policy, existing only as material to fertilize capitalist culture and civilization. And when they talk of handing out mandates over colonies, we know very well that it means handing out mandates for spoliation and plunder—handing out to an insignificant section of the world's population the right to exploit the majority of the population of the globe.[3]

That majority, which up till then had been completely outside the orbit of historical progress, because it could not constitute an independent revolutionary force, ceased, as we know, to play such a passive role at the beginning of the twentieth century. We know that 1905 was followed by revolutions in Turkey, Persia, and China, and that a revolutionary movement developed in India. The imperialist war likewise contributed to the growth of the revolutionary movement, because the European imperialists had to enlist whole colonial regiments in their struggle. The imperialist war aroused the East also and drew its peoples into international politics. Britain and France armed colonial peoples and helped them to familiarize themselves with military technique and up-to-date machines. That knowledge they will use against the imperialist gentry. The period of the awakening of the East is being succeeded in the contemporary revolution by a period in which all the Eastern peoples will participate in deciding the destiny of the whole world, so as not to be simply objects of the enrichment of others. The peoples of the East are becoming alive to the need for practical action, the need for every nation to take part in shaping the destiny of all mankind.

That is why I think that in the history of the development of the world revolution—which, judging by its beginning, will continue for many years and will demand much effort—that in the revolutionary struggle, in the revolutionary movement, you will be called upon to play a big part and to merge with our struggle against international imperialism. Your participation in the international revolution will confront you with a complicated and difficult task, the accomplishment of which will serve as the foundation for our common success. For here the majority of the people for the first time begin to act independently and will be an active factor in the fight to overthrow international imperialism.

Most of the Eastern peoples are in a worse position than the most backward country in Europe—Russia. But in our struggle against feudal survivals and capitalism, we succeeded in uniting the peasants and workers of Russia; and it was because the peasants and workers united against capitalism and feudalism that our victory was so easy. Here contact with the peoples of the East is particularly important, because the majority of the Eastern peoples are typical representatives of the working people—not workers who have passed through the school of capitalist factories, but typical representatives of the working and exploited peasant masses who are victims of medieval oppression. The Russian revolution showed us how the proletarians, after defeating capitalism and uniting with the vast diffuse mass of working peasants, rose up victoriously against medieval oppression. Our Soviet republic must now muster all the awakening peoples of the East and, together with them, wage a struggle against international imperialism.

In this respect you are confronted with a task which has not previously confronted the Communists of the world. Relying upon the general theory and practice of communism, you must adapt yourselves to specific conditions such as do not exist in the European countries. You must be able to apply that theory and practice to conditions in which the bulk of the population are peasants, and in which the task is to wage a struggle against medieval survivals and not against capitalism. That is a difficult and distinctive task, but a very gratifying one, because masses that have taken no part in the struggle up to now are being drawn into it, and also because the organization of Communist cells in the East gives you an opportunity to maintain the closest contact with the Third International. You must find specific forms for this alliance of advanced proletarians from around the world with the laboring and exploited masses of the East whose conditions are in many cases medieval.

We have accomplished on a small scale in our country what you will do on a big scale and in big countries. And that latter task you will, I hope, perform with success. Thanks to the Communist Organizations of the East, of which you here are the representatives, you have contact with the advanced revolutionary proletariat. Your task is to continue to ensure that communist propaganda is carried on in every country in a language the people understand.

It is self-evident that final victory can be won only by the proletariat of all the advanced countries of the world, and we, the Russians, are beginning the work which the British, French, or German proletariat will consolidate. But we see that they will not be victorious without the aid of the working people of all the oppressed colonial peoples—first and foremost, of the peoples of the East. We must realize that the transition to communism cannot be accomplished by the vanguard alone. The task is to arouse the working masses to revolutionary activity, to independent action and to organization, regardless of the level they have reached; to translate the true communist doctrine, which was intended for the Communists of the more advanced countries, into the language of every people; to carry out those practical tasks which must be carried out immediately, and to join the proletarians of other countries in a common struggle.

Such are the problems whose solution you will not find in any communist book, but will find in the common struggle begun by Russia. You will have to tackle that problem and solve it through your own independent experience. In that you will be assisted, on the one hand, by close alliance with the vanguard of the working people of other countries, and, on the other, by ability to find the right approach to the peoples of the East whom you here represent. You will have to base yourselves on the bourgeois nationalism which is awakening, and must awaken, among those peoples, and which has its historical justification. At the same time, you must find your way to the working and exploited masses of every country. You must tell them in a language they understand that their only hope of emancipation lies in the victory of the international revolution, and that the international proletariat is the only ally of all the hundreds of millions of the working and exploited peoples of the East.

Such is the immense task which confronts you. Thanks to the era of revolution and the growth of the revolutionary movement—of that there can be no doubt—this task will, by the joint efforts of the Communist Organizations of the East, be successfully accomplished and crowned by complete victory over international imperialism.

APPENDIX 4
JULY 28, 1920

Theses on the national and colonial questions

Adopted by the Second Congress of the Communist International

1. An abstract or formal conception of the question of equality in general and of national equality in particular is in the very nature of bourgeois democracy.[1] Under the guise of the equality of individuals in general, bourgeois democracy proclaims the formal, legal equality of the property owner and the proletarian, the exploiter and the exploited, thereby grossly deceiving the oppressed classes. Claiming to uphold the supposed absolute equality of individuals, the bourgeoisie transforms the idea of equality, which itself reflects the relations of commodity production, into a tool in the struggle against the abolition of classes. The real meaning of the demand for equality consists in its being a demand for the abolition of classes.

2. As the conscious expression of the proletarian class struggle to shake off the yoke of the bourgeoisie, the Communist Party, in line with its basic task of struggling against bourgeois democracy and exposing its lies and duplicity, should not base its policy on the national question on abstract and formal principles. Instead, it should be based

first on an exact appraisal of specific historical and above all economic conditions. Second, it should clearly differentiate between the interests of the oppressed classes, the toilers, the exploited, and the general concept of the so-called interests of the people, which means the interests of the ruling class. Third, it should with equal precision distinguish between the oppressed, dependent nations that do not have equal rights and the oppressor, exploiting nations that do, in order to counter the bourgeois-democratic lies that conceal the colonial and financial enslavement of the immense majority of the entire world population by a narrow minority of the richest, most advanced capitalist countries—a characteristic feature of the epoch of finance capital and imperialism.

3. The imperialist war of 1914 revealed with particular clarity to all enslaved nations and oppressed classes around the world the deceitfulness of bourgeois-democratic rhetoric. The war was justified by both sides with platitudes about national liberation and self-determination. Nonetheless, both the treaties of Brest-Litovsk and Bucharest and those of Versailles and St. Germain showed that the victorious bourgeoisie ruthlessly sets even "national" borders according to its economic interests.[2] For the bourgeoisie even "national" borders are objects of trade. The so-called League of Nations is nothing but the insurance policy with which this war's victors mutually guarantee their loot. The attempts to reestablish national unity, to "reunify with detached portions of land,"[3] are for the bourgeoisie nothing but attempts by the vanquished to assemble forces for new wars. The reunification of nations artificially torn apart is also in the interests of the proletariat. However, the proletariat can achieve genuine national liberation and unity only through revolutionary struggle and by overpowering the bourgeoisie.

The League of Nations and the entire postwar policy of the imperialist states expose this truth ever more clearly and sharply, strengthening everywhere the revolutionary struggle of the proletariat of the advanced countries, as well as of all toiling masses of the colonies and dependent countries, and hastening the collapse of petty-bourgeois illusions about the possibility of peaceful coexistence and the equality of nations under capitalism.

4. It follows from these principles that the entire policy of the Communist International on the national and colonial questions must be based primarily upon uniting the proletarians and toiling masses of all nations and countries in common revolutionary struggle to overthrow the landowners and the bourgeoisie. Only such a unification will guarantee victory over capitalism, without which it is impossible to abolish national oppression and inequality.

5. The international political situation has now put the dictatorship of the proletariat on the order of the day. All events in world politics necessarily focus on one single central issue: the struggle of the world bourgeoisie against the Russian Soviet Republic, which rallies around itself both the soviet movement of the advanced workers of all countries and all national liberation movements of the colonies and oppressed peoples. These peoples are learning through bitter experience that their only salvation lies with the revolutionary proletariat and in the victory of Soviet power over world imperialism.

6. Consequently, we cannot limit ourselves at this time merely to recognizing or proclaiming the friendship of the toilers of various nations. Rather we must pursue a policy of implementing the closest possible alliance of all national and colonial liberation movements with Soviet Russia. The forms of this alliance will be determined by the level of development of the Communist movement

within the proletariat of each country or of the revolutionary liberation movement in the backward countries and among the backward nationalities.

7. Federation is a transitional form toward full unity of the toilers of all nations. Federation has already shown its usefulness in practice—in the Russian Soviet Federated Socialist Republic's relations to the other Soviet republics (the Hungarian, Finnish, and Latvian in the past, the Azerbaijani and Ukrainian at present), and also within the Russian Soviet Federated Socialist Republic itself toward the nationalities that formerly had neither a state nor self-government (for example, the autonomous Bashkir and Tatar republics in the Russian Soviet Federated Socialist Republic created in 1919 and 1920).

8. The task of the Communist International in this respect consists not only in further perfecting these developing federations based on the Soviet order and the Soviet movement but also in studying and testing their experiences. Recognizing the federation as a transitional form toward complete unification, we must strive for an ever closer federal association. We must take into consideration first, that the Soviet republics, surrounded by imperialist states of the whole world that are considerably stronger militarily, cannot possibly exist without close association with each other. Second, a close economic alliance of the Soviet republics is necessary, without which it is impossible to restore the productive forces destroyed by imperialism and ensure the well-being of the toilers. Third, that there is a tendency to create a world economy unified according to a common plan, controlled by proletarians of all countries. This tendency has already begun to appear quite openly under capitalism and is bound to develop further and be completed under socialism.

9. In the field of relations between states, the national policy of the Communist International cannot stop at the bare, formal recognition of the equality of nations. Such lip service, carrying no obligation to act, is the limit to which the bourgeois democrats confine themselves—both those who frankly admit to being such and those who call themselves "Socialists."

Both within parliament as well as outside it, the Communist parties must incessantly expose in their entire propaganda and agitation the continually repeated violations of the equality of nations and guaranteed rights of national minorities in all capitalist countries despite their "democratic" constitutions. In addition, it must be explained persistently that only the Soviet order can ensure true national equality by uniting first the proletariat and then the whole mass of the toilers in struggle against the bourgeoisie. Moreover, all Communist parties must directly support the revolutionary movement among the nations that are dependent and do not have equal rights (for example Ireland, the Negroes in America, and so forth), and in the colonies.

Without this last, especially important condition, the struggle against oppression of the dependent nations and colonies and recognition of their right to a separate state remains a dishonest facade, such as we see in the parties of the Second International.

10. Recognizing internationalism in word only, while diluting it in deed with petty-bourgeois nationalism and pacifism in all propaganda, agitation, and practical work, is a common practice not only among the centrist parties of the Second International but also among those that have left that International, and often even among parties that now call themselves Communist.

The fight against this evil, against the most deeply rooted petty-bourgeois, nationalist prejudices (which are expressed in all possible forms, such as racism, national chauvinism, and anti-Semitism) must be given all the more priority as the question becomes more pressing of transforming the dictatorship of the proletariat from a national framework (that is, a dictatorship that exists only in one country and is incapable of carrying out an independent international policy) into an international one (that is, a dictatorship of the proletariat in at least several advanced countries, capable of exercising a decisive influence on all of world politics).

Petty-bourgeois nationalism declares that internationalism consists of the mere recognition of the equality of nations (although this recognition is strictly verbal) and considers national egoism to be sacrosanct. Proletarian internationalism, on the contrary, requires subordinating the interests of the proletarian struggle in one country to the interests of this struggle on a world scale. It also requires that the nation that has overthrown its bourgeoisie has the ability and willingness to make the greatest national sacrifices in order to overthrow international capitalism.

Therefore, in the already fully capitalist countries that have workers' parties truly constituting a vanguard of the proletariat, the first and most important task is the fight against the opportunist and petty-bourgeois pacifist distortions of the concept and policies of internationalism.

11. With respect to the states and nations that have a more backward, predominantly feudal, patriarchal, or patriarchal-peasant character, the following points in particular must be kept in mind:

a) All Communist parties must support with deeds the revolutionary liberation movement in these countries. The form the support should take must be discussed with the Communist Party of the country in question, if there is such a party. This responsibility of most energetic assistance applies above all to the workers of the country upon which the backward country is colonially or financially dependent.

b) A struggle absolutely must be waged against the reactionary and medieval influence of the clergy, the Christian missions, and similar elements.

c) It is necessary to struggle against the pan-Islamic and pan-Asian movements and similar currents that try to link the liberation struggle against European and American imperialism with strengthening the power of Turkish and Japanese imperialism and of the nobles, large landowners, clergy, and so forth.

d) It is especially necessary to support the peasant movement in the backward countries against the landowners and all forms and vestiges of feudalism. We must particularly strive to give the peasant movement the most revolutionary character possible, organizing the peasants and all the exploited into soviets where feasible, and thereby establishing the closest connection between the Western European Communist proletariat and the revolutionary peasant movement in the East, in the colonies, and in the backward countries in general.

e) A resolute struggle is necessary against the attempt to portray as communist the revolutionary liberation movements in the backward countries that are not truly communist. The Communist International has the duty to support the revolutionary movement in the colonies and the backward countries only on condition that the components are gathered in all backward countries for future proletarian parties—communist in fact and not only in name—and that they are educated to be conscious of their particular tasks, that is, the tasks of struggling against the bourgeois-democratic movement in their own nation. The Communist International should arrive at temporary agreements and, yes, even establish an alliance with the revolutionary movement in the colonies and backward countries. But it cannot merge with this movement. Instead it absolutely must maintain the independent character of the proletarian movement, even in its embryonic stage.

f) It is necessary continually to expose and explain to the broadest masses of toilers of all countries and nations, and especially the backward ones, that the imperialist powers, with the help of the privileged classes in the oppressed countries, are perpetrating a fraud. They are creating state structures that pose as politically independent states but are economically, financially, and militarily totally dependent upon the imperialist powers. The Palestine affair is a crass example of Entente imperialism and the bourgeoisie of the relevant country working together to swindle the working classes of an oppressed nation. Under the cover of creating a Jewish state in Palestine, Zionism actually delivers the Arab working population of Palestine, where the toiling Jews constitute only a small minority, to exploitation by Britain. In the present international situation, there is no salvation for the dependent and weak nations other than in alliance with Soviet republics.

12. The age-old, ongoing enslavement of the colonies and weak peoples by the imperialist great powers left the toiling masses of the enslaved countries with feelings not just of bitterness but of mistrust toward the oppressor nations in general, including against the proletariat of these nations. Socialism was despicably betrayed during the years 1914–19 by the majority of the official leaders of this proletariat, when the social patriots used "defense of the fatherland" to conceal the "right" of "their" bourgeoisie to enslave the colonies and plunder financially dependent countries. Such a betrayal could only rein-

force this completely justified mistrust. Abolishing such mistrust and national prejudices can proceed only very slowly. They can be eradicated only after imperialism is destroyed in the advanced countries and after the entire basis of economic life of the backward countries is radically transformed. The class-conscious Communist proletariat of all countries therefore has a responsibility to give particular care and attention to the survivals of national feelings in the long-enslaved countries and peoples, while making concessions to overcome more rapidly this mistrust and these prejudices. The victory over capitalism cannot be successfully accomplished without the proletariat and with it all working people of all countries and the nations of the entire world voluntarily coming together in a unified alliance.

APPENDIX 5
SEPTEMBER 1920

A new world

*by the Baku City Executive Committee,
Communist Party of Azerbaijan*

To the Congress of the Peoples of the East:[1]

A new world is awakening to life and struggle: the world of the oppressed nationalities, grouped—not entirely correctly—under the heading of the "East." This involves the peoples not only of Asia, but also of Africa, America (the Mexicans and the Negro population of the United States), etc.

Until today the white race has claimed, with little justification, to represent all humanity. Even by their numbers the oppressed peoples (the colored races) are at least two times greater than the white race. We need not go into the fact that the civilization of the East is older than ours. We must not forget that when we speak of the immobility of the East, this is often simply the fruit of our unfamiliarity with a way of life and social relations that we do not understand. The East has lived, and lives on today. True, its development has been arrested by the violence of the European conquerors and the colonial policy of capital, which have intentionally destroyed the productive forces of the East or, at least, fettered their natural development. This very violence, however, has awakened the oppressed peoples to resistance and struggle and has given the fighting international proletariat a new, powerful ally.

The Second International was, by its very essence, incapable of calling forth a revolutionary movement among the oppressed peoples or even of availing itself of the already existing movements. While condemning the colonial policy of the bourgeoisie in words, the parties of the Second International supported the overall policies of their bourgeoisies and, consequently, their colonial policies as well. Moreover, among the German, Belgian, and Dutch Socialists a tendency existed that applauded the colonial policy of capital, cleansed of its "extremes." These gentlemen even had the effrontery to preach these views at congresses of the International.[2]

The platonic protests of the Second International against colonial policy remained on paper alone. In deeds Social Democracy undertook nothing to oppose this policy of exploitation and strangulation of the hundreds of millions of inhabitants of the colonies. It did not fight in a revolutionary manner against the bourgeoisie at home; still less did it consider arousing the revolutionary protest of the oppressed peoples themselves, or actively supporting the revolutionary movements that flared up sporadically among them. Is it surprising that the oppressed peoples, when all is said and done, extend their hostility to and distrust of the European and American bourgeoisie even to the workers of these countries? For the bourgeoisie this is cause only for celebration.

The Communist International acts differently. Even the very existence of Soviet Russia and the policy it has applied on the national question have aroused the oppressed peoples to new outbursts of resistance to world capital. The Second Congress of the Communist International will play a decisive role in this liberation movement, in the same way that it is coming to the assistance of the revolutionary struggle of the European and American working class. The Third International does not just stand in solidarity with the revolutionary uprisings of the oppressed peoples against capitalist domination. In addition it obligates Communist parties in all countries, and especially in the oppressor countries, to render active support to the revolutionary movement in the colonies directed against the bourgeoisie of these oppressor countries.

In this way international solidarity of the working people finds its full realization. Until today the English worker, for example, could think that he had carried out his international duty by adopting a resolution protesting Entente attacks on Soviet Russia, or by signing a pledge of support to strikers in some European country. Now the Communist International tells him that if he wants to free himself from the yoke of capital, his elementary proletarian duty is to actively support both proletarians of all other countries and oppressed peoples, especially those oppressed by his own bourgeoisie. The same applies to the French, American, Belgian, and Dutch workers and to all workers living in countries that possess colonies and oppress other peoples. That is, this applies to the workers in all the big capitalist or, as they call themselves, "great" powers.

When news of the decisions of the Second Congress of the Communist International reaches the hundreds of millions of Indians, Chinese, Negroes, Malays, and other oppressed peoples, it will be music to their ears—the signal for an intensified struggle against capital, which exploits them. The hope of active support from the proletariat's international organization will lead the peasant and worker masses of the colonies and semicolonies to redouble and multiply their efforts many times over in desperate resistance to the murderous yoke of bourgeois exploitation. The proletarian struggle in the old capitalist countries can only gain from the awakening of revolutionary struggle amidst the oppressed peoples.

It remains to be seen where the first decisive blows to the world bourgeoisie will be struck—in the metropolitan centers, or in the colonies. In either case the struggle against capital is being extended across the entire face of the planet. The many millions of the East, who have until now lain like a dead weight on the highway of history, are being drawn into this struggle. For the first time it is taking the form of a movement breaking out onto a truly world scale. All this will accelerate the maturing collapse of capitalism and will bring nearer the day that bourgeois domination perishes.

The enlistment of the colossal masses of the oppressed peoples opens a new epoch in the history of the world struggle against oppression. The Communist International was the first to openly raise the banner of this struggle and to call on all the oppressed peoples and the entire organized international proletariat to rally to it. That will remain an enduring contribution of the Communist International.

Proletarians of all countries, unite!

APPENDIX 6
SEPTEMBER 1920

Workers of Armenia have cemented an alliance with toiling Azerbaijan

Declaration of the representatives of the working masses of Armenia

For many centuries the toiling masses of Armenia lived under the despotic power of the tsars and the sultans.[1] They languished under a heavy burden of oppression and slavery, bathed in sweat to satisfy the insatiable greed of the ruling classes and ruling nationalities. Yet the toiling masses of Armenia were exploited to no less a degree by the Armenian commercial-industrial bourgeoisie, despite the soothing voice of its nationalist phraseology.

Barbarous absolutism and its bloodthirsty agents, together with the possessing classes of both dominant and oppressed nationalities, constantly fostered national animosity and hatred between brothers, taking advantage of the backwardness and lack of consciousness of the broad popular masses. This they did to better defend their own narrow class interests and prevent the toiling masses of these peoples from uniting against their common parasites and oppressors.

These mutual hostilities and hatreds, continually fanned into life, were utilized to an even greater degree by the Western imperialists. Contesting for dominion over Turkey, the world plunderers cultivated national hostilities and incited bloody clashes by supporting the national movement of the oppressed peoples. At the same time, with their other hand, they protected the throne of the Eastern despot. When one competing plundering power, striving to transform Turkey into a colony, succeeded in buying the sultan's government, the other powers, pretending to defend the national interests of the oppressed, clutched at the small oppressed peoples, using them to carve out their own spheres of influence.

The ruling classes of Turkey, the immediate enemy of the peoples inhabiting that country, were beholden to German imperialism and drew Turkey into the imperialist war. Seizing on this fact, the imperialists of the Entente carved up Turkey, with flowery phrases about the liberation of small peoples. Turkish Armenia was essentially handed over to the Armenian bourgeoisie, agents of British finance capital who had already managed to create a small corner for themselves in Russian Armenia.[2] In the very heart of the East, which has set out on the revolutionary road, the Entente created a counterrevolutionary base for Western imperialism's struggle against the revolutionary East, and against the guiding light of the revolution in the East—Red Baku. Imperialism's primary goal is to deprive the toiling masses of Azerbaijan of their socialist conquests.

To this end, as revolutionary moods broaden and deepen in the lower layers of the oppressed peoples of the East, the Entente extravagantly flings about empty promises that the Armenian bourgeoisie and bourgeois-nationalist intelligentsia find more and more enticing. The intelligentsia, through the intransigent and warlike Dashnaktsutiun Party, has been transformed into an instrument for realizing the aims of the Entente imperialists and the Armenian bourgeoisie. The Dashnaks emerged from within Armenian capital as a brutal defender of its interests. For decades they conducted a struggle against the despotism of Turkey, appealing for assistance to absolutist Russia and the Western European imperialists. Their goal was to remake Turkish Armenia into an "Armenian Turkey," where the Armenian bourgeoisie's capital would predominate just as it did in Transcaucasia under the aegis of the two-headed eagle [of the tsars]. The victims of these wars were the working peasants of Turkish Armenia.

The Dashnaks, backed by the Mausers of their bandits, buried alive the working peasantry of Turkish Armenia and erected a new calvary for the worker and peasant masses of Transcaucasian Armenia.

Together with the bankrupt Musavat party [of Azerbaijan] and with the unfortunately still flourishing Mensheviks of Georgia, the Dashnaks have forcibly separated us from our brothers, the toiling masses of Azerbaijan and Georgia, and above all from the revolutionary proletariat of Soviet Russia. They have created on the territory of Russian Armenia a bourgeois-national power whose sole objective purpose is to defend Western finance capital's exploitation and feed the appetite of the Armenian capitalists. This party and its government carry out their counterrevolutionary policy with fire and sword, with blood and iron. Zangezur, Karabakh, Akulis, Agbaba, and Zangibasar [Razdan] bear living witness to the brutal, imperialist policy of the Dashnaks and their kindred party, the Musavats.

From the moment of its birth, this government sacrificed the lives of many of the Armenian people to protect and consolidate its rule, in the interests of the Entente and the Armenian bourgeoisie—sometimes in war outside of Armenia, sometimes in nightmarish bloody clashes between nationalities in Armenia itself. Already devastated by the invasion of the Turkish imperialists, the country under the rule of the Dashnak imperialists has been brought to complete ruin.

Armenia has completely degenerated both economically and morally; it is hurtling toward the brink of extinction. Under the bandits' domination the worker and peasant Muslim masses are being exterminated in the name of an independent and unified Armenia. The Turkish sultan's policy of cleansing Turkey of Armenians is now being applied by the Dashnaks to the Muslims of Armenia. Under the rule of these hangmen, worker and peasant rebels in Armenia are being executed.

But the first thunder of the revolution in May this year shook the contemptible, criminal government. Masses of working people in Armenia rose up in their thousands, determined that they—now awakened—would not give themselves over in servitude to the government of oppression and violence.

Their response to the uninterrupted nationalist wars, to the murderous policy of the Entente and its Dashnak hirelings, and to their own disenfranchised position, was the general uprising in May, led by the Communist Party, which proclaimed a Soviet Armenia.

The combined forces of the armed bandits and of Denikin's officers once again imposed darkness on Armenia, transforming it into a graveyard for the hundreds and thousands of those gunned down in the fields and of the Red rebels and their Communist leaders languishing in the prisons.

With their own blood the revolutionary working masses of Armenia have cemented an alliance with toiling Azerbaijan in the struggle against the Dashnaks and Musavats. The White terror currently raging in Armenia, carrying away its best sons, forces us to appeal to you, brothers, workers and peasants of the revolutionary East, to you, workers and peasants of the Soviet republics, to put an end to the counterrevolutionary cravings of the Armenian bourgeoisie once and for all.

Armenia must be liberated from the centuries-old oppression of the international plunderers; it must be freed from the power of their mercenaries. Armenia must be transformed into the beloved socialist homeland of the peoples inhabiting it, irrespective of their nationality.

Armenia's toilers know that all this can be realized if the power of the Entente's agents and the Armenian bourgeoisie is overthrown and replaced by the power of the toilers, by the dictatorship of the workers and peasants; if a Soviet government is created in Armenia. We are striving for this, we must strive for this. In our difficult revolutionary struggle we pin all our hopes on assistance and support from both the Soviet countries and the revolutionary peoples of the East. On our part, we will come to the assistance of the oppressed revolutionary masses of Turkey and Persia struggling for their liberation.

We cannot allow Armenia to become a base of operations for the West against Soviet Azerbaijan and the revolutionary East. Such would be to our eternal disgrace before the world revolution. We cannot allow our common enemy, Entente imperialism, to walk victoriously right through us—or behind our backs—against the revolutionary masses of the East. We will merge our forces with those of our neighboring peoples for final victory over our common enemy, for the overthrow of the dominion of world imperialism, for the final triumph of social revolution under the banner of the Communist International.

Long live the alliance of the revolutionary masses of the East with the workers of the West!

Long live the Third, Communist International!

APPENDIX 7
ZIONISM: AN EXCHANGE OF VIEWS AT THE
BAKU CONGRESS

7A
Thousands of Jewish toilers need land

Declaration of the delegation of Mountain Jews

For centuries the community of Mountain Jews got along peacefully and amicably with the surrounding Muslim population, adopting their spoken language and many of their customs.[1] Together with them it shed its blood for the mountains and gorges of the common homeland.

High mountains and broad plains closed off the Mountain Jews from their brothers, from others of their kind scattered across all the countries of the old world and the new. Nonetheless, the Mountain Jews never for a moment lost touch with them, responding keenly to their joys and sorrows. The explosion in recent years of the great world revolution brought us closer still to our western brothers.

When the cries and groans of our brothers in Ukraine and Poland, tormented and tortured by the White Guard bands, reached the inaccessible heights of Dagestan, we ourselves were facing a most difficult situation. This underscored yet again the commonality and singularity of economic and ideological needs of Jewish working people around the world. Jewish people everywhere are marked by a quite distinctive economic and class structure. Among Jews the peasantry is absent; workers are few in number.

The main bulk of the laboring Jewish community has hitherto been drawn into trade and services. That is why the destructive processes of world revolution have had a particularly sharp effect on the Jewish people, one that finds expression in deformed ways.

Just like the Jews of Russia and Ukraine, the Mountain Jews have faced the full force of the challenge of entering production, of integrating themselves into healthy productive labor. Convinced that their only salvation lies in revolution, the Mountain Jews look with hope to this great congress of workers and peasants of the East, who have gathered here to deal a powerful and decisive armed rebuke to world imperialism. Jewish workers and toilers of all countries have a vital interest in the overthrow of world capital and will work for this end with all their might.

British imperialism, now fastening its grip on the Near East, poses an insurmountable obstacle to the achievement of our ancient aspiration—the radical solution of our labor question. For decades the Jewish poor have been adapting to new, developing ways of life. During the course of this accommodation, the idea has developed and matured of Jewish immigration to and colonization of the Near East, chiefly of Palestine. This idea resonated powerfully among the broad working masses of Jews who had already watered Palestine's fertile pastures and fields with their sweat and blood, laying a basis there for a new life of free labor.

The Mountain Jewish community has empowered us to declare from this authoritative platform that it expects the congress to come up with a positive solution to this painful question. When the agrarian question comes up here for discussion, it will be essential to bear in mind the hundreds of thousands of Jewish toilers who need land and are prepared for any sacrifice in order to make the transition to new forms of collective, productive labor in

Palestine—where we have lived in fraternal friendship with Arab workers and toilers.

The Mountain Jews form part of the East. As in the past, they express their complete readiness, now and in the future, to fight with all their might, hand in hand with all the working people of the East, against the common enemy—the Entente—and for complete economic and ideological liberation.

Only the victory of the oppressed over the oppressors will bring us to our sacred goal—the creation of a Jewish communist society in Palestine.

Long live the unity of the toilers of the whole world! Long live the revolutionary East! Long live victory over world capital!

Long live the economic and ideological emancipation of the Jewish proletarian nation!

Long live the Third, Communist International!

7B
Settle and colonize Palestine on communist principles

Declaration of Jewish Communist Party (Poale Zion) delegation to the Baku congress

The British bourgeoisie stands at the head of the colonial predators in the oppression of the peoples of the East.[2] The interests of British imperialism demand possession of Mesopotamia and Syria in order to connect India with Egypt, and thereby with the metropolitan center. In the same way, Palestine's advantageous location gives it particular value in the eyes of the British imperialists, who are openly striving to transform it into their colony.

This endeavor, however, is meeting stubborn resistance from Palestine's population. For capitalist Britain, which exhausted its economic resources in the war and ruined its industry to a significant degree, is unable to supply its colonies with goods even in prewar quantities. Britain's colonial policy now takes the form of open economic plunder and unrestrained violence, based on military force. All in all, therefore, Britain is incapable of doing anything to help the country.

These facts compel the British bourgeoisie to seek allies in Palestine among the local population. The series of diplomatic steps that led to the notorious document signed in San Remo were an insidious maneuver to win the sympathies of the Jewish population.[3]

The Jewish population, after having lived through the nightmarish tyranny of Jemal Pasha, at first reacted favorably to this crafty maneuver, greeting the British as saviors announcing a new era.[4] But subsequently British imperialism's policy found expression in a prohibition of the immigration of Jewish working people from other countries, because of fear that they would bring in Bolshevism. The growth and development of Jewish colonization was openly obstructed. Moreover, British imperialism supported the self-seeking endeavors of the Jewish propertied classes there to the detriment of the vital interests of the Jewish working masses. All this brought a rapid sobering up of the working layers of Palestinian Jews, who have now entered into a determined struggle against the British occupiers.

In response to this, British diplomacy began to resort to tried and tested means of suppression of any revolutionary movement in the country. They began to incite nationalist feelings among the Jewish and Arab masses, turning one against the other, in an attempt to create in this fratricidal struggle a basis for their rule.

The criminal character of this policy of the British occupiers found clear confirmation in the bloody events that followed in Palestine. The April pogrom in Jerusalem bears a deliberate political character.[5] It results from the furious agitation of the Arab effendis and the agents of "King" Faisal, a buffoon, acting on the orders of the British administration and "influencing" the urban mob with the help of British gold.

It must be stressed that after forty years of Jewish colonization under Turkish rule, this is the first time Palestine has witnessed brutality and pogroms against Jews. Such are the precious "flowers" of the European capitalist civilization that British imperialism has brought into the country, along with oppression and enslavement. In Jerusalem we see once again the old familiar story from tsarist times. While the pogrom raged, British troops stood by, under command of their officers, protecting the perpetrators and disarming and arresting members of the Jewish self-defense organization. Meanwhile the Arab police, side by side with the pogromists, took part in the pogrom and in the sharing out of the spoils.

This brutal policy of the British occupiers is actively supported by the Arab sheikhs and landlords, who deeply hate the Jewish working masses, viewing them as dangerous and harmful elements. This hatred is not only the result of British gold; it is also dictated by their class, economic, and political interests. The Jewish masses undermine the patriarchal order of the country, arouse the indigenous wage slaves against their rule, and organize the Arab agricultural day laborers around demands for the nationalization of the land.

The Arab sheikhs and emirs consider themselves the rightful heirs of the sultan's lands, which amount to nearly 30 percent of the cultivated land in Syria and Mesopotamia. Yet the Jewish working masses conduct a struggle to take these lands for the needs of the poor—both indigenous and settlers. All these sheikhs, emirs, and other parasites see the communal farms and production cooperatives founded by Jewish workers as dangerous economic competitors. The Jewish labor collectives are communizing the Arab poor, clearly showing them the way out of their bondage.

Faced with this danger, the Arab propertied classes have launched a merciless struggle against the Jewish working masses, one which finds full sympathy and support in the camp of the Jewish landowners, who are equally afraid of the Jewish worker. The Jewish kulak exploits the undemanding and submissive Arab poor as cheap wage slaves. This exploitation of the Arab poor by Jewish landowners imparts to class oppression a national form, thereby creating fertile ground for the chauvinist agitation of pan-Islamism.

Bourgeois Zionism in turn is a reliable ally of British imperialism's colonial policy in Palestine. Like pan-Islamism, bourgeois Zionism strives to utilize for its own class purposes the Jewish working masses' efforts toward liberation. Just like the bourgeoisie of every oppressed nation, the Zionist bourgeoisie, with its talk of national rebirth, seeks to seize out of the hands of the foreign bourgeoisie the monopoly it holds in the exploitation of the Jewish working masses.

The reactionary nature of Zionist politics became especially clear to the Jewish working masses recently with the intensification of the civil war [in Russia]. The Zionist bourgeoisie, who in the Soviet federation lost all their class privileges, were seized with terror before the impending triumph of the proletarian dictatorship in all of Eastern Europe. Worried about the fate of their ill-gotten gains, they are striving to create a sanctuary for themselves in Palestine. The Zionist bourgeoisie hail the British occupation of Palestine because they see in it a real force on which they can depend in the struggle with the Jewish working masses.

The settlement of Jewish working masses in Palestine is introducing into the country the Red specter of communism, which threatens both the Zionist bourgeoisie and the British imperialists and Arab feudalists. That is why the Zionist bourgeoisie is giving the occupation forces every form of help in hindering this immigration. Last year one of the leaders of the world Zionist organization, Dr. Weizmann, published a semiofficial document on the necessity of restricting Jewish emigration to Palestine and subjecting this matter to the bourgeoisie's control. In this regard, Zionist policy in Palestine is blatantly reactionary.

The language of the Jewish popular masses has been declared to have no standing. Funds collected from Jewish working people in various countries for the rebirth of Palestine are spent on subsidies for Jewish landowners and on improvements in the bourgeois quarters in Jaffa and other cities. Their economic policy has led to a staggering increase in unemployment and poverty among Jews. They have not hestitated even to create a White Guard base for themselves in the country in the form of special Jewish regions. The Zionist leaders are striving to transform Palestine into a country of exploitation and profiteering.

As a consequence of all this, it is evident that due to the World War, the efforts of Anglo-French imperialism, the alliance of the Arab effendis with the Jewish colonialists, and the reactionary policy of the Zionist bourgeoisie, Palestine has been transformed into an arena of imperialist, nationalist, civil, and religious struggle. Only a close alliance of the Jewish and Arab working masses can genuinely overcome these obstacles, liberate the country forever from these dark reactionary forces, and bring Palestine a new and free life.

The Jewish proletarian masses, who in the process of the socialist revolution have been compelled to rebuild their economy on new principles of labor, who are striving to settle and colonize Palestine on communist principles, decisively disassociate themselves from this adventure. They base themselves and their movement exclusively on their own revolutionary struggle in Palestine itself, hand in hand with the Arab working masses. They base it on the objective factors of world revolution and on the fraternal assistance of the international proletariat and its highest leading body, the Third, Communist International.

The Jewish proletariat has no other road. Only in the tireless struggle against world capital and in close unity with working people around the world will it achieve full realization of its ideas.

Down with the imperialists and their bourgeois stooges! Long live the fraternal unity of the oppressed and enslaved of the whole world!

Long live the general staff of the world proletarian struggle, the Third International!

7C
The slogan of the Jewish proletariat must be 'Hands off Palestine!'

Declaration by Central Bureau of Jewish Sections, Communist Party of Russia

1. It is the policy of the Entente (and particularly Britain) regarding the creation of a Jewish state in Palestine, where

the overwhelming majority of the population is Arab—a policy backed by the Yellow Second International—that provides the basis for the bourgeois Zionist party's agitation among the Jewish popular masses in favor of Zionism.[6] Under the given conditions, this agitation favors the Entente, especially Britain.

2. Jews are being provocatively identified as initiators and culprits in the parceling out of Arab lands among the victorious powers, including the handing over of Palestine to Britain. This identification serves British imperialism in Palestine and throughout the East as a means to ignite national passions among the working people of the East and to sow hatred between Arabs and Jews. This found expression in the three-day-long pogrom of Jews in Jerusalem in April this year, which enjoyed the open sympathy of the British occupying authorities.

3. The Entente's whole policy is a typical example of colonial domination. It finds striking expression in the "constitution" of Palestine adopted by the San Remo conference of the League of Nations. At the same time this policy endeavors to utilize the capital of the small and middle Jewish bourgeoisie of all countries and to hitch them to the chariot of British imperialism, "the herald of the peoples' liberation."

Under this constitution, the government in Palestine aims to include the Jewish capitalists (through the Zionist party) in the intensified exploitation of the Arab peasantry and to implicate them in this plunder. It aims to ignite a national dispute between Jewish and Arab cliques in the legislative bodies. By this it seeks to retard the awakening of the masses of the East.

Britain's entire policy on Palestine aims at maintaining power wholly in the hands of the British occupiers and ideologically subordinating the Jewish community in all countries to Britain's interests. With the assistance of imperialism's Zionist servants, Britain's policy aims at drawing away from communism a portion of the Jewish proletariat by arousing in it national feelings and sympathies for Zionism. This policy of the Entente is actively supported by the Jewish bourgeoisie. In matters of exploitation and oppression, they solidarize fully with the capitalists of other nationalities. Their own class interests lead them to strive to participate in the plunder of the Arab peasant.

4. In the name of the Jewish proletariat and the working masses, we therefore most vigorously protest that, on the pretense of national liberation, a privileged Jewish minority is being artificially implanted in the population of Palestine. Such a policy is a direct violation of the rights of the Arab working masses in their struggle for independence and for complete possession of the land and of all the products of their labor.

The slogan of the Jewish proletariat, and of every friend of the toiling masses and every fighter for national liberation, must be "Hands off Palestine!"

We also sharply condemn the attempts by certain Jewish left-Socialist groups to combine communism with adherence to Zionist ideology. This is what we see in the program of the so-called Jewish Communist Party (Poale Zion). We believe that in the ranks of fighters for the rights and interests of the working people there is no place for groups that have in one form or another maintained Zionist ideology, concealing behind the mask of communism the nationalist appetites of the Jewish bourgeoisie. They are using communist slogans to exert bourgeois influence on the proletariat.

We note that during all the time that the mass Jewish workers' movement has existed, the Zionist ideology has been foreign to the Jewish proletariat. The social-Palestinian parties have been insignificant groups.[7] We declare that the Jewish masses envision the possibility of their social-economic and cultural development not in the creation of a "national center" in Palestine, but in the establishment of the dictatorship of the proletariat and the creation of socialist Soviet republics in the countries where they live.

We call on the Jewish working masses of all countries to take part actively in the unfolding socialist revolution and to join the ranks of the Third International through the Communist parties of their respective countries.

> A. Merezhin,
> *delegate to the Congress of the Peoples of the East from the Central Bureau of the Jewish Section of the Russian Communist Party (Bolsheviks)*

This declaration was endorsed by delegates to the Congress of the Peoples of the East from:
1. The general assembly of working indigenous Jews of Tashkent
2. The branch of indigenous Jews in the Tashkent organization of the Communist Party of Russia
3. The Jewish branch of the Communist Union of Youth of Samarkand
4. The Baku branch of the Communist Bund
5. The Kuba branch of the Azerbaijan Communist Party
6. The Mountain Jews branch of the Baku organization of the Communist Bund

APPENDIX 8
CORRECTING ABUSES OF SOVIET POWER IN ASIA

8A
Corrections must be made, and made quickly

Resolution submitted to the Baku Congress by 21 delegates

1. The Communist Party has firmly established that victory over capital is impossible without the liberation of the colonies and semi-colonies.[1] The Second Congress of the Comintern and, following it, the Congress of the Peoples of the East have clearly set forth the theoretical bases for future stages in the development of the revolutionary movement in the East. The international situation that has now arisen, as a result of complications on the battlefronts and in the East, demands that we focus our attention most seriously on the Eastern question and related issues, without restricting ourselves to purely theoretical considerations. In short, it requires that we move to practical implementation of the tasks of struggle thrust forward by life.

Any omission, any unconsidered policy that we apply in the East may not only repel the East from us but even, in certain circumstances, turn it into the main threat possessed by the imperialists against the social revolution.

2. There are two sides to Soviet Russia's tasks in the development of revolution in the East. One involves carrying through, efficiently and correctly, the revolutionary

tasks facing Soviet Russia in the Eastern countries where the bourgeoisie and imperialism still hold sway. The other concerns the relations between Soviet Russia and the Eastern Soviet republics and regions that are arising or are already in existence—the majority of which form part of the Russian Soviet Republic [RSFSR], for example Turkestan, the Caucasus, etc.—and the role of these states in the East.[2] These two tasks facing Soviet Russia in the East are closely related. They are interdependent, and neither can be carried out without the other. The Soviet order's three-year period of struggle has also provided experience in the Eastern borderlands, throwing up a whole range of both errors and positive factors. Indeed this experience relates to the whole of the East.

3. In terms of their special customs and the ethnographic makeup of the peoples living in them, the Eastern borderlands of Soviet Russia form an indivisible part of the East, having suffered still worse conditions of colonial exploitation. These Eastern borderlands are important as specific economic and strategic factors in the struggle with capital. In addition, the governmental forms developed there, through experience, provide examples of structure and of effective campaigning that can be carried over to the East as a whole: to Central Asia and Turkestan; to the Caucasus, Azerbaijan, and the Near East; and to Siberia, Mongolia, and the Far East. This is why these borderlands form the gates to the East and are so dangerous to world imperialism.

4. Soviet Russia needs to support the bourgeois-democratic movement in the East and make use of it as a powerful force that can promote the decay of imperialism. But at the same time it has to transform this movement into a social struggle that will culminate in the seizure of power in the East by the masses of the peasants and workers.

Conditions imposed by the colonialists' imperial policy placed the revolutionary proletarian masses of the East in a position where they were unable to organize in the manner of the working class in Europe; today they lack the sources of arms available to workers there. It is therefore inevitable that they initially fall under the influence of the bourgeois-national movement.

In Soviet Russia the Communist Party is gaining strength and resilience, and the armed forces of the international proletariat are being created, primarily for the West. In the Eastern countries, on the other hand—both inside and outside Soviet Russia—strong parties have yet to be created, and the indigenous toilers have yet to be armed, so as to be able to serve as a resource and support for the toiling masses in the process of a revolution in the East from within.

5. The fundamental error in the approach to the Eastern peoples during the three years of Soviet power has been the failure to pay sufficient attention to these tasks, or to the enormous significance of the colonial East in the struggle for world social revolution. The commissions and commissars sent from the center to the hastily declared "Eastern republics" and "regions" saw their task as being to abolish as quickly as possible the "autonomies of the Eastern peoples"—despite the fact that this autonomy had not yet had time to develop—and to implant communism there immediately.

In doing this they completely disregarded a number of factors. The first of these was the special nature of the Eastern borderlands, as former colonies relating to the former imperial power. A mistrust and hatred of the oppressor nation had been instilled in the soul of these peoples, as a result of tsarism's activity, and remained there. The important role played by such feelings toward the former oppressor nation was evident in our struggle with White Poland, where it became clear that here too the working class has not yet overcome these prejudices. What, then, can we demand of the backward Eastern peoples? These feelings continue to influence the uneducated and enslaved masses of indigenous peoples.

Further, there are the colonizing elements of the settler populations, tsarist officials, and agents of Russian industrial capital—products of tsarism now cut adrift. To save their own skin, they quickly turned partisans and supporters of the proletarian revolution. But at the same time, they support "centralization," understanding it as the continuation of the old tsarist policy and implementing it in essentially just this way.

6. Written and oral reports made at delegation meetings at the Congress of the Peoples of the East have already been relayed to the central bodies of the RSFSR by various delegations, including those from Turkestan, the Caucasus, the Kalmyk region, and the non-Russian peoples of Siberia, Persia, and elsewhere. They all testify to the same problems. The main issues raised in all of these reports are as follows:

a) Representatives of the center, special emissaries, commissars, and commissions have failed to implement the "autonomies of the peoples of the East" proclaimed by the Soviet government—in the sense of a genuine transfer of power to indigenous toilers from the exploiters. Where this autonomy has been implemented, it has been gradually eliminated by these representatives.

These emissaries, commissions, and bureaus from the center have been transformed into the effective power in the regions, thus gradually undermining in the eyes of the masses all the authority of the local government and indigenous Communist organizations and all initiatives that they take. The masses get the impression that these bodies are intended to function in the borderlands just like the tsarist governors. The significance of the constitution and the elected authorities is reduced to virtually nothing in the eyes of the masses. And so on.

b) The center displays an irresolute attitude to Russian colonial officials and merchants who, climbing aboard the Soviet administrations, continue to oppress the indigenous population in the name of Soviet power. For these colonizers, the revolution is useful precisely in that it gives them the opportunity to enrich themselves still further by robbing the indigenous people, thus holding back the process of class differentiation.[3] The interests of these colonizers, as persons of property, conflict with those of Soviet power, and they represent a constant counter-revolutionary danger.

c) Indigenous Communist organizations are allowed no initiative and are not trusted. Their role in revolutionizing and organizing the masses is eliminated, under pressure from officials of the center and with the encouragement of colonizers and indigenous nationalist elements. These Communist organizations are persecuted, and all independent activity of the toilers is undermined.

d) There has been an almost complete failure to recruit indigenous toilers into the Red Army, owing to a low evaluation of their quality and a mistrust of them. Indigenous military units that exist are dispersed among Russian units drawn predominantly from the local European population. Inappropriate elements are appointed as officers, and there is no attempt to form command staffs and a body of political commissars from among the indigenous population. Military administration is monopolized absolutely by officials from the center, around whom the mass of petty officials concentrate.

e) The Cheka (Special Section), whose agencies are found in every region, generally recruits the most negative elements, and its tactless conduct terrorizes the population, not to speak of the well-off. It shows a disrespectful attitude to the local authorities, commits outrages against the indigenous people's residual religious customs, and persecutes indigenous workers with special zeal.

f) When various social reforms are implemented, no proper account is taken of the precise nature of a given people's customs and of their conditions—errors that alienate the masses. Economic policy is frequently thoughtless and unjustified, and more often than not harms the national economy, providing virtually nothing for the organization of the indigenous toilers. In most cases, aspects of life such as the education, political instruction, and organization of the toiling masses are disregarded.

g) As a result of "centralization" along these lines and of the dispatch of emergency bodies from the center to these areas, a "special caste" of adventurist elements has developed, inserted between the central bodies and the indigenous Communist organizations. These elements hold no defined views and attach themselves to officials from the center in order to win their trust and gain power through appointment. Such persons are necessary to officials from the center to counter talk of a concentration of dictatorial powers in their hands. For this "intermediate caste," the opinions of the masses are a matter of total indifference. These elements are forming a wall that gradually takes power out of the hands of the masses, etc.

7. As far as external relations are concerned, the entire policy has now turned away from broad views on self-determination, away from the development and organization of the revolutionary movement in neighboring countries. Now, on the contrary, all the old slogans

are ignored and replaced with the idea that it is necessary for the Russian Red Army units to move into the East, in order to artificially create a revolution in the neighboring countries.

8. The application of this kind of policy by representatives of the center in the Eastern borderlands, appeared—in its essence—everywhere, and the results are already apparent. Because the policy has been applied so inconsistently, and because of the failure to acknowledge the special features of the customs and interests of the indigenous toiling masses, these masses have gradually become alienated from Soviet power. Strong dissatisfaction has arisen among the indigenous Communist organizations, along with conditions in which it is impossible to work.

In addition, an aggressive military policy has been pursued in the East that cannot be considered in any way appropriate. It has now reached an impasse, with the creation of a whole number of external Eastern battlefronts: on the one hand, the Fergana-Bukhara-Afghanistan front, and the Persian front on the other.[4] These fronts opposing Soviet power are held by Eastern peoples, a fact that grieves us, but that must be taken seriously into consideration. Of course, correcting the errors of the past will demand great efforts, but the corrections must be made, and made as quickly as possible.

Proceeding from the above points, and taking into account the demands put forward in the reports by representatives of different regions, the delegation to the Congress of the Peoples of the East proposes the following specific measures:

On the Eastern question in general:

1. Soviet Russia's way forward in the East should be recognized as lying, firstly, through the Eastern Soviet countries, both inside and outside the RSFSR. In these countries indigenous Communist parties must be created, organized, and strengthened, and the indigenous peasants and workers armed and educated as quickly as possible. Around them must be united the revolutionary underground forces of the neighboring countries. Taken together, these countries will provide toilers in the East with a genuine resource and support for their revolution from within.

Secondly, the way forward lies through a very careful, correct, and persuasive approach to these Eastern Soviet borderlands, which must not in any way be treated in the same manner as the general run of provinces of central Russia. Distortions of the principles of Soviet power and errors such as those committed in these regions by many officials from the center must not be tolerated, for the East will take its education from the experience of these borderlands.

2. On the basis of the theses on the Eastern question adopted by the Second Congress of the Communist International and the Congress of the Peoples of the East, practical ways forward for revolutionary work in the East should be devised as a matter of urgency. Specifically, some of the practical aspects of these tasks that are of particular interest to us could be defined as follows.

In the countries where a feudal order prevails or class differentiation is weak, and where the revolution is being achieved with our cooperation, our tactics must proceed in the following practical sequence:

a) The revolution's most immediate task is to organize and support any kind of revolutionary movement, even if it is nationalist in character, against imperialism and economic exploitation.

The Communist Party may enter into government in order to use its authority for agitation, propaganda, and organization of the revolutionary masses and for leadership of the revolutionary movement.

b) Communists must make use of this period of struggle, firstly, to rapidly organize and strengthen their party by intensively recruiting into it the truly revolutionary forces. Secondly, they must develop intensive agitation among the masses against the princes, beys, khans, large landowners, and manufacturers—the agents of European imperialism. They must call on the middle bourgeoisie, intelligentsia, and progressive clergy to support the new power. Thirdly, they must intensively organize everywhere soviets of smallholders, landless peasants, and—where they exist—industrial workers. They must organize cooperatives and unions of artisans, and intensively recruit toilers into the Red Army units. Fourthly, they must increase the strength of their position further, and prepare for gradual revolution and for the creation of Soviet power of the true toilers.

In all these steps the initiative must be fully in the hands of the indigenous Communists. Dictatorship by individuals appointed from above cannot be tolerated here, for this would undermine the profoundly mass character of events.

The errors committed by our side during recent events in Persia must not now be repeated. This is possible, provided that individual RSFSR commissars do not proceed each with his own special program for the East, rather than drawing up a comprehensive plan beforehand and implementing it in an organized manner.

3. To ensure more efficient and successful work in the East, three "Councils for Action and Propaganda" should be set up. These should be based in the cities of Baku,

Tashkent, and Irkutsk, thus dividing the East into three parts. The first part will be the Near East, including Turkey, Arabia, Syria, Egypt, Armenia, Georgia, Azerbaijan, Dagestan, and Terek; the second will be Central Asia, including India-Afghanistan, Turkestan, Bashkiria, western Chinese Turkestan, Kashmir, and Altai; the third will be the Far East, including China, Korea, Mongolia, Manchuria, Siberia, and Japan.

The need to organize three councils stems primarily from the geographical and other conditions that make it impossible to cover the whole of the East from a single center.

Regarding relations between the center and the surrounding Eastern Soviet republics and regions that form part of the RSFSR:

1. The entire policy pursued by the center recently in relation to the Eastern borderlands should be fundamentally altered, giving these regions a broader basis of autonomy. The "autonomy" initially granted to the Eastern nations has effectively failed to achieve its aims, since virtually no indigenous toilers have been drawn into authority. Moreover, as a result of the "centralization" of power in the hands of a few representatives of the center, the indigenous toilers have been unable to organize into soviets and to pass through the whole revolutionary school and education that the soviets offer. For in the eyes of the masses the soviets have lost their significance, as the power of the soviets and their executive committees in the borderlands has been replaced by simple agents of officials from the center, who dictate to everyone.

2. The borderlands are currently governed by special commissars, commissions, bureaus, and the like, at the behest of the center, in order to guarantee that it is rep-

resented there. These institutions should be abolished. Workers sent from the center should simply enter local bodies to carry out communist cooperation with local workers, rather than dictating to them.

Centralization could be carried out without dispatch of commissars with special powers.

3. The authority and weight of the local government, local soviets, and indigenous Communists should be increased. Rather than being reduced to the role of simple petitioners, constantly traveling to the center with appeals, they should become genuine leaders of the indigenous toilers, providing support for the revolution in the regions. Full initiative in Soviet construction should be given to the local authorities and Communist organizations.

4. The struggle against patriarchal-feudal relations and for a class differentiation among the indigenous population should be conducted exclusively among the indigenous toilers and Communist organizations. Moreover, economic enterprises should be broadly based. This is the only way to get results in the areas of agriculture, food production, and so on. This cannot be done by ignoring the importance of the indigenous population and attempting to carry out the task of class differentiation through the Cheka and special envoys, as was done for example in Turkestan. A high degree of success in class differentiation will be achieved if the indigenous toilers in the region themselves feel that they have power over the exploiters.

5. The violent grip of colonial settlers and tsarist officials over indigenous people in the borderlands should be abolished once and for all. They should be set on an equal level with the local population. Further, the prevailing opinion among officials from the center, albeit concealed, is that these colonizers could form a base of support for Soviet power against a pan-Islamic movement (or

something of that sort). This opinion must be eradicated.

Until this layer of colonizers is abolished, there can be no talk of having created true Soviet power based on the indigenous toilers, and Soviet power will not be secure against counterrevolution.

6. Rather than leaving things as they have been up to now, indigenous toilers should be recruited into the Red Army on a broad scale. Military staffs and political commissars should be drawn from among indigenous peoples. As for organizing military units from among the indigenous population, here again full initiative should be given to the local authorities.

7. We should eliminate the practice of the Cheka in these borderlands of recruiting, for the most part, from the most negative elements—sometimes even clearly counterrevolutionary ones—among the local Europeans and indigenous peoples. Eliminate the focusing of the whole of the Cheka's activity on struggling against the local Communists rather than against the counterrevolution. Revolutionary justice in these Eastern borderlands should be administered by bodies drawn mainly from the indigenous toilers, although strictly subordinated to the center.

8. A central bureau for the Eastern republics and regions within the RSFSR should be set up, reporting to the All-Russia Central Executive Committee. A central bureau is also needed for Communist organizations in these Eastern borderlands, reporting to the Central Committee of the Russian Communist Party. These bodies should be independent of the People's Commissariat of Nationalities. Before each all-Russia congress, Soviet and especially party congresses of these Eastern republics and regions must be called to outline the practical ways forward for Soviet construction in the Eastern regions, and to elect these bodies, which are subordinate to the All-Russia Central

Executive Committee and the Central Committee of the party. In addition, participation in all-Russia congresses is assumed to be understood.

These steps will stimulate the independence of the masses. More effectively than forcible centralization, these steps will contribute to a stronger union of the Eastern peoples in Soviet Russia.

Mountain peoples:
M. Eneyev, N. Magarik, A. Tagiyev, N. Gikalo, K. Varukayev, Ye. Ramonov, Kostoyev, Goykov, Soliyer, Agayev, Khudoiratov, Sersanov

Turkestan delegation:
Ryskulov, Azizkhanov, Kultasov, Irurbayev

Representatives of Kalmyk region:
Amur Sanan, Kochirov

Representatives of Persia and India:
Emakhundov, Eyvazov, N. Qadir

8B
Communist tasks among Eastern peoples

Excerpt from minutes of Political Bureau, Communist Party of Russia, October 14, 1920

9. Tasks of the Communist Party of Russia in areas inhabited by Eastern peoples[5]

The politburo of the Central Committee has discussed the reports and communications made at its meeting with twenty-seven delegates from the Baku Congress of the Peoples of the East from the Mountain peoples of the Caucasus in the districts of Terek and Dagestan (Chechens, Ingushes, Ossetians, Kabardians, Balkars, Karachays, and Mountain Jews) and from Turkestan, the Kalmyk region, Persia, India, Mongolia, the Buryat region, Tibet, and the Indian association.[6] The Political Bureau has decided the following:

1. To publish in the name of the Supreme Soviet a manifesto reaffirming the principles of the national policy of the Russian Soviet Republic (RSFSR) and establishing genuine control over its implementation in real life.

2. On the agrarian question, to recognize the necessity of providing the landless Mountaineers of the Northern Caucasus with land at the expense of the kulak elements of the cossack population. To charge the Council of People's Commissars to prepare appropriate decrees immediately.[7]

3. To recognize the necessity of implementing autonomy, in forms appropriate to the concrete conditions, for Eastern nationalities that do not yet possess autonomous

institutions—first and foremost for the Kalmyks and Buryat Mongols. The Commissariat of Nationalities will be assigned the task of drafting a decree on Kalmyk autonomy, and the Commissariat of Foreign Affairs will communicate with the fraternal Far Eastern Republic about taking such measures in relation to the Buryat Mongols.[8]

4. To conduct the strictest investigation into abuses and acts of violence committed by the local Russian population toward the Eastern peoples (especially the Kalmyks, Buryat Mongols, and so on) and to punish the offenders.

5. To propose to the meeting's participants that they give the party Central Committee a list of persons belonging to the Eastern nationalities who, in their opinion, should be amnestied.

6. To recognize the need to organize a school under the Commissariat of Nationalities for preparing Soviet and party cadre from among the workers and peasants of the Eastern nationalities.

7. To cut to a minimum the number of emissaries sent by various central institutions to regions of the RSFSR inhabited by Eastern peoples; to give these emissaries detailed instructions stipulating above all the necessity of conducting all their work through local organizations and appropriate Soviet institutions.

8. To direct the attention of the All-Russia Cheka to the need in the outlying regions, in particular in localities inhabited by Eastern nationalities, to select Cheka personnel with particularly painstaking care.

9. To recognize that representatives of the Central Committee of the Communist Party of Russia in regions of the RSFSR inhabited primarily by Eastern nationalities (and also in party organizations in these regions) have as their chief task to struggle against bourgeois and pseudo-Communist groups among the local population, while at

the same time supporting the really Communist groups and elements.

10. To strengthen the work of the Soviet of Nationalities under the People's Commissariat of Nationalities. A report on this work is to be made at the next meeting of the Council of People's Commissars.

8C
Appeal to Red Army soldiers fighting in the East

Council for Propaganda and Action of the Peoples of the East, late 1920

To Red Army men fighting for the proletarian revolution in the East
Red Army comrades!

The victorious Red Army is advancing, penetrating deeper and deeper into the countries of the East.[9]

Why is the Red Army marching to the East?

Certainly not in order to seize new lands and subject the peoples who inhabit them to Russian rule. The Red Army marches into the East in order to liberate the peoples there—and with them the whole world—from the yoke of imperialism, from the dominion of the bourgeois exploiter governments of Britain and France.

We, the Russian workers and peasants, who have thrown off the rule of our own bourgeoisie, must also free other peoples from bourgeois rule. This we must do not simply because we want all working people to be free, so that the bourgeoisie will never dare exploit the workers and peasants anywhere. Even more, we do this because if we do not overthrow bourgeois rule throughout the world, it will strangle our Soviet republic, and the bourgeoisie will restore its rule in Russia.

Particularly important for the success of the world revolution is liberating the countries of the East from the yoke of Entente imperialism. For it is from these rich countries that the capitalist governments of Britain and France draw their main strength.

The Eastern countries, such as India, Persia, Mesopotamia, Egypt, and Turkey, serve Britain and France as a storehouse of the bread, raw materials, and fuel needed for the operation of their factories. These countries are a source of gigantic profits for the Entente capitalists, enabling them to accumulate colossal wealth, to maintain enormous armies, to bribe the top layers of their workers, and in this way delay the development of the proletarian revolution in Europe.

Without the proletarian revolution in Europe, the Russian revolution will suffocate in the clutches of the bourgeois countries, and the Russian peasants and workers will be turned into abject slaves of the British and French capitalists. To keep this from happening and to avoid delaying the movement toward proletarian revolution, the Eastern countries must be broken free of the bourgeois governments' rule. All the Eastern peoples—Turks, Persians, Indians, Arabs, Egyptians, and others—must be liberated from British exploitation.

Thus, we must cut away from the capitalists of Britain and France the very foundations of their power—their colonies. We must liberate the Eastern peoples from the shameless exploitation of Western European capitalists, thus saving both them and ourselves from bourgeois slavery. It is in order to do this that the Red Army is advancing into the East, rooting itself in the Eastern countries.

The Red Army comes to the Eastern peoples not as an enemy, but as a friend and liberator. This is not always understood by the peoples of the East, who sometimes greet the Red Army with fear and hostility. They are accustomed to the Russia of the tsar, which for centuries was an imperialist power, seizing for itself other lands and other peoples and enslaving them. The peoples of the East are accustomed to see the arrival of a Russian army bringing them oppression and enslavement. They view the Red Army with suspicion, expecting that it too, like the former Russian army, will bring ruin, bondage, and suffering.

That is why it is the responsibility, the revolutionary duty, of every Red Army fighter to prove by his behavior and his treatment of the indigenous peoples that they have nothing to fear from the Red Army. He must prove that the Red Army is not the former Russian army; it is an army of conscious revolutionary fighters, bringing freedom, light, and happiness to the peoples of the whole world. This must be shown not just by words but by deeds, since words prove nothing if actions speak offensively.

Each fighter of the Red Army must prove to the peoples of the countries to which the Red Army comes, by his deeds, that he arrives not as an enemy and conqueror, but as a friend and liberator. That means that every Red Army soldier is obliged to treat the local inhabitants with the greatest care and to try to cause them neither harm nor offense, neither loss nor destruction.

Each Red Army soldier must treat the local inhabitants not as a conquered people, but as his own brothers. The Red Army soldier must bear in mind, first, that working people of all countries are brothers, and that only by preserving this brotherhood will their common liberation from the capitalist yoke be possible. In addition, he must remember that the peoples of the East must be drawn into the proletarian revolution and shown in life that this revolution is really liberating the working peoples of the entire world from every kind of oppression, that it will establish well-being for all.

Each Red Army soldier must treat the local inhabitants in such a way that they will not curse but will instead be thankful for the arrival of the Red Army. In this way, its fame will spread rapidly and far, throughout all the East. The revolutionary Red Army will liberate all the working people from all kinds of oppression and slavery, and its glory will light a revolutionary fire everywhere.

Yes, the Red Army must go forth and light the fires of revolution everywhere, in order to save both the whole world and Soviet Russia itself from the horror of endless wars, from slow death in the midst of torment, famine, destitution, and ruin.

But to ignite the flame of revolution, you must know how. You cannot ignite it by brute force; you cannot employ everywhere one and the same method, one and the same technique.

Every Red Army soldier knows that at the front victory is gained not only by attacking all along the line. The struggle must also be waged with complex and diverse stratagems: in one situation, rush to the attack; in another, simulate an offensive; in a third, remain on the defensive; and in a fourth, even carry out a deliberate retreat.

It is the same thing in a revolution. We must obtain the common success and victory of the proletarian revolution throughout the world. But this does not mean that we must quickly install communism in its entirety in every corner of the globe.

Our Communist Party says that in carrying out a revolution it is necessary to consider, first of all, the level of historical development of each country, and employ in that country whatever revolutionary method is appropriate to that situation.

In the East it must be borne in mind that these are primarily agricultural and peasant countries, in which large-scale industry and an industrial proletariat do not yet exist. A clear class differentiation has not yet taken place there. No deep gulf has yet opened up between the layers of working people and the bourgeoisie. The producers have not yet been torn away from the means of production. Each handicraftsman sells the objects he produces; consequently he is also a merchant. Commerce has not yet been concentrated in the hands of a few large-scale merchants and bankers. Instead, it rests in the hands of millions of small traders, who cannot in any way be called capitalists, because each of them only has a penny's worth of goods.

Given all these conditions, the rapid implementation of communism in the Eastern countries by such measures as we have carried out in Russia is impossible. Expropriation of the entire bourgeoisie, nationalization of all trade, nationalization of handicraftsmen and artisans, would injure the interests of many millions—perhaps the majority of the population—and would incite the whole country against the revolution.[10] To implement such revolutionary measures in the East is impossible at this time, first of all because there is no one who could carry them out. In the Eastern countries there is no unified revolutionary industrial proletariat. Consequently, there are no forces to provide support, with whose help we might bring around the petty bourgeoisie, who have influence among the peasant masses and lead them.

That is why waging a war against the petty bourgeoisie and abruptly implementing purely communist measures not only does not help the world revolution but is positively harmful. Such measures would alienate from the revolution the Eastern countries as a whole, forcing them to break off the struggle with the imperialist countries of the West. The most important role of the Eastern countries in the world revolution lies in their conducting a struggle against the imperialist countries, one that undercuts the power of their bourgeois governments and thus facilitates the struggle of the Western workers against those governments. Extending, continuing, and developing the struggle of the national liberation movement in the Eastern countries is a hundred times more necessary and more useful for the world revolution than the rapid introduction there of class stratification, civil war, and communist measures.

Communism can become firmly established in the backward agricultural countries of the East only after it becomes firmly established in the industrialized countries of Europe. Then the backward agricultural countries of the East will be drawn into communism by the industrialized countries of the West in a common world communist economy, just as, in Russia today, the proletarian industrial city draws the peasant agricultural countryside into the revolution.

Until the moment of victory of the proletarian revolution in Europe, our main task in the East will be drawing the Eastern countries into the struggle against the Western European imperialists, and strengthening by all the forces and means at our disposal the support rendered by this struggle. It follows that we must, through the organization of our economy and the conduct of our glorious Red Army in the countries it occupies—by this living example—prove to the peoples of the East the superiority of the communist over the bourgeois system, the need for unity of the working masses, and the establishment of their power over the bourgeoisie.

We must recognize that the peoples of the East—even including their own bourgeoisie temporarily—are our allies. With them we shall fight the common foe: the imperialist Entente, which seeks to enslave both the Russian and the Eastern peasants and workers. Together we shall fight for the victory of the world proletarian revolution, which brings the laboring masses of all peoples total liberation from any kind of oppression or exploitation.

And every Red Army soldier, fighting in the East in the name of the victory of the world revolution, must recognize in himself not only a fighter of the Russian army but a fighter of the international Red Army, representing the military power of a worldwide federation of Soviet republics. Every country of the East that he enters must be seen by the Red Army soldier as a new friend, a new member of this federation, newly liberated from under the imperialist yoke. He must see it as a member of a socialist fatherland—his homeland—that embraces the whole world. The Red Army soldier must conduct himself in this country just as he would in his own homeland.

The glorious Red Army has set out to light a conflagration of revolution in the East. The glorious Red Army will do this not only with its courage but also with its tact, its self-control, and its understanding of the tasks of the revolutionary movement in Eastern countries.

Notes

Introduction

1. For documents of the struggle within the Second International on this question and Lenin's assessment, see John Riddell, ed., *Lenin's Struggle for a Revolutionary International* (New York: Pathfinder, 1986 [2019 printing]), pp. 38–57, 83–86, 133–46, 169–75, and 736–48. V.I. Lenin's articles of 1913, "The Awakening of Asia" and "Backward Europe, Advanced Asia," can be found in this collection, pp. 169–71.

    An analysis of the Socialist International's achievements and shortcomings can be found in Farrell Dobbs, *Revolutionary Continuity: The Early Years*, (New York: Pathfinder, 1980), pp. 39–43 and 120–30.

2. For Lenin's report, see Riddell, ed., *Workers of the World and Oppressed Peoples, Unite!* (New York: Pathfinder, 1991 [2021 printing]), vol. 1., pp. 271–78.

3. An important discussion on this point took place in the Second Congress. Two leading Communists, M.N. Roy of India and Ahmed Sultanzadeh of Iran, argued initially against supporting "bourgeois-democratic" movements in Asian countries with some degree of capitalist development. Lenin's report to the congress clarified the nature of the "national-revolutionary" movements deserving support. For the record of this discussion, including the changes made in theses proposed by Lenin and Roy, see Riddell, *Workers of the World*, vol. 1, pp. 76–77, 271–368, and vol. 2, pp. 1077–99.

4. The revolution triumphed on October 25, 1917, by the Julian (old style) calendar used in prerevolutionary Russia. All dates in this book are given according to the Gregorian calendar, predominant in the world today, which was introduced in Russia in February 1918.

5. Alfred Rosmer, *Moscow under Lenin* (New York: Monthly Review Press, 1971), p. 86.
6. Yelena Stasova, *Vospominaniya* (Memoirs) (Moscow: Mysl', 1969), p. 177.
7. On the significance of the subbotnik movement, see Lenin, "A Great Beginning," in *Collected Works* (Moscow: Progress Publishers, 1960–71), vol. 29, pp. 411–34; "Report on Subbotniks," in vol. 30, pp. 283–88; "From the Destruction of the Old Social System to the Creation of the New," in vol. 30, pp. 516–18, and "From the First Subbotnik . . . to the All-Russia May Day Subbotnik," in vol. 31, pp. 123–25.
8. M.N. Roy, the most prominent Communist from India, had been assigned to help establish a Comintern bureau in Tashkent, and did not attend the Baku congress.

    The Moscow newspaper *Pravda* (Truth) reported September 8 that representatives of the one million Chinese in Turkestan spoke in Baku September 4, stating that they were in contact with revolutionary forces in north China.
9. *Kommunistische Internationale* (Communist International), no. 14 (October 1920), p. 292.
10. *De Tribune*, November 3, 1920.
11. J.T. Murphy, *New Horizons* (London: John Lane The Bodley Head, 1941), p. 121.
12. Stasova recalls that on some occasions, such as in the agrarian report, the question of women's equality was raised when many considered it out of order. Stasova, *Vospominaniya*, p. 179. Such a passage is not found, however, in the text of the agrarian report that was printed in the congress proceedings.
13. Lenin, "Question of Nationalities," in *Collected Works*, vol. 36, p. 606.
14. G. Safarov, *Kolonial'naya revolyutsiya (opyt Turkestana)* (Colonial revolution—the Turkestan experience) (Moscow: State Publishing House, 1921), p. 133. The Central Committee's comments formed part of a circular letter it sent to the Turkestan Communist Party membership early in 1920.

15. Matushev, speaking in session 5, specified that the term did not properly apply to Africa south of the Sahara. On the other hand, the greetings of the Azerbaijan Communist Party, printed in appendix 5, defined the East to include the subject peoples of the Americas.
16. Lenin, speech to chairmen of Moscow-area soviet executive committees, October 15, 1920, in *Collected Works*, vol. 31, p. 330.
17. From a discussion with Samad Yerevani in Rasht, 1983. Babayev died in 1987.
18. It was on this occasion that Lenin defended this slogan against detractors who saw it as an unwarranted alteration of the words with which Marx and Engels concluded their statement of principles in 1848. "Of course, the modification is wrong from the standpoint of the *Communist Manifesto*," Lenin replied, "but then the *Communist Manifesto* was written under entirely different conditions. From the point of view of present-day politics, however, the change is correct." Lenin, "Speech at a Meeting of Activists," in *Collected Works*, vol. 31, p. 453.
19. Diplomatic note of Curzon to Chicherin, quoted in Stephen White, "Communism and the East: The Baku Congress, 1920," in *Slavic Review*, vol. 33, no. 3 (September 1974), pp. 502–3.
20. The proceedings are found in *The First Congress of the Toilers of the Far East* (London: Hammersmith Reprints, 1970).
21. Lenin, "The Question of Nationalities or 'Autonomisation,'" in *Collected Works*, vol. 36, pp. 610–11. This and other writings of Lenin during the last months of his political activity will be contained in the forthcoming Pathfinder collection, *Lenin's Final Fight*.
22. For the record of the struggle to defend Lenin's course against this petty-bourgeois current, see Leon Trotsky, *The Challenge of the Left Opposition* (New York: Pathfinder, 1975–81), 3 vols., and Trotsky, *The Third International after Lenin* (New York: Pathfinder, 1970).

23. For a discussion of the Communist International's policy in the 1925–27 revolution in China, see *Leon Trotsky on China* (New York: Pathfinder, 1976) and Jack Barnes, "Their Trotsky and Ours," in *New International*, no. 1 (Fall 1983), pp. 9–89.
24. The following editions of the Baku congress have been previously published:
    - *Pervyy s"ezd narodov vostoka: Baku 1–8 sent. 1920 g.* (First Congress of the Peoples of the East: Baku 1–8 Sept., 1920). Petrograd: Communist International Publishing House, 1920.
    - *Le premier congrès des peuples de l'Orient, Bakou 1920: L'Internationale Communiste et la libération de l'Orient* (First Congress of the Peoples of the East, Baku 1920: the Communist International and the Liberation of the East). Petrograd: Communist International Publishing House, 1921. Reprint. Paris: Maspéro, 1971.
    - *Birinci dogu halklari kurultayi: Baku 1–8 eylül 1920* (First Congress of the Peoples of the East: Baku 1–8 September, 1920). Istanbul: Koral, 1975.
    - *Congress of the Peoples of the East: Baku, September 1920, Stenographic Report*. Translated and annotated by Brian Pearce. London: New Park Publications, 1977.

    In addition, the manuscript for a projected two-volume collection of documents relating to the congress, prepared by Solmaz Rustamova Tohidi and Bakhtiar Rafiyev, is available in the Central State Archives of Political Parties and Social Movements of the Republic of Azerbaijan.

Call to the Baku congress

1. *Kommunisticheskiy Internatsional* (Communist International), no. 12 [July 1920], cols. 2259–64.
2. The opening of the congress, originally planned for August 15, was later postponed to the beginning of September. Both dates are given in this call.
3. The reference to the shariat, found in the German edition of the Communist International magazine, is absent from the version printed in *Kommunisticheskiy Internatsional*.

4. Under the Anglo-Iranian Agreement of 1919, London was to furnish the Iranian government with a loan of £2 million. In return, the British government received sweeping privileges in Iran, including a monopoly in supplying its government with arms, military instructors, and administrative advisers. Because of strong popular opposition, the treaty was not ratified by Iran's parliament, and was abrogated by Iran early in 1921.
5. Anatolia is the name for the part of Turkey in Asia between the Black and the Mediterranean seas.
6. Before 1914, about 1.75 million Armenians lived in Turkey. Armenian peasants in northeast Turkey were harshly oppressed by Kurdish nobles acting for the Ottoman regime. During World War I, many Armenian political leaders refused to back the Turkish government in its war against Russia. This helped provide the Ottoman government with a pretext to deport the entire Armenian population, an operation that was carried out with a brutality bordering on genocide. About a third of the Armenian population perished.

Opening rally

1. "Turkic" refers here to the closely related languages and dialects of the Caucasus and Central Asia, including Azerbaijani, Uzbek, Kirghiz, Turkmen, and Kumyk. The congress later chose Azerbaijani as the standard language of Turkic translation. Translations were also made at the congress into "Turkish," the more distantly related language of what is now the Republic of Turkey.
2. The events referred to are the 1905 workers' and peasants' uprising against tsarism and the February and October revolutions of 1917.
3. S.G. Shaumyan (b. 1878) and Ilya Dzhaparidze (b. 1880) were leaders of the Baku Soviet government, which was overturned in July 1918 by an alliance of Socialist Revolutionaries, Dashnaks (an Armenian petty-bourgeois nationalist party), and other forces. Shaumyan, Dzhaparidze, and

twenty-four other leaders of the soviet were executed in September 1918, with the complicity of the British army.

4. In the French edition of the congress proceedings, this sentence reads, "But, comrades, not two weeks have passed since then, and our armies have recovered and are standing firm under the walls of Brest-Litovsk."

5. The Polish government, backed by France and other Allied powers, attacked Soviet Ukraine on April 25. The Red Army repulsed the invading forces and pursued them deep into Poland, but suffered a reverse in August as it approached Warsaw. An armistice was signed in October 1920.

6. For the Second Congress appeal, "Let No Ship, No Train Leave for White Guard Poland," see Riddell, *Workers of the World*, vol. 1, pp. 178–82.

7. In fact, ten of the thirty-seven national delegations at the Second Congress represented countries in Asia.

8. In the French edition, the sentence that follows begins, "At this precise moment, when the guns of the Red Army are about to roar once again before Warsaw."

9. The Russian text refers to "the American Horthy." The translation here follows the French text.

10. In August 1920 trade unions in Britain formed a joint Council of Action, which threatened a general strike if the British government intervened militarily in the Polish government's war against Soviet Russia. Shaken by the massive protest campaign and by unrest among its soldiers, the government publicly undertook not to send troops to Poland.

11. In March 1919, French soldiers along the Black Sea coast began refusing to fight, and in April the French Black Sea fleet mutinied. By the end of May, French armed forces in the region had been withdrawn.

12. Rail workers in France struck in February and again in May 1920. The May walkout called forth a mass solidarity strike, which at its peak embraced 1.5 million workers. Nonetheless, the railway workers went down to defeat. More than 10 percent of the strikers were fired, and many revolutionaries were jailed.

13. At this point, among the audience "the solemn faces were suddenly shaken with laughter," notes Rosmer, from whose account the wording of Reed's question is taken. See Rosmer, *Moscow under Lenin*, p. 87.
14. The original text refers here not to "Reed" but to "Radek," an evident misprint.

Session 1: Tasks of the congress

1. It was in the commission on the colonial question at the 1907 Stuttgart congress that a majority of delegates endorsed a statement backing a reformed colonialism. This stand was rejected, however, by a narrow majority of congress delegates, including the Menshevik delegates from Russia. Zinoviev uses the term *Menshevik* here to apply to the Socialist International majority leadership as a whole. For excerpts of the congress debates, see Riddell, *Lenin's Struggle for a Revolutionary International*, pp. 35–50.
2. See Riddell, *Workers of the World*, vol. 2, p. 893.
3. In place of this sentence, the French edition reads, "The French bourgeoisie has sent blacks into Germany."
4. Zinoviev, *Voyna i krizis sotsializma* (Petrograd: State Publishing House, 1920). For excerpts from this book published in English, see "The Social Roots of Opportunism," in *New International*, no. 2 (winter 1983–84); and "Wars: Defensive and Aggressive," in *Three Study Guides on Lenin's Writings* (Pathfinder: New York, 2017).
5. See Lenin, "Report on the World Political Situation," in Riddell, *Workers of the World*, vol. 1, pp. 108–11.
6. See Lenin, "Report on the National and Colonial Questions," in Riddell, *Workers of the World*, vol. 1.
7. The movement led by Mustafa Kemal sought to unify all Turks against the Allied invaders while avoiding an open break with the sultan, who favored submission to Allied dictates. When the Grand National Assembly convened by Kemal met in Ankara in April 1920, delegates reaffirmed

their loyalty to the sultan and resolved to rescue him from the Allied forces occupying Istanbul. Subsequently, the Assembly abolished the sultanate (1922) and the caliphate (1924).

8. In a report given after the congress, Zinoviev specified that the Turkish politician in question was Enver Pasha. See *Kommunistische Internationale*, no. 14 [October 1920], p. 293.

9. The main White Guard activity northward of Baku during the congress was an offensive in the Kuban, north of the Caucasus Mountains. White forces were also active near Maikop in the Northern Caucasus foothills. Major fighting elsewhere at that time took place north of Crimea and on the Polish front.

10. R.E.H. Dyer was the British general who in April 1919 ordered troops in Amritsar to fire on a crowd assembled to hear speakers for Indian national rights. Almost four hundred persons were killed. In a later incident, Dyer ordered that any Indian using the street where a woman missionary had allegedly been attacked must do so crawling on all fours, and posted a guard to see to this.

Session 2: World political situation

1. In 1906 a mass uprising in Iran succeeded in broadening democratic rights and forced the shah to convene a national assembly. In June 1908 troops commanded by Lyakhov spearheaded a reactionary coup against the assembly. Lyakhov headed the shah's Cossack Brigade, a mercenary force led by officers supplied under contract by the tsar. Successful in Tehran, the coup provoked armed resistance in Tabriz and elsewhere in the country. Revolutionary forces soon retook Tehran, and a constitutional government was proclaimed. In 1909 a brutal assault on Tabriz by the Russian tsar's troops helped give reactionary forces the upper hand. The revolutionary movement was gradually suppressed as British and Russian government troops occupied much of the country.

2. The Young Turks were a bourgeois-nationalist movement formed 1899 and based on the younger generation of the officer caste. They aimed to reform and modernize Turkish society and secure an independent Ottoman Turkish state by replacing the sultan's despotism with a constitutional monarchy. In 1908 a rebellion by Young Turk army officers led to the establishment of a parliamentary regime in which the Young Turks were the dominant force.
3. On January 21, 1920, Turkish forces attacked the French army garrison in Marash in southern Turkey, killing hundreds of Armenians who lived in the area. After three weeks of fighting, a French relief column advancing toward Marash turned back without explanation. The French army garrison was then evacuated, triggering a general exodus of Armenians from southern Turkey. In the whole operation about eight thousand Armenians were killed.
4. Curzon, G.N., *Persia and the Persian Question* (London: Cass, 1966). The original date of publication is 1892.
5. Radek is probably referring to Lloyd George's speech of March 18, 1920, in which he proposed that the Liberals and the Conservatives, the two main parties of the British bourgeoisie, unite in a "common front" against the rising "menace" of working-class "anarchy, subversion, and autocracy."
6. During 1919–20 Italy experienced wave after wave of mass strikes and peasant land occupations; police retaliation left more than a hundred dead. During the Baku congress this upsurge reached its peak as factory occupations swept across the country.
7. See notes 11 and 12 on page 378.
8. See J.R. Seeley, *The Expansion of England: Two Courses of Lectures* (Boston: Roberts Bros., 1883), pp. 233–34.
9. The Czechoslovak contingents, recruited during World War I into the Russian army from among Czech and Slovak prisoners of war, revolted against the Soviet government in May 1918. The Allied powers backed the rebellion.

10. The Treaty of Brest-Litovsk, containing the terms ending the war between Soviet Russia and the German-led Central Powers, was signed in March 1918.
11. Benefiting from the diplomatic support of Britain and the other major powers of Europe, the Italian government attacked Tripoli (Libya), a Turkish possession, in the fall of 1911.
12. The Russian text contains here the word *gandzhamina*, apparently a rendering of *anjoman*, the Farsi word for "council" or "soviet."

Session 3: Discussion—Turkestan, Mountain republic

1. Tsarist authorities had inaccurately applied the term "Kirghiz" to the Kazakh peoples, and in the first years of Soviet rule, this term was still used to refer to the republic approximating present-day Kazakhstan. The Kirghiz people, in fact, lived in what was then eastern Turkestan.
2. An international one-day protest strike was organized on July 21, 1919, on the initiative of the Communist International, to defend the Soviet republics of Russia and Hungary. The strike, which took place as the Allied assault on Hungary reached its climax, was undercut by the opposition of key sectors of the opportunist trade union leadership. For the Comintern Executive Committee's assessment of the strike, see Riddell, *Workers of the World*, p. 125.
3. For the text of the appeal, see appendix 2, pp. 299–302.
4. The "Mountain poor" belonged to various peoples inhabiting the northern foothills of the Caucasus Mountains. The Volunteer Army was the main body of counterrevolutionary forces in southern Russia.
5. During the struggle described by Korkmasov, revolutionary workers and peasants in the North Caucasus, which included Dagestan, were opposed by two mutually hostile forces: right-wing nationalist Muslims led by the imam Najmuddin Gotsinsky and backed by Turkey's government; and counterrevolutionary, Russian-chauvinist White

Guards led by Denikin and L.F. Bicherakhov and backed by British imperialism.
6. Shamyl (1797–1871) led the peoples of Dagestan in an extended war to maintain independence from tsarist Russia. Gotsinsky headed the nationalist Muslim forces that in September 1917 proclaimed the independence of the "United Mountaineers" of the North Caucasus.
7. Soviet power was proclaimed in Petrovsk, capital of Dagestan, in December 1917, and prevailed over most of Dagestan by May 1918.
8. Following an incursion by British-backed White Guards led by Bicherakhov, the Turkish army took control in Dagestan in October 1918. Anti-Soviet nationalist Muslim forces were installed as the Mountain government, under the tutelage of Enver Pasha's Committee of Union and Progress, the party then ruling Turkey.
9. Turkey's surrender to the Allied powers in October 1918 and the reentry of British army units permitted Denikin's White Guards to occupy most of the region early in 1919. They soon faced an uprising by a coalition encompassing Bolsheviks, other pro-Soviet forces, and Muslim nationalist currents, including adherents of Enver Pasha.
10. Following the triumph of the revolutionary forces in March 1920, the Soviet Mountain Republic was constituted as an autonomous unit within the Soviet federation of Russia. A revolt led by Gotsinsky, which began in August, had not yet been put down as the congress convened.

Session 4: Guest speakers; India; Turkey

1. The report from the U.S. delegate (Reed) is found on pages 156–62. For the report of the Dutch Communist Party, see Pearce, *Congress of the Peoples of the East*, pp. 183–86. No other such reports have come to light.
2. In the years just prior to the Baku congress, Britain, moving out from its bases in Egypt and India, had seized Palestine, Jordan, and Mesopotamia, advanced its troops to Iran's northern frontier, occupied the Transcaucasus, set

up a flotilla on the Caspian Sea, garrisoned Transcaspia from Krasnovodsk to the Afghan frontier, and waged war to subjugate Afghanistan.

3. In the French-language version of the proceedings, this paragraph concludes with an additional sentence: "And why is France now carrying on a war in Cilicia [in Turkey] and Syria in order to enlarge her empire by adding a piece of Asia?"

4. While a military attaché in Berlin, Enver volunteered in 1912 to serve with Turkish forces defending Tripoli against the army of Italy. The phrase regarding Enver's "comfortable life" is taken from Ali Fuat Cebesoy, *Moskova hatiralari* (Memoirs of Moscow) (Ankara, 1982), p. 31. The Russian text reads "the quiet life of a refugee."

5. In 1912 Turkey withdrew its armed forces from Tripoli (or Tripolitania) and recognized Italian rule. Armed resistance of the Arab population to Italian occupiers continued, however, into the 1920s, and during World War I Italian forces were driven back to the principal seaports.

   Azerbaijan was controlled during most of 1918 by a supposedly independent force under Ottoman command that was built around contingents of the Turkish army.

6. Enver made three unsuccessful attempts to break through the Allied blockade of Soviet Russia: twice in airplanes that had to land prematurely, leading to his jailing by pro-Allied governments, and once in a boat driven back by a storm.

7. The Transvaal or Boer War (1899–1902) saw Britain conquer Transvaal and the Orange Free State in what is now South Africa.

8. Enver is referring to the "Union of Revolutionary Islamic Organizations" that he wished to form with the aid of the Bolsheviks. After the Baku congress, he returned to Western Europe, where he held a conference of the organization that winter.

9. The "monstrous decision" to partition Ottoman Turkey was originally taken in secret treaties among the Allied powers during World War I. Its implementation began in the months following Turkey's surrender, as Allied armies

seized wide areas of its territory. The proposals for partitioning the country were codified in the Treaty of Sèvres, signed August 10, 1920.

10. The revolts in Anatolia led by these and other counter-revolutionaries took place between August 1919 and the summer of 1920. In April 1920 the sultan's government in Istanbul, which favored submission to the dictates of the Entente, organized an assault on supporters of the national independence movement led by Kemal, proclaiming the killing of its adherents to be a religious duty.

11. The text of Reed's speech, not delivered at the congress because of shortage of time, was appended to the Russian edition of the proceedings. No English text has been found.

12. Although the United States promised in 1916 to grant independence to the Philippines, no such action was taken. Japanese occupation authorities proclaimed the Philippines an independent republic in 1943. Following its reconquest by the United States, the Philippines gained its formal independence in 1946.

13. As a condition for recognizing Cuba's formal independence, Washington in 1902 imposed on Cuba the right to oversee Cuban foreign relations, maintain a military base on Cuban soil, and intervene in Cuban internal affairs at any time.

14. On July 12, 1917, more than 1,100 strikers at the Phelps-Dodge mines in Bisbee, Arizona, were rounded up by armed company agents, loaded into freight cars, and shipped into the desert, where they were held until the strike ended.

Session 5: National and colonial questions

1. French premier Georges Clemenceau left office in January 1920.
2. During the first Balkan War (October 1912–May 1913), a coalition of the governments of Bulgaria, Greece, Serbia, and Montenegro defeated Turkey and forced it to cede most of its territories in Europe. In June 1913 war broke out among the victors over division of the spoils. For a Marxist account written at the time, see Leon Trotsky,

The Balkan Wars 1912–13 (New York: Pathfinder, 1981).

3. The first "People's Republic," of which Simon Petlyura was a central leader, was overturned by the soviets after two months of rule in January 1918, only to take office again when the German government occupied Ukraine in March. The German authorities soon replaced it with a puppet regime headed by P.P. Skoropadsky. The next government in which Petlyura figured ruled Ukraine under sponsorship of the Allied powers from November 1918 until February 1919. In December 1919 Petlyura signed an agreement with the Polish government by which the latter would conquer Ukraine, and Petlyura would then rule it as a satellite unit within the Polish state.

4. The Zaporozhian Camp was the cossack headquarters on the Dnieper, from which struggles were waged in the sixteenth and seventeenth centuries against the Polish rulers of this region. Bogdan Khmelnitsky (1595?-1657), hetman of the Zaporozhian cossacks, led the great Ukrainian peasants' revolt against Polish rule in the 1650s.

5. Charles Dumas, *Libérez les indigènes; ou, renoncez aux colonies* (Free the indigenous peoples; or, give up the colonies) (Paris: E. Figuière et Cie., 1914).

6. The Geneva congress of the Second International was held July 31–August 5, 1920.

7. The Constitutional Revolution in Iran won significant democratic gains during the period 1906–1909. In 1908 the Young Turk uprising forced the Turkish sultan to grant a constitution. The revolution that established the Chinese republic began in 1911.

8. The partition of Poland between the Russian, Prussian, and Austrian monarchies took place between 1772 and 1795.

9. An August 10, 1920, agreement between the governments of Armenia and Soviet Azerbaijan placed the disputed border areas of Karabakh and Zangezur under Azerbaijan's temporary control. No record is available of the letter of General Dro, who commanded Armenian troops in the fighting preceding the August 10 settlement.

10. A military union between Soviet Russia, Ukraine, and other adjoining Soviet republics existed since these republics' formation. In September 1920 federated structures were being established among the republics to unify overall economic policy, finance, foreign trade, communications, and other services; treaties to this effect were signed in late 1920 and in 1921. The formation of the Soviet Union followed at the end of 1922. The Tatar, Bashkir, and other autonomous republics originated differently, through being structured within the Russian republic.
11. The congress proceedings do not record any translation into Russian of Najiye Hanum's remarks. Najiye spoke again—with translation—in session 7 (see pp. 243–46).
12. The party that came to power in the Turkish revolution of 1908, known in the West as the Young Turks, was called the "Committee of Union and Progress."
13. See "Program of the Russian Communist Party (Bolsheviks)," in Riddell, ed., *The German Revolution and the Debate on Soviet Power* (New York: Pathfinder, 1986 [2021 printing]), pp. 633–34.
14. In his poem, "The Dispute," Mikhail Lermontov imagines a conversation between Elbruz and Kazbek, the two highest peaks in the Caucasus, in which Elbruz warns Kazbek to beware of the "teeming, powerful East." The quotation here is from Kazbek's answer, which concludes, "No, I have no great need to fear/The old, decrepit East."
15. The first four statements referred to here are found in appendixes 6 and 7. The fifth statement is reprinted in the Turkish edition of the Baku congress, *Birinci dogu halklari kurultayi* (Istanbul: Koral, 1975), pp. 259–60.

Session 7: Council for Propaganda and Action; women of the East; concluding remarks

1. For the list of council members, see pp. 247–49.
2. In August 1920 an uprising took place in Bukhara organized by Young Bukharans, members of a revolutionary nationalist organization formed in 1909. In response to

their request for aid, the Red Army advanced on the city of Bukhara, which was taken after a five-day battle on September 2.
3. Stanislavsky Street was one of the dividing lines in 1918 fighting between forces from the Armenian and Muslim quarters of Baku.
4. The two Iranian governments were the monarchy based in Tehran and the revolutionary government of Gilan.

Manifesto to the peoples of the East

1. *Kommunisticheskiy Internatsional*, no. 15 [December 1920], cols. 3141–50. The introductory five paragraphs are taken from Sorkin, G.Z., *Pervyy s"ezd narodov vostoka* (First Congress of the Peoples of the East) (Moscow: Eastern Literature Publishing House, 1961), pp. 57–58. These paragraphs appeared in the version of the manifesto first printed in *Narody Vostoka*, but not in the *Kommunisticheskiy Internatsional* version.
2. The British government used its victory in the 1840–42 Opium War against China to force China, where opium had been illegal, to open its ports to exports of the drug from British India and to grant Britain other economic privileges. Several decades later, in 1902, the British government signed an alliance with Japan.

Appeal to the workers of Europe, America, and Japan

1. *Kommunisticheskiy Internatsional*, no. 15 [December 1920], cols. 3151–56.
2. For the pre-1914 Socialist International's stand on immigrant workers from Asia, see Riddell, *Lenin's Struggle for a Revolutionary International*, pp. 51–57, 88.
3. The original text reads "Tripoli," an evident misprint.

Composition of the congress

1. Information from this list is summarized by Sorkin in *Pervyy s"ezd*, pp. 21–22.

Appendix 1: Declaration on rights of peoples of Russia

1. Klyuchnikov, Yu.V. and Sabanin, Andrey, *Mezhdunarodnaya politika noveyshego vremeni v dogovorakh, notakh i deklaratsiyakh* (Contemporary international politics: treaties, notes, and statements) (Moscow: Commissariat of Foreign Affairs Publishing House, 1926), vol. 2, pp. 90–91.

Appendix 2: Appeal to all toiling Muslims

1. Klyuchnikov and Sabanin, *Mezhdunarodnaya politika*, vol. 2, pp. 94–96.

Appendix 3: Address to Communist organizations of the East

1. Lenin, *Collected Works*, vol. 30, pp. 151–62. The Communist Organizations of the Peoples of the East originated March 1918 as the Socialist-Communist Muslim Party, uniting pro-Communist groups among the primarily Islamic peoples of the old tsarist empire. After affiliating to the Communist Party of Russia in November 1918, the organization broadened its framework early in 1919 to encompass Communists living in the Soviet republics from all the Asian peoples, changing its name accordingly.
2. See "Program of the Russian Communist Party (Bolsheviks)," in Riddell, *German Revolution*, p. 627.
3. In parceling out colonies of Germany and parts of the former Ottoman Turkish Empire to the victorious powers, the League of Nations termed the territories' new status a "mandate," in which the League retained a formal supervisory role.

Appendix 4: Theses on national and colonial questions

1. Riddell, *Workers of the World*, vol. 1, pp. 361–68.
2. The Treaty of Bucharest (May 1918) contained the terms by which the war between the Central Powers and Romania was ended. The Treaty of St. Germain (September 1919)

did the same for the war between Austria and the Allied powers.
3. The "detached portion of land" in question is East Prussia, which by decision of the Allied powers was separated off from the rest of Germany after World War I by a band of Polish territory.

Appendix 5: A new world

1. Archives of the Russian Documents Center.
2. It was at the 1907 Stuttgart congress of the Socialist International that the mentioned delegations backed a resolution favoring a reformed colonialism.

Appendix 6: Workers of Armenia

1. "Declaration of the Representatives of the Working Masses of Armenia," submitted to the Baku congress and first printed in *Kommunist* (Baku), September 8, 1920. Published here courtesy of the Azerbaijan State Archives.
2. The Entente's plan to hand over Turkish Armenia to the Dashnak government of Armenia was never put into action.

Appendix 7: Zionism: an exchange of views

1. "Declaration of the Delegation of Mountain Jews to the First Congress of the Peoples of the East," published courtesy of the Azerbaijan State Archives.
2. "Declaration of Jewish Communist Party (Poale Zion) Delegation on the National-Colonial Question," first printed in *Kommunist* (Baku), September 8, 1920; published here courtesy of the Azerbaijan State Archives.

   Poale Zion (Workers of Zion) was a coalition of Jewish nationalist organizations whose stated aim was to combine the ideas of socialism with Zionism. Its Russian branch, which claimed 15,000 members in 1917, opposed the October revolution. A left wing of this branch split in August 1919, taking the name Jewish Communist Party (Poale

Zion); it was represented at the Comintern's Second Congress. A number of members of this party joined the Communist Party of Russia in December 1922.

    For the debate on Zionism at the Second Congress, see Riddell, *Workers of the World*, vol. 1, pp. 341–58.

3. A conference of six Allied powers, meeting in San Remo, Italy, in April 1920, awarded the British government a mandate over Palestine while endorsing London's support for establishment there of a "Jewish national home."
4. Until 1917, Palestine was ruled by Ottoman Turkey. Jemal (Cemal) Pasha, a close associate of Enver Pasha in the Ottoman government, was Ottoman army commander in Syria and Palestine during World War I.
5. Early in 1920 the British government declared that it intended to maintain control over Palestine and promote Zionist settlement there. The Arab inhabitants protested, tensions grew, and during the first week of April violent clashes took place that left five Jews and four Arabs dead.
6. "Declaration on Palestine by the Central Bureau of Jewish Sections of the RCP," first printed in *Kommunist* (Baku), September 8, 1920; published here courtesy of the Azerbaijan State Archives.
7. The term "social-Palestinian parties" refers here to Zionist organizations functioning within the Socialist and labor movements.

Appendix 8: Correcting abuses of Soviet power

1. "General Resolution of Delegates to the Congress of the Peoples of the East," archives of the Russian Documents Center.
2. Only the North Caucasus was an integral part of the Russian Soviet Republic; the Republic of Azerbaijan was independent, linked to Russia by treaties.
3. "Class differentiation" refers here to the separating out of a working class and a bourgeoisie from among the mass of artisans and petty merchants in the population.

4. The Fergana region in Turkestan was the center of the Basmachi insurgency, an anti-Soviet movement allied to counterrevolutionary forces abroad that won peasant support around slogans such as "Turkestan for the natives." The conflict spread to Bukhara after a pro-Soviet uprising there in August 1920. Afghanistan's government gave military supplies and political support to the Basmachis, but was not directly involved in the fighting.

   In northern Persia, where the tsarist regime had long stationed troops, the Red Army occupied Enzeli in May 1920, driving out British detachments. The insurgent Jangalis in this area, who were fighting the armies both of Britain and of the Iranian shah, received supplies from the Red Army.

5. "Excerpt from Proceedings of the Politbureau of the CC, 14/10/20," archives of the Russian Documents Center. A draft of this resolution written by Lenin is found in Lenin, *Collected Works*, vol. 42, pp. 218–19.

6. The Buryat region lies in central Siberia just west of Lake Baikal.

7. Lenin's draft of this paragraph reads, "to consider it necessary to restore to the Mountaineers of the Northern Caucasus the lands they were deprived of by the Great Russians, at the expense of the kulak elements of the Cossack population . . ."

8. The Kalmyks established an autonomous region by the end of 1920; the Buryats in 1923. By 1924, almost all the peoples mentioned in this resolution had set up autonomous governments.

9. "To Red-Army Soldiers Fighting for Proletarian Revolution in the East," archives of the Russian Documents Center.

10. Subsequently, leaders of the Communist Party called into question whether "a rapid implementation of communism" in the sense described had been possible even in Russia. "Partly owing to the war problems that overwhelmed us and partly owing to the desperate position in which the Republic found itself when the imperialist war ended," Lenin wrote in October 1921, "we made the mistake of de-

ciding to go over directly to communist production and distribution. . . . Brief experience convinced us that that line was wrong, that it ran counter to what we had previously written about the transition from capitalism to socialism, namely, that it would be impossible to bypass the period of socialist accounting and control in approaching even the lower stage of communism." Lenin, "The New Economic Policy and the Tasks of the Political Education Departments," in *Collected Works*, vol. 33, p. 62.

Glossary of names and terms

Abdul Hamid II (1842–1918) – sultan of Ottoman Turkey 1876–1909.

Abdur Rabb Barq, Mohammed (1875–1960s) – from Peshawar, India; pan-Islamist; went to defend Turkey at outbreak of World War I; made his way to Moscow 1919; went to Kabul as part of Soviet mission 1919; chairman of Indian Revolutionary Association founded there at beginning of 1920; did not join CP of India; later settled in Turkey.

Ambali – laborer, longshoreman.

Anzavur Pasha – led revolts in Anatolia late 1919 and early 1920 against national resistance movement led by Kemal.

Aul – settlement in the Caucasus or Central Asia.

Bahaeddin Shakir – see Shakir, Bahaeddin.

Bey – provincial governor in Ottoman Empire; courtesy title for members of upper classes.

Bicherakhov, L.F. (b. 1882–1952) – tsarist colonel; joined, then betrayed defense of Baku soviet 1918; later allied with British and led White Guard forces in North Caucasus.

Bismarck, Otto von (1815–1898) – prime minister of Prussia 1862–71; chancellor of Germany 1871–90.

Black Hundreds – rightist gangs formed by tsarist police that organized pogroms against Jews and carried out attacks on revolutionaries.

Bulach Tatu – delegate from Dagestan; one of three women elected to Baku congress Presiding Committee.

Bund – see Communist Bund.

Buniatzadeh, Dadash (1888–1938) – participated in Iran Constitutional Revolution 1908–09; leader of Hümmet-Muslim

Social Democrats; founding member of Azerbaijan CP 1920; leader in Azerbaijan Soviet government from 1920; killed during Stalin frame-up purges.

Carranza, Venustiano (1859–1920) – a leader of 1913–14 revolution that overthrew Mexican dictator Victoriano Huerta; president of Mexico 1914–20.

Chabanoglu (Çapanoglu) – a family of feudal chieftains in central Anatolia.

Cheka – abbreviated name of Soviet police force set up after October revolution to combat counterrevolutionary terror and sabotage.

Chermoyev – a Chechen oil millionaire.

Communist Bund – left-wing majority in 1919 split of Russian wing of Bund (General Union of Jewish Workers in Lithuania, Poland, and Russia), a non-Zionist party whose leadership opposed 1917 October revolution; most members of Communist Bund joined CP of Russia 1920.

CP – Communist Party.

Dashnaktsutiun (Dashnaks) – nationalist petty-bourgeois party in Armenia; headed anti-Soviet government of Armenia 1918–20.

Dehkhan – peasant in Central Asia.

Denikin, A.I. (1872–1947) – commander-in-chief of main counterrevolutionary army in southern Russia 1918–20.

Derebeys – feudal chieftains in Anatolia.

Dro (Drastamat Kanayan) – general commanding Armenian forces fighting in Karabakh, Zangezur, and other border territories.

Efendiyev – either Sultan Mejid Efendiev (1887–1938), a leader of Azerbaijan Soviet government; or Najmuddin Efendiev-Samurski, leader of Dagestan CP. Both were victims of Stalin purges.

Effendi – landowner; courtesy title in Arab countries for members of upper classes.

Entente – see Triple Entente.

Enver Pasha (1881–1922) – leader of Young Turk revolution 1908; leader of Turkish government 1913–18; went to Moscow and declared solidarity with Soviet regime August 1920; joined anti-Soviet Basmachi revolt in Bukhara 1921; killed in action.

Faisal I (1885–1933) – led Arab forces that occupied Damascus 1918; forced out by French 1920; installed as king of Iraq with British support 1921.

Fellahin – peasants and agricultural laborers in Arabic-speaking countries.

Gegechkori, Yevgeniy (1879–1954) – foreign minister of 1918–21 Menshevik government of Georgia.

Ghazavat – in Muslim tradition, a holy war.

Gladstone, W.E. (1809–1898) – Britain's prime minister during four periods from 1868 to 1894.

Gotsinsky, Najmuddin (c. 1865–1925) – landowner; imam (spiritual and temporal ruler) in North Caucasus 1917; leader of anti-Soviet Mountain Republic May 1918; headed revolt in Dagestan against Soviet government August 1920–March 1921; tried by Soviet court and executed.

Gracia, Ramón Merino – see Merino Gracia, Ramón.

Hajis – those who have made pilgrimage to Mecca; title of honor for privileged classes.

Haydar Khan 'Amu 'Ughli (1880–1921) – founding member of Iranian Social Democratic Party 1904; participant in Iran Constitutional Revolution; joined Iran Communist movement early summer 1920; became its chairman October 1920; killed in Gilan during civil war.

Hervé, Gustave (1871–1944) – held ultraleft antimilitarist views in French Socialist Party until 1914, then became extreme chauvinist; opponent of Soviet republic.

Hrushevsky, Mikhailo (1866–1934) – Ukrainian historian; briefly president of republic of Ukraine 1918; emigrated 1918; returned to Ukraine 1924; expelled 1930.

Ibrahim Tali – see Tali, Ibrahim.

Imam – Muslim spiritual authority; Islamic ruler holding both spiritual and temporal power.

Ismail Hakki, Arap (d. 1921) – Turkish educator; brother of Najiye Hanum; in Germany during World War I; won to revolutionary socialism by Spartacist movement; member of Turkish CP Central Committee; murdered together with Subhi on return to Turkey.

Jewish Communist Party (Poale Zion) – left-wing split-off from Russian branch of Poale Zion, a Zionist organization in labor movement.

Karayev, A.A. (1896–1938) – joined CP 1919; member of Azerbaijan CP Central Committee 1920; secretary of Azerbaijan CP 1925–29; victim of Stalin purges.

Kemal Pasha, Mustafa (Atatürk) (1881–1938) – led Turkish independence struggle and establishment of Turkish republic 1919–23; president of provisional government 1920; remained head of Turkish state until death.

Kerensky, A.F. (1881–1970) – headed Russian Provisional Government overthrown by October 1917 revolution.

Kishlak – village of predominantly Muslim peoples in Central Asia.

Kolchak, A.V. (1873–1920) – head of counterrevolutionary armies in Siberia and "supreme ruler" of Russian White forces 1918–19.

Korkmasov, Jalaluddin (1879–1938) – joined CP of Russia 1917; leader of revolutionary wing of Dagestan soviets 1917; chairman of Dagestan regional executive committee of CP of Russia 1918; led defense of Dagestan autonomy in Dagestan CP November 1920; head of Dagestan government 1921–32; shot during Stalin frame-up purges.

Kotsov – Kabardian horsebreeder from Terek region.

Kulak – wealthy peasant exploiting farm laborers and smallholders.

Kulturträger – upholders of civilization.

Kun, Béla (1886–1939) – headed Hungarian Soviet government March–June 1919; worked in Comintern apparatus from 1920; arrested and killed during Moscow frame-up trials.

Lagrosillière, Joseph (1872–1950) – born in Martinique; later settled in Paris; Socialist Party deputy 1910–24 and 1932–42.

League of Nations – alliance created by Allied powers to defend division of world codified in Versailles treaty 1919.

Left Socialist Revolutionaries – see Socialist Revolutionary Party.

Lenin, V.I. (1870–1924) – central leader of Bolshevik Party, Soviet state, and Communist International.

Madero, Francisco (1873–1913) – led revolution that overthrew dictatorial regime of Porfirio Díaz 1911; president of Mexico 1911–13; overthrown and murdered in coup.

Makharadze, Pilipe (Filipe) (1868–1941) – joined Bolsheviks 1903; leader of CP of Georgia 1920; opposed Stalin on national question 1922–23; removed from responsible posts during frame-up purges late 1930s.

Matushev, Akhmed – chairman of Bukhara delegation to Baku congress and member of congress Presiding Committee.

Merezhin, A.N. (b. 1880–1937) – Menshevik 1905–16, then member of Bund; joined Bolsheviks 1919; member of Central Bureau of Jewish Sections of CP of Russia.

Merino Gracia, Ramón – general secretary of CP of Spain.

Mirza – courtesy title for members of upper classes in Iran.

Mohammed Abdur Rabb Barq – see Abdur Rabb Barq, Mohammed.

Molkdar – landowner or propertied person in Persia.

Mujtahid – in Shia branch of Islam, an interpreter of religious law.

Musavat Party (Equality) – party of Azerbaijani nationalist bourgeoisie; headed anti-Soviet government 1918–20.

Najiye Hanum (Naciye Hanim) – member of CP of Turkey; reported to Baku congress on struggle for women's equality.

Narbutabekov (d. 1938) – left-wing nationalist reformer in Turkestan; prominent among Soviet leaders of Muslim origin; leader of nonparty fraction and cochairman at Baku congress; elected to Council for Propaganda and Action; executed during Stalin frame-up purges.

Narimanov, Nariman Kerbalai Najaf-oglu (1871–1925) – member of Social Democrats of Russia 1905; founder of Hümmet-Muslim Social Democrats 1905; headed Azerbaijan Soviet government from 1920; member of Central Committee of CP of Russia 1923–25; posthumously denounced as "enemy of people" during Stalin frame-up purges.

Nicholas II (1868–1918) – tsar of Russia 1894–1917.

Noske, Gustav (1868–1946) – leader of Social Democratic Party of Germany; as war minister, organized suppression of workers' uprisings in Berlin and central Germany 1919.

Ordzhonikidze, G.K. (1886–1937) – joined Bolsheviks 1903; leading Communist on Caucasus front in civil war; subsequently chairman of CP Caucasus Bureau; was shot or committed suicide during frame-up purges.

Ostrovsky – representative at Baku congress of indigenous Jewish population of Turkestan; elected to Council for Propaganda and Action; teacher at council's cadre school.

Palais Bourbon – seat of French national assembly.

Pan-Islamism – movement originating in 19th century purporting to unify all Islamic peoples in resisting Christian and Western encroachment; promoted by Turkish sultanate.

Pan-Turkism – movement originating in late 19th century purporting to unify peoples in Turkey, the Caucasus, Russia, Central Asia, and elsewhere who speak a Turkic language.

Pasha – man of high rank or office in Turkey or northern Africa.

Pavlovich, Mikhail (1871–1927) – Menshevik from 1903; internationalist during World War I; rallied to Bolsheviks 1917; joined Commissariat of Foreign Affairs November 1917; leader of Council for Propaganda and Action established by Baku congress.

Petlyura, S.V. (1877–1926) – leader of anti-Bolshevik forces in Ukraine 1918–19; participated in Polish offensive against Soviet Ukraine 1920.

Pood – Russian unit of weight; about 36 pounds.

Qajar – ruling dynasty of Iran 1794–1925.

Quelch, Thomas (1886–1954) – leader of British Socialist Party, which fused with other groups to form CP of Great Britain summer 1920.

Radek, Karl (1885–1939) – leader of revolutionary Social Democrats in Poland and Germany; joined Bolshevik Party 1917; leader of Communist International from 1920; supported Communist opposition to Stalin 1923–29; capitulated to Stalin 1929; arrested 1937 during Moscow frame-up trials; died in prison.

Rayat – peasant in Iran; subject of a king or country.

Reed, John (1887–1920) – radical U.S. journalist; supported IWW from 1913; won to Communist movement while in Russia 1917; founding leader of U.S. Communist movement; died of typhus in Soviet Russia.

Rosmer, Alfred (1877–1964) – French revolutionary unionist; joined CP on its formation 1920; expelled as supporter of Communist opposition to Stalin led by Trotsky.

Roy, Manabendra Nath (1887?–1954) – active in anti-British protests in India 1910–15; won to communism in Mexico 1919; founded Indian CP in Tashkent 1920; member Comintern Executive Committee 1922–27; expelled with Bukharin supporters 1929.

RSFSR – Russian Soviet Federated Socialist Republic.

Ryskulov, Turar (1894–1938) – took part in uprising of Kazakh nomads against tsar 1916; joined CP 1917; led current in Turkestan CP that sought to expand autonomy of Soviet Asian peoples; chairman of Turkestan Soviet Executive Committee 1920; member of Central Committee of Russian CP and head of Turkestan government 1923–24; fell into disfavor under Stalin; executed during frame-up purges.

Sepoy – Indian serving in the British army.

Shabanova-Karayeva, Khaver (1901–1958) – joined CP 1919; medical school graduate; served in Red Army; active in organizing revolutionary women in Azerbaijan from 1920; elected to Council for Propaganda and Action; jailed during frame-up purges 1937; later freed and readmitted to CP.

Shablin, Nikolai (Ivan Nedelkov) (1881–1925) – Central Committee member of CP of Bulgaria from 1919.

Shakir, Bahaeddin (Baha; Sakir) (1874–1922) – leader of Young Turks and Committee of Union and Progress; organizer of Armenian deportation 1915; associate of Enver Pasha in exile from 1918; assassinated by Armenian nationalist.

Shariat – body of Islamic law.

Shevchenko, Taras (1814–1861) – artist, poet, and advocate of Ukrainian national rights; wrote against serfdom and tsarist autocracy.

Skachko, A.E. (1892–1964) – Menshevik, later joined CP; secretary of Comintern commission on the East; leader of Council for Propaganda and Action; wrote many works on China, where he was posted 1925–27.

Skoropadsky, P.P. (1873–1945) – general; head of German puppet government of Ukraine 1918.

Socialist Revolutionary Party (SRs) – main peasant-supported party in Russia during 1917 revolution; majority leadership opposed October revolution and backed Whites in civil war; left wing allied briefly with Bolsheviks but went into opposition mid-1918; minority currents split and continued to support Bolshevik-led government.

Stalin, Joseph (1879–1953) – Bolshevik from 1903; Soviet people's commissar of nationalities from November 1917; presided over bureaucratic degeneration of Russian CP and Comintern and their rejection of Lenin's revolutionary course.

Steinhardt, Karl (J. Gruber) (1875–1963) – leader of CP of Austria 1918–21; remained member until death.

Subhi, Mustafa (1883–1921) – organized Communist group among Turkish war prisoners 1918; chairman of CP of Turkey 1920; murdered upon return to Turkey.

Sultanov, G.G. (1889–1938) – joined Bolsheviks 1907; leader of Hümmet-Muslim Social Democrats from 1913; leader of economic construction in Azerbaijan 1920–38; victim of Stalin purges.

Sultanzadeh, Ahmed (Avetis Mikaelian) (1889–1938) – born in Iran; Armenian; joined Bolsheviks 1912; Iranian CP founder 1920; Central Committee member 1920–23; perished in Stalin purges.

Tajiyev, Kari – chairman of delegation to Baku congress from Samarkand in Turkestan; elected to Council for Propaganda and Action.

Tali, Ibrahim (Öngören) (1875–1952) – Turkish army medical officer; collaborator of Mustafa Kemal in launching national resistance movement 1919; political counsel for this movement's delegation to Moscow 1920; subsequently ambassador and parliamentary deputy.

Tamerlane (c. 1336–1405) – Mongol conqueror of Central Asia, Iran, Syria, and much of India.

Tarkovsky, Prince Nukh-Bek – also known as the Shamkhal of Tarki; principal feudal chieftain among Kumyks of Dagestan.

Timur – see Tamerlane.

Triple Alliance – secret treaty linking governments of Germany, Austria-Hungary, and Italy, signed 1882 and periodically renewed until World War I.

Triple Entente – alliance of governments of France, Russia, and Britain formed 1907; later known as "Entente," including other Allied powers in World War I.

Trotsky, Leon (1879–1940) – joined Bolsheviks 1917 and elected to Central Committee; commissar of foreign affairs 1917–18; organized and led Red Army 1918–25; from 1923 led opposition to the retreat from Lenin's communist course; assassinated on Stalin's orders.

Tskhakaya, Mikha (1865–1950) – leader of Russian Social Democrats in Caucasia from 1898; leader of CP in Georgia 1917–20 and of Georgian Soviet republic from 1921; denounced but not arrested during Stalin purges.

Ulema – body of clerics who interpret and elaborate Islamic law.

Venizelos, Eleutherios (1864–1936) – Greek premier several times between 1910 and 1923; led Greece into World War I on Allied side 1917; premier during first stage of Greek army's invasion of Turkey 1919–20.

Verst – Russian measure of distance; 0.66 miles.

Vilayet – administrative division of Turkey.

Vinnichenko, V.K. (1880–1951) – a leader of counterrevolutionary Ukrainian Directory government 1918–19; briefly held posts in Soviet government 1920.

Waqf lands – lands placed in trust to provide support for charitable or religious activities.

Weizmann, Chaim (1874–1952) – early leader of Zionist movement; president of Israel 1948–52.

Wilhelm II (1859–1941) – German kaiser 1888–1918.

Wrangel, P.N. (1878–1928) – baron, general of White armies in south Russia 1917–20, commanding them April–November 1920.

Yegorov, V.G. (1899–1938) – joined CP and elected to its Baku city leadership 1917; took part in Baku Soviet government 1918; member Azerbaijan CP Central Committee 1920; executed during Stalin purges.

Yudenich, N.N. (1862–1933) – commander of counterrevolutionary Russian army in Baltic states 1917; led unsuccessful drive against Petrograd 1919.

Zamindar – in colonial India, landowner holding large tracts through paying part of income from peasants to British administration.

Zhordania, N.N. (1870–1953) – headed Menshevik government in Georgia 1918–21.

Zinoviev, Gregory (1883–1936) – member of Russian Social Democratic Central Committee from 1907; Bolshevik; chairman of Communist International 1919–26; joined Trotsky in United Opposition to bureaucratic current led by Stalin 1926–27; convicted at first Moscow frame-up trial and executed.

Index

Abas Haji, 249
Abdul Hamid II, 123, 395
Abdul Hamid Yumusov, 71
Abdulayev, 71, 248, 278
Abdur Rabb Barq, Mohammed, 143, 395
Abdur Rashidov, 70, 247, 277
Abkhazia, 183
Acharya, 70, 248
Adana, 267
Afghanistan, 193, 223, 392
Africa, 13–14, 16, 30–31, 88, 164, 264, 284–87, 329, 375
Agayev, 363
Agazadeh, 71, 247, 277
Agrarian question
  and capitalism, 229–31
  and collective farming, 228, 233–36
  Communist program for, 233–36
  and land to toilers, 81–83, 224–27, 233–34, 364
  report on, 219–31
  social revolution in East, 191–92, 210–11, 223–25, 237–38
  Soviet policy on, 228
  theses on, 231–38
  See also Peasants; Soviets and Soviet power, peasant-based
Ahmed Khan, 71
Alexandropol, 182

Algeria, 167
Ali Fuat Cebesoy, 384
Aliyev, 71, 128, 277
Alliance of workers and oppressed peoples, 14–15, 18–20, 36, 45–47, 52, 56–60, 63–64, 77–85, 178–80, 184–86, 230–31, 264, 274–76, 279–87
All-Russia Soviet Central Executive Committee, 362
Amritsar massacre, 89–90, 282, 380
Amur Sanan, 71, 248, 277, 363
Anatolia. *See* Turkey
Anglo-Iranian Agreement of 1919, 101, 377
Anti-Semitism, 324, 339
Anzavur Pasha, 152, 395
Arabia, 44, 90, 97–99, 269
Armenia, 34, 150, 182–83, 223
  and Azerbaijan, 386
  and ethnic violence, 26–27, 175, 333–38
  imperialism and, 43–44, 100–101, 159–61, 171, 334–37
  and Turkey, 44, 159–60, 301, 334–36, 377, 381, 390
Artmasov, 113
Asia, 13–16, 30–31, 88, 138, 164–65, 264–65, 284–87, 329

Asia Minor. *See* Turkey
Austria, 67
Autonomy, national, 353–54, 360, 364–65, 375
Avis, 248
Azerbaijan, 26, 37, 182–83, 391
  Soviet republic of, 32, 116, 252–53, 337
  Turkish invasion of, 115–17, 182
Azerbaijan Communist Party, 11
Azerbaijan Revolutionary Committee, 53
Azim, 71, 278
Azizkhanov, 363

Babayev, 33, 375
Baku, 25–26, 61–62, 250–52
  battle for Soviet power in, 26–27, 54, 252–53, 377–78
  soviet in, 51, 58
  Turkish occupation of, 182
Baku congress
  appeal adopted by, 279–87
  call to congress, 41–48
  and Comintern Second Congress, 13, 72–74
  Communist fraction, 23–24, 70–71
  composition of, 23–25, 73–75, 255, 263, 289–91
  efforts to block, 22–23
  guiding precepts, 15–20
  historic significance, 11, 37–38, 73, 252–55
  impact of, 32–35
  manifesto of, 263–78
  murder of leaders under Stalin, 36

Baku congress (*continued*)
  nonparty fraction, 24, 70–72, 124
  preparations for, 21–23
  Presiding Committee, 70–72, 277–78
  resolutions adopted, 153–54, 215–19, 231–38, 240–42
  secretaries at, 71
  translation at, 27–28, 136
  See also Council for Propaganda and Action
Balabanoff, Angelica, 47
Balkan Communist Federation, 65, 143
Balkans, 114, 171
Balkan Wars (1912–13), 164, 385–86
Baluchistan, 193
Bashkir Soviet Republic, 167
Basmachi insurgency, 392
Basra, 269
Bibinur, 11–12, 246–47
Bicherakhov, L.F., 129–31, 382–83, 395
Bilan, Alexander, 47
Bismarck, Otto von, 115, 395
Black Hundreds, 126, 395
Blacks, in U.S., 31, 158–60, 323, 329
Black troops, 78, 379
Boer (Transvaal) War, 147, 384
"Bolshevik," 86
Bolsheviks. *See* Communist Party of Russia
Bombacci, Nicola, 47
Bourgeois democracy, 211, 216, 319–20
Bourgeois revolutions, 54, 201, 214

Brest-Litovsk Treaty, 110, 308, 320, 382
Britain, 34, 60–61, 183
  class divisions in, 80–81, 381
  Communist Party of, 138
  working class of, 105, 138–39, 378
British imperialism, 22–23, 30–31, 86, 193, 264–74, 382
  aims of, 164–65, 265–68
  in China, 269–70, 388
  in India, 89–90, 95–97, 106–7, 119, 138, 193, 223, 265–68
  in Iran, 42, 101–2, 119, 268–69, 392
  and Ireland, 105–6, 138
  in Palestine, 269, 341–43, 346–48, 391
  and Soviet Russia, 34, 59–60, 139–40
  and tsarist Russia, 95–96
  in Turkey, 267–68
  as victor in World War I, 98, 265
Buchanan, George W., 96
Bucharest Treaty, 320, 389
Bukhara, 177, 223, 242–43, 392
Bukharin, Nikolai, 47
Bulach Tatu, 189, 395
Bulgaria, 181
Buniatzadeh, Dadash, 36, 92, 112–16, 395–96
Buryats, 364–65, 392

Calendars, Julian-Gregorian, 373
Caliphate, 23, 85, 380

Capitalism
  postwar crisis of, 12, 37, 103, 176–77, 186–87
  and underdevelopment, 219
  and world war, 182–83, 281
  See also Imperialism; National bourgeoisie
Capitalist stage of development
  not inevitable in East, 19, 82–83, 178, 211–12, 230, 236–38
Caribbean, 31, 157
Carranza, Venustiano, 158, 396
Central America, 158, 160
Central Asia, 95, 138
Central Committee of National Muslim Unions, 25
Central Executive Committee of Russian Soviet Republic, 53
Central Powers, 382, 389–90
Chabanoglu (Çapanoglu), 152, 396
Chador, 243
Chauvinism, 28–29, 284, 312, 324
  See also National hostilities; Nationalism; Zionism
Cheka, 356, 361, 365, 396
Cherkas, 248
Chermoyev, 131, 396
China, 13, 31–32, 177, 374
  imperialist oppression of, 89–90, 388
  revolution in, 35–37
Chkheidze, N.S., 256
Churchill, Winston S., 311

Civilization
  "defenders" of, 172, 197
  old vs. new, 111–12
Clemenceau, Georges, 105, 164, 385
Clergy, 220, 225, 325
Comintern. *See* Communist International
Commissariat of Foreign Affairs, 365
Communism, transition to, 52, 123, 178, 214–15, 219, 230–31, 315–17, 369–72, 392–93
Communist Bund, 349, 396
Communist International (Comintern), 39–42, 73–75, 263, 286–87
  and Chinese revolution, 35
  in Europe, 19–20
  Executive Committee of, 13, 46–48, 53, 69, 240–41
  and federation of nations, 322
  First Congress, 56
  and July 21, 1919, strike, 125, 382
  on national and colonial questions, 173–74, 183, 199, 321–24, 330–31
  and peoples of the East, 13–14, 18–20, 57–58
  Third Congress, 34–35
Communist International Second Congress, 13, 56, 58–59, 67, 72–73, 178, 351
  and Baku congress, 15, 72–73
  composition of, 263–64, 378
Communist International Second Congress (*continued*)
  manifesto of, 77–78
  on national and colonial questions, 15–20, 319–27
Communist Manifesto (Marx and Engels), 15, 375
Communist Organizations of the Peoples of the East, 316–17, 389
Communist parties in the East, 24, 33–34, 354–57, 361
  need to create, 88, 202
Communist Party of Azerbaijan, 329–32
Communist Party of Bulgaria, 143
Communist Party of Greece, 143
Communist Party of Hungary, 52
Communist Party of Romania, 143
Communist Party of Russia, 13, 195
  Political Bureau on abuses in East, 29, 364–72
Communist Party of Turkestan, 126–27
Communist Party of Yugoslavia, 143
Conference of Youth of Asia, 26
Constantinople. *See* Istanbul
Consumers' cooperatives, 235–36
Council for Propaganda and Action, 30, 33–35, 239–41, 250, 259, 286, 359–60

Council for Propaganda and
Action (*continued*)
dissolved, 34–35
membership of, 247–49
resolution on, 240–41
Council of Action (Britain),
64, 180, 378
Council of People's
Commissars, 127, 296–97,
299, 301, 364
Cuba, 38, 157, 159, 167, 385
Culture, under Soviet rule,
169–70, 191, 193–95
Curzon, George Nathaniel,
101, 375
Czechoslovak contingents, in
Russian civil war, 107, 381

Dagestan, 130–32, 339
Damascus, 99
Dashnaks (Dashnaktsutiun),
44, 151, 216, 335–37, 377,
396
Delinières, Lucien, 47
Denikin, A.I., 60, 62–63, 76,
107–8, 129, 304, 307, 312,
336, 383, 396
Dictatorship of the
proletariat, 185, 198,
210–11, 321, 324
See also Soviets and Soviet
power
Digurov, 70, 277
Dodge, Cleveland, 159, 385
Dominican Republic, 158
Dro (Drastamat Kanayan),
183, 386, 396
Dumas, Charles, 174, 386
Dyer, R.E.H., 89–90, 282, 380
Dzhaparidze, Ilya, 54, 377–78

East Prussia, 320, 390
Efendiyev, 115, 396
Egypt, 64, 90, 97, 105–6, 269
Emakhundov, 363
Eneyev, M., 363
Engels, Frederick, 15, 193
Entente, 20–21, 44–45, 60, 66,
89, 96, 113–14, 146, 151,
172, 260, 385, 390, 404
Enver Pasha, 24–25, 86, 115,
131–32, 144–49, 182, 380,
383–84, 397
ERK (Will), 25
Erzurum, 151, 183
Estonia, 12, 161
Eyvazov, 363

Faisal I, 99, 207, 343, 397
Fazil al Qadir, 142
Federation
of oppressed nations, 186
of Soviet republics, 172, 185,
200, 213, 230–31
as transition to unification,
18, 195, 322
Feudalism, 61, 232, 315
Finland, 12, 161
First Congress of the Peoples
of the East. *See* Baku
congress
First Congress of the Toilers
of the Far East (1922), 35,
375
Fraina, Louis, 47
France, 98–103, 114, 150, 265,
310, 381
Communists in, 140
workers' upsurge in, 65–66,
105, 378
French Revolution, 61

Gajinsky, Isa-Bek, 251
Gajiyeva, 204
Gandhi, Mohandas, 31
Gegechkori, Yevgeniy, 76, 256, 397
Genghis Khan, 112, 123, 196
Genikoy, 248
Georgia, 34, 182–83
　Menshevik regime in, 75–76, 171
Germany
　as imperialist power, 96–99, 163–64
　revolution in, 20
　and Soviet Russia, 110, 386
　and Turkey, 115–19, 145–46, 182, 334
　and Versailles Treaty, 104, 389
　working class in, 67
Ghazavat. *See* Holy war against imperialism
Gikalo, N., 363
Gladstone, W.E., 95, 397
Gobiyev, 248
Gogol, Nikolai, 170
Gorodetsky, 197
Gotsinsky, Najmuddin, 130, 382–83, 397
Goykov, 363
Gracia, Ramón Merino, 399
Graziadei, Antonio, 47
Greece, 98, 150, 170–72, 181, 183
Grey, Edward, 96
Group of Turkestan Socialists, 25
Guseinov, M.D., 21, 247

Haavis Mahomed, 71, 277
Haiti, 158

Haydar Khan 'Amu 'Ughli, 71, 118–19, 247, 277, 397
Hervé, Gustave, 172, 397
Herzen, A.I., 257
Hodo-Yoshiharo. *See* Yoshiwara Gentaro
Holy war against imperialism, 33, 88, 90–91, 94, 129, 132, 186, 260–61, 274–76
Horthy, Miklós, 63, 378
Hrushevsky, Mikhailo, 169, 397
Hungary, 160–61, 207, 382
　Soviet, 21, 62–63

Ibrahim Tali. *See* Tali, Ibrahim
Ibrahimov, 248
Imperialism, 43–44, 61, 186–87, 282–83
　colonies and, 206–7, 279–82, 325–27
　as monopoly capitalism, 197–98, 320
　and national feelings of oppressed, 326–27
　and national ruling classes, 17–18, 154, 157–58, 183–84, 334–35
　need to fight, 89–92, 273–76
　See also British imperialism; Holy war against imperialism; Interimperialist rivalries
India, 61, 171
　British oppression of, 89–90, 95–97, 119, 193, 223, 265–67
　industrial development of, 177

India (*continued*)
  peasants in, 219–20, 223–24, 265–66
  rebellion in, 106–7, 119, 267
Indian National Congress, 31
Indian Revolutionary Association, 23, 142–43
Indian soldiers in British army, 90, 143
Indochina, 167
Interimperialist rivalries, 96–98, 101–4, 163–65, 259–60, 264–65, 281, 309–10
Internationalism, 17–19, 36–38, 323–24
  See also Alliance of workers and oppressed peoples
Iran, 90, 177
  Constitutional Revolution, 114, 118, 179, 380, 386
  Gilan uprising, 34, 388
  imperialist oppression of, 42, 61, 95–97, 119, 268–69, 392
  oppression of peasants in, 42, 193, 221
  and Soviet Russia, 13, 301
Iraq, 44, 90, 97–100, 269
Ireland, 64, 180–81, 323
  rebellion in, 105–6, 138
Irurbayev, 363
Islam, 23, 33, 190
  and land question, 219–21, 224–25
  See also Caliphate
Ismail Hakki, Arap, 154, 247, 398
Istanbul, 90, 98, 151–52, 267–68, 301–2

Italo-Turkish war, 113, 145, 384
Italy, 113, 382
  workers' upsurge in, 104–5, 381

Jabarzadeh, 243, 248
Jansen, 72, 277
Januzakov, 248
Japan, 164, 269–70, 283, 388
Jemal (Cemal) Pasha, 342, 391
Jerusalem, 343, 347
Jewish Communist Party. *See* Poale Zion
Jewish sections of Russian Communist Party, 27, 204, 346–49
Jews, 27, 269, 326, 339–49, 390–91
Jurabayev, 247

Kalmyks, 365, 392
Karabakh, 183, 335, 386
Karayev, A.A., 52–53, 62, 64–65, 398
Kari Tajiyev, 71, 348–50, 278
Karid, 277
Kariyev, 70, 277
Karpov, 248
Kartmyzov, 112
Kastonyan, 70
Kasumov, 53
Kautsky, Karl, 174
Kazakh people, 382
Kemal Pasha, Mustafa (Atatürk), 25, 34, 44, 84–85, 230, 379–80, 385, 398
Kerensky, A.F., 115, 122–23, 301, 398
Khajan Kuliyev, 249

Khemzatov, 249
Khmelnitsky, Bogdan, 168, 386
Khudoiratov, 363
Kirghiz republic, 248, 382
Kirov, S.M., 249
Kizizadeh, 243
Klinger, Gustav K., 47
Kochirov, 363
Kolchak, A.V., 32, 60, 107–8, 146, 304–7, 398
Koran, 225
Korea, 270
Korkmasov, Jalaluddin, 36, 70, 128–33, 142, 277, 398
Kostanyan, 277
Kostoyev, 363
Kotsov, 131
Krasnyy Dagestan (Red Dagestan), 83
Krimazov, 248
Kubeyev, 71
Kubse Osman, 249
Kuleyev, 278
Kultasov, 363
Kulturträger, 124, 169, 398
Kun, Béla, 52, 62–63, 68, 72, 153–54, 205–18, 277, 399
Kurds, 43–44

Lagrosillière, Joseph, 175, 399
Landlords, 17, 42–43, 82, 102, 130, 207, 215–26, 233–34, 237, 268, 321, 343–44
 See also Agrarian question; Peasants
Latvia, 161
League of Nations, 320–21, 347, 389, 399

Left Socialist Revolutionaries. *See* Socialist Revolutionaries
Lenin, V.I., 72, 250, 295–97, 303–17, 399
 on chauvinism, 28–29, 35–36, 392
 on civil war, 304–7
 on impact of 1905 revolution, 314
 on imperialism, 303–4, 307–8, 310–12
 on introduction of communism, 392–93
 on invasion of Soviet Republic, 311–12
 on national and colonial questions, 14
 on national-revolutionary movements, 14, 202–3, 373
 on peoples of the East, 312–17
 on results of Baku congress, 32–33
 on revolutionary war, 306–7
 on self-determination, 127, 296–97
 on socialist revolution, 14
 on soviets in East, 17, 178
 on Subbotnik movement, 374
 on United States, 309–10
 on war as reflection of domestic policy, 304–5
Lermontov, Mikhail, 170, 196, 387
Le Temps, 101–2
Lloyd George, David, 99–101, 105, 381

London Stock Exchange, 95
Lozovsky, S.A., 47
Lyakhov, 96, 114, 380

Madero, Francisco, 158, 399
Magarik, N., 363
Mahmud Khan, 71
Mahmudov, 71, 248, 277
Makharadze, Pilipe (Filipe), 71, 248, 277, 399
Malta, 267
Mamedov, 248
Manchester Guardian, 101
Mansurov, 248
Marchlewski, Julian, 48
Marx, Karl, 15, 26, 68, 138, 193, 260–61
Marxism, 193
  continuity of, 36
Matushev, Akhmed, 190–97, 375, 399
McLaine, William, 47
Mehmet Emin, 149
Melikov, 71
Mensheviks, 55, 75, 173, 216, 305, 335, 379
Merezhin, A.N., 349, 399
Merino Gracia, Ramon, 399
Mesopotamia. *See* Iraq
Mexico, 66
  revolution in, 31, 158
Mohammed Abdur Rabb Barq. *See* Abdur Rabb Barq, Mohammed
Mongolia, 34
Montenegro, 181
Morocco, 114, 167
Moscow, 54–55, 170, 196
Mosul, 269
Mountain Jews, 204, 339–41

Mountain republic, 128–33, 382
Muhamedov, 70, 277
Muhammad Ali Shah, 114
Mullah Bekkhan Rakhmanov. *See* Rakhmanov, Bekkan
Murphy, John T., 47
Musavat Party, 87, 132, 335–36, 399
Musayev, 71, 248, 278
Musazadeh, 113–15
Muslim East, 190

Najiye Hanum (Naciye Hanim), 12, 189, 243–46, 399–400
Napoleon Bonaparte, 61
Narbutabekov, 24, 28–29, 36, 71, 121–28, 137, 248, 277, 400
Narimanov, Nariman Kerbalai Naja-foglu, 21, 24, 36, 53, 69–71, 112–13, 137, 247, 252–53, 277, 400
Narody Vostoka (Peoples of the East), 34, 240
National and colonial questions, 163–204
  Comintern on, 15–20, 173–76, 183–84, 198–99, 319–26, 330–32
  limited self-rule, 217–18
  national independence and, 181–82, 202–3, 216, 229–31
  and Soviet Russia, 165–66
  and working-class movement, 173–74
National bourgeoisie, 17–18, 216–17, 236–37, 333

National bourgeoisie (*continued*)
  alliances with, 18, 86, 229, 237
  and imperialist powers, 17–18, 154, 157–58, 184, 334–35
  need to fight, 229–31, 237–38, 321
  See also National-revolutionary movements
National exclusiveness, 18, 83–85, 125–26
National feelings, 19, 326–27
National hostilities, 18, 27, 158, 175–76, 326–37, 333–37, 345, 347–48
National independence, 16–17, 99–100, 180–84, 202, 216–17, 229–30, 325–27
  See also Self-determination
Nationalism, 18, 323–24, 326–27, 348
National-revolutionary movements, 30–31, 90, 358–59, 373
  and class independence, 16, 18, 153–54, 202, 229–30, 325–26
  Communist stance toward, 18, 84–87, 153–54, 183–84, 201–2, 236–38, 324–26, 330–31
  petty-bourgeois character of, 199, 201
Nazir Sidiq, 71, 248, 278
New Armenia, 100
Nicholas II, 114, 122, 130–31, 400
Niyas Kuli, 71, 278

Nomadic tribes, 235
Noske, Gustav, 76, 400
Nurijanian, Avis, 248
Nuri Pasha, 131–32

Oil, 66–67, 99–100
Opium War, 388
Oppressed and oppressor nations, 15–16, 77–81, 166–67, 175–76, 184, 276, 320
Ordzhonikidze, G.K., 21, 248, 400
Ostrovsky, 71, 144, 149, 247–48, 278, 400

Pahlavi dynasty, 34
Palestine, 27, 90, 326, 340–49
Pan-Asianism, 325
Pan-Islamism, 87, 130, 325, 344, 400
Pan-Turkism, 130, 400
Pavlovich, Mikhail, 65, 140, 163–89, 248, 401
Peasants
  agrarian revolution and, 17, 82, 202–3, 214–15, 216–17
  in Armenia, 223
  cancellation of debts, 82, 226–27, 235
  and collective labor, 228
  exploitation of, 219–26, 231–34
  indebtedness of, 222, 226–27, 232–33, 235
  in India, 218, 220, 223, 265–67
  in Iran, 42, 193, 221
  as majority of Eastern population, 210, 219–20

Peasants (*continued*)
  taxation of, 82, 222, 226–27, 232, 235
  in Turkey, 117, 149–52, 153–54, 191–93, 221–23
  See also Agrarian question; Soviets and Soviet power, peasant-based
People's Commissariat of Nationalities, 362–66
Peoples of the East, 29–30, 329–30, 376
  and agrarian revolution, 216–17
  capitalism and, 57–58, 69–70, 94–96
  class struggle among, 16–17, 86–88, 153–54, 176–78, 183–85, 230–32
  and imperialist powers, 206–9, 264–67, 279–83, 324–27
  independence, 12, 16, 236–37
  mistrust of oppressor nations, 19, 353–54
  proletarianization of, 272–73
  Russian revolution and, 32–33
  and Soviet republics, 19, 108–11, 170–73, 237–38, 321–22, 351–52, 386
  See also Alliance of workers and oppressed peoples; Baku congress; Oppressed and oppressor nations
Persia. *See* Iran
Pestaña, Angel, 47
Petlyura, Simon V., 168–69, 386, 401

Petrograd (St. Petersburg), 53–54, 108, 170
Petrov, Peter, 27–28, 64, 66, 138
Philippines, 157, 167, 385
Pichon, Stéphane, 99
Poale Zion, 27, 204, 341–46, 348, 390, 398
Poland, 181, 354, 386
  war against Soviet Russia by, 55–56, 60, 108, 378
Pushkin, A.S., 170

Qadir, N., 363
Qajar, 401
Quelch, Thomas, 27–28, 47, 63–64, 72, 138–40, 277, 401

Radek, Karl, 11, 47, 52, 59–62, 68, 72, 93–112, 277, 381, 401
Rakhmanov, Bekkhan, 24, 70, 247, 277
Rákosi, Mátyás, 48
Ramishvili, Noe, 182
Ramonov, Ye., 363
Red Army, 55–56, 249–50
  composition of, 32
  defeat of Whites by, 21, 108, 304–7
  Eastern toilers in, 355, 359, 362
  intervention of in East, 356–57, 366–72
Reed, John, 27, 31, 66–67, 72, 156–62, 277, 401
Reisler, 48
Renaudel, Pierre, 174
Riga, 54
Rojabov, 242–43

Rosmer, Alfred, 22, 47, 65–66, 72, 140–41, 277, 379, 401
Roy, Manabendra Nath, 373–74, 401
Rudnyánszky, Endre, 48
Russian civil war, 21, 31–34, 107–8, 304–7
Russian revolution (1905), 179
 impact of in East, 30, 114, 258–59, 314
Russian revolution (1917), 20, 299
 impact of in East, 30, 114–15, 165–66, 258–59
 nature of, 205–6
 See also Soviet Russia; Soviets and Soviet power
Ryskulov, Turar, 24, 28, 36, 70, 197–203, 248, 277, 363, 401–2

Sadoul, Jacques, 47
Safarov, G., 374
Said Gabiev, 21
St. Germain Treaty, 320, 389–90
San Remo conference, 342, 347, 391
Second International, 35, 74, 184, 286, 305, 323, 386
 collapse of, 14, 76–77
 colonial policy of, 13, 75–76, 174–76, 198–201, 330, 346–47, 379, 390
 as International of white race, 57, 77
Seeley, J.R., 106–7
Self-determination, 12–13, 28–29, 127, 202, 208–9, 295–97, 300–301, 356

Serbia, 181
Sersanov, 363
Sèvres Treaty, 385
Shabanova-Karayeva, Khaver, 36, 189, 243, 248, 402
Shablin, Nikolai, 48, 65, 72, 143–44, 277, 402
Shakir, Bahaeddin, 117–18, 248, 402
Shamyl, 130, 383
Shariat, 42, 220, 225–26
Shaumyan, S.G., 54, 377–78
Sheikh Eshref, 152
Sheikh Rejeb, 152
Shevchenko, Taras, 168–69, 402
Sidajedin Kardash Ogly, 71, 278
Skachko, A.E., 219–38, 248, 402
Skoropadsky, P.P., 168, 386, 402
Smyrna, 98, 150–51, 267
Sneevliet, Henk, 26
Socialist-Communist Muslim Party, 389
Socialist International. *See* Second International
Socialist Revolutionaries, 55, 305, 377, 402
Soliyer, 363
South Africa, 97, 147, 384
Soviet republics, 32, 130–33
 abuses in, 28–29, 123–27, 166, 255–58, 351–72
 class differentiation in, 361, 370–71, 391
 federation of, 12, 172, 185, 200, 213, 230–31
 formation of USSR, 36, 387

Soviet Russia
  aid to colonial struggle, 19, 321–22
  attempts to crush, 21, 107–8, 311–12
  blockade of, 20–21, 34, 179
  and British imperialism, 34, 59–60, 139
  centralization of, 353–56, 359–61
  and Eastern peoples, 108–11, 171, 321, 351–53, 387
  national policy of, 166–67, 169
  and national-revolutionary movements, 352–53
  and right to self-determination, 12–13, 28–29, 127–28, 208–9, 295–97, 300–1, 356–57
  war with Poland, 55–56, 60, 108, 378
Soviets and Soviet power
  and dictatorship of proletariat, 210–12
  as new form of state, 122, 194, 208–11, 217
  peasant-based, 17, 83–84, 178, 186, 210–12, 226–27, 233, 325, 359–60
  report on, 205–15
  as road for peoples of East, 45–46, 81–84, 123–26, 180, 200–201, 237–38, 246
  theses on, 215–18
Spanish-American War (1898), 157, 167
Stalin, Joseph, 36, 72, 297, 403

Stalinism, 36–37
Stasova, Yelena, 21–22, 248, 374
Steinhardt, Karl, 67–68, 72, 277, 403
Stoklitsky, Alexander I., 47
Straus, Oscar Solomon, 159–60
Subbotniks, 22, 374
Subhi, Mustafa, 21, 70, 277, 403
Suleiman Nuri, 247
Sultanate, 42–44, 85, 98, 104, 151, 207, 379–80, 381
Sultanov, G.G., 63, 403
Sultanzadeh, Ahmed, 24, 67, 189–90, 247, 373, 403
Syria, 44, 98–99, 150, 164

Tabriz, 96, 380
Tagiyev, A., 363
Tajiyev, Kari, 128, 248–49, 403
Takhsim Baari, 71, 277
Tali, Ibrahim (Öngören), 149–52, 403
Tamerlane, 123, 196, 403
Tanner, Jack, 47
Tarkovsky, Prince Nukh-Bek, 131, 403
Tatar Socialist Soviet Republic, 167, 169
Tehran, 96, 380
Third International. *See* Communist International
Thomas Aquinas, 194
Timur. *See* Tamerlane
Tolstoy, Leo, 170
Trade Union Congress of Azerbaijan, 51
Trebizond, 183

Triple Alliance, 96–97, 113–14, 384–85, 403
Triple Entente. *See* Entente
Tripoli, 114
Tripolitania, 114
Trotsky, Leon, 68, 72, 250, 375–76, 404
Tskhakaya, Mikha, 256, 404
Tukhareli, 183
Tunisia, 141
Turkestan, 121–28, 392
  abuses of Soviet power in, 29, 124, 126, 256–57
Turkey
  and Armenians, 43–44, 301, 334–37, 377, 381, 390
  character of Kemalist government, 84–85, 151, 153–54
  Communist movement in, 192
  imperialist oppression of, 42–44, 95–99, 115–16, 301, 334–36, 384–85
  national-revolutionary movement in, 34, 44–45, 150–52, 171, 385
  peasants in, 117, 149–54, 192, 221–23
  ruling class in, 43, 117, 151–52, 181
  and Soviet republics, 147–48, 153–54, 183, 383–84
  in World War I, 24–25, 115–19, 145–47, 334–36, 383, 391
  Young Turk movement in, 24–25, 97–98, 131–32, 207–208, 381
Turkic languages, 377

Ukraine, 168–70, 386–87
Union of Revolutionary Islamic Organizations, 148, 384
United States
  blockade of Soviet republics by, 160
  class struggle in, 105, 385
  "humanitarian" aid by, 160–61
  as imperialist power, 31, 66–67, 103–4, 156–62, 309–10, 385
  See also Blacks, in U.S.

Vandervelde, Emile, 174
Varukayev, K., 363
Venizelos, Eleutherios, 150, 171–72, 185, 404
Versailles Treaty, 30–31, 103–4, 196, 308–9, 320
Vinnichenko, V.K., 169, 404
Volunteer Army, 128, 131–32, 382
Vorovsky, V.V., 47
Voyenmor (Fighting Navy), 197

Wang, 70–71, 249, 277
Waqf lands, 220, 227, 234, 404
War and the Crisis of Socialism, The (Zinoviev), 80
Warsaw, 54–56
Weizmann, Chaim, 345, 404
White Guard armies, 21–22, 107–8, 304–7, 382–83
  See also Volunteer Army
Wijnkoop, David, 48
Wilhelm II, 182, 404
Wilson, Woodrow, 149

Women, 243–47
  at Baku congress, 28, 137, 189, 374
  communist demands for, 245–46
Working class
  in imperialist countries, 15, 19–21, 63–67, 78–79, 105, 138–40, 175–76, 179–80, 279–87
  in oppressed nations, 17–18, 105–6, 176–77, 210–11, 218–20, 272–74
  See also Alliance of workers and oppressed peoples
World War I, 320
  causes of, 20, 114, 163–64, 281–82
  results of, 20, 97–99, 102–5, 140–41, 176–77, 199, 264–66
  and social revolution, 198
  See also Entente; Versailles Treaty
Wrangel, Baron P.N., 66, 108, 171–72, 404

Yegorov, V.G., 250–52, 404
Yelchiyev, 71, 248, 278
Yeleyeva, 248
Yenikeyev, 71, 277
Yoshiwara Gentaro, 72, 277
Young Bukharans, 387–88
Young Turks, 24, 97–98, 131–32, 207, 381
Yudenich, N.N., 60, 107–8, 146, 304, 307, 311–12, 405
Yusuf Izet Pasha, 131
Yuzgada, 152

Zangezur, 183, 335
Zaporozhian Camp, 168–69, 386
Zhordania, N.N., 76, 173, 182–83, 255, 405
Zinoviev, Gregory, 13, 15, 24, 28–29, 47, 53–59, 71–91, 277, 405
Zionism, 27, 326, 344–49
  and communism, 348–49, 390–91

THE COMMUNIST INTERNATIONAL IN LENIN'S TIME SERIES

Workers of the World and Oppressed Peoples, Unite!
Proceedings and Documents of the Second Congress of the Communist International, 1920

The debate among delegates from 37 countries takes up key questions of working-class strategy and program and offers a vivid portrait of social struggles in the era of the October Revolution. Two volume set. $45

Lenin's Struggle for a Revolutionary International
Documents, 1907–1916; the Preparatory Years

The debate among revolutionary working-class leaders, including V.I. Lenin and Leon Trotsky, on a socialist response to World War I. $30

The German Revolution and the Debate on Soviet Power
Documents, 1918–1919; Preparing the Founding Congress

A day-to-day account of the 1918–19 German revolution in the words of its main leaders, including Rosa Luxemburg and Karl Liebknecht. $27

Founding the Communist International
Proceedings and Documents of the First Congress, March 1919

Delegates from 20 countries discuss the revolutionary upsurge that swept Central Europe and Asia following World War I. Includes manifesto announcing founding of new revolutionary International. $25

THE WORKING CLASS AND THE FIGHT AGAINST JEW-HATRED

The Fight Against Jew-Hatred and Pogroms in the Imperialist Epoch
Stakes for the International Working Class

V.I. LENIN, LEON TROTSKY
FARRELL DOBBS, JAMES P. CANNON
JACK BARNES, DAVE PRINCE

Jew-hatred and pogroms—such as Hamas carried out on October 7, 2023—are part of the social convulsions and wars of the imperialist epoch. The authors explain why fighting Jew-hatred is decisive to the working class and oppressed nations of the world—and *what is to be done to end it*. $10. Also in Spanish, French, Greek.

Imperialism's March Toward Fascism and War
JACK BARNES

"There will be new Hitlers, new Mussolinis. That is inevitable. What is not inevitable is that they will triumph. The working-class vanguard will organize our class to fight back against the devastating toll we are made to pay for the capitalist crisis. The future of humanity will be decided in the contest between these contending class forces." In *New International* no. 10. $14. Also in Spanish, French, Farsi, Greek.

The Jewish Question
A Marxist Interpretation

ABRAM LEON

The battle against reactionary forces aiming to exterminate the Jews remains central to world politics, as shown by the genocidal October 2023 pogrom in Israel. Why is Jew-hatred still raising its ugly head? What are its class roots? Why, as Abram Leon explains, is there no solution "independent of the world proletarian revolution"? Revised translation, new introduction, 40 pages of illustrations and maps. $17. Also in Spanish, French, Greek.

PATHFINDERPRESS.COM

CUBA'S SOCIALIST REVOLUTION

New!
Revolution and the Road to Peace in Colombia
The Example of the Cuban Revolution
FIDEL CASTRO

"No crime can be committed in the name of revolution," Fidel Castro declares, drawing from the example set by working people of Cuba as they took state power out of the hands of its capitalist rulers. In 2008, as part of efforts to end six decades of armed conflict in Colombia, he shared the exemplary record of Cuba's revolutionary struggle with the Revolutionary Armed Forces of Colombia (FARC) and the world. $10. Also in Spanish.

Cuba and the Coming American Revolution
JACK BARNES

This is a book about the example set by the Cuban people that socialist revolution is not only necessary—it can be made. A book about the struggles of workers and other exploited producers in the imperialist heartland, and the youth attracted to them. About the class struggle in the US, where the revolutionary capacities of working people are as utterly discounted by the ruling powers as were those of the Cuban toilers. $10. Also in Spanish, French, Farsi.

Women in Cuba: The Making of a Revolution Within the Revolution
VILMA ESPÍN, ASELA DE LOS SANTOS, YOLANDA FERRER

The integration of women in the ranks and leadership of the Cuban Revolution was intertwined with the proletarian course led by Fidel Castro from the start. This is the story of that revolution and how it transformed the women and men who made it. $17. Also in Spanish, Farsi, Greek.

THE RUSSIAN REVOLUTION'S WORLD EXAMPLE

Lenin's Final Fight
Speeches and Writings, 1922–23
V.I. LENIN

In 1922 and 1923, V.I. Lenin, central leader of the world's first socialist revolution, waged what was to be his last political battle—one that was lost after his death. At stake was whether that revolutionary government and the world communist movement it led would remain on the revolutionary proletarian course that brought workers and peasants to power in Russia in 1917. $17. Also in Spanish, Farsi, Greek.

The Revolution Betrayed
What Is the Soviet Union and Where Is It Going?
LEON TROTSKY

In 1917 workers and peasants of Russia were the motor force of one of the deepest revolutions in history. Yet within ten years a political counterrevolution by a privileged social layer, whose chief spokesperson was Joseph Stalin, was being consolidated. The classic study of the Soviet workers state and its degeneration. $17. Also in Spanish, Farsi, Greek.

The History of the Russian Revolution
LEON TROTSKY

How, under Lenin's leadership, the Bolshevik Party led millions of workers and farmers to overthrow the state power of the landlords and capitalists in 1917 and bring to power a government that advanced their class interests at home and worldwide. Unabridged, 3 vols. in one. Written by one of the central leaders of that socialist revolution. $30. Also in French and Russian.

PATHFINDERPRESS.COM

PROGRAM AND COMMUNIST CONTINUITY

The Low Point of Labor Resistance Is Behind Us
The Socialist Workers Party Looks Forward

JACK BARNES
MARY-ALICE WATERS, STEVE CLARK

The global order imposed by Washington is shattering. A long retreat by the working class and unions has come to an end. The bosses and their government are stepping up attacks on our wages, conditions, and constitutional rights. This book highlights opportunities for building a mass proletarian party able to lead the struggle to end capitalist rule, opening a socialist future for humanity. $10. Also in Spanish, French, Greek.

U.S. Imperialism Has Lost the Cold War
JACK BARNES

The collapse of regimes across Eastern Europe and the USSR claiming to be communist did not mean workers and farmers there had been crushed. In today's sharpening class conflicts and wars, these toilers are joining working people the world over in the class struggle against capitalist exploitation. In *New International* no. 11. $14. Also in Spanish, French, Farsi, Greek.

The Communist Manifesto
KARL MARX AND FREDERICK ENGELS

Communism, say the founding leaders of the revolutionary workers movement, is not a set of ideas or preconceived "principles" but workers' line of march to power. It springs from a "movement going on under our very eyes." $5. Also in Spanish, French, Farsi, Arabic.

$12 $20

$15

Three books to be read as one ...

about building a party that's working class in program, composition, and action. One that recognizes, in word and deed, the most revolutionary fact of our time ...

... that working people have the power to create a different world as we act together to defend our own class interests—not those of the privileged classes who exploit our labor, not of those who fear us as "deplorables," or just plain "trash."

As we advance along a revolutionary course toward workers power, we will transform ourselves and awaken to our own worth. Also in Spanish, French, Farsi, Greek.

Special Offer!
All three $30

The Turn to Industry and Tribunes of the People and the Trade Unions $20

Either book plus Malcolm X, Black Liberation, and the Road to Workers Power $25

PATHFINDERPRESS.COM

CAPITALIST CRISIS AND THE FIGHT FOR WORKERS POWER

The Teamster Series
FARRELL DOBBS

Four books on the 1930s strikes, organizing drives, and political campaigns that transformed the Teamsters into a militant industrial union movement. Written by the organizer of these battles and leader of the Socialist Workers Party. A tool for workers seeking to use union power and advance the fight for a party of labor. $16 each, series $50. Also in Spanish. *Teamster Rebellion* is also available in French, Farsi, Greek.

Capitalism's Long Hot Winter Has Begun
JACK BARNES

Today's global capitalist crisis is but the opening stage of decades of economic, financial, and social convulsions and class battles. Class-conscious workers confront this historic turning point for imperialism with confidence, Jack Barnes writes, drawing satisfaction from being "in their face" as we chart a revolutionary course to take power. In *New International* no. 12. $14. Also in Spanish, French, Farsi, Arabic, Greek.

Are They Rich Because They're Smart?
Class, Privilege, and Learning Under Capitalism
JACK BARNES

Exposes growing class inequalities in the US and the self-serving rationalizations of well-paid professionals who think their "brilliance" equips them to "regulate" working people, who don't know what's in our own best interest. $10. Also in Spanish, French, Farsi, Arabic, Greek.

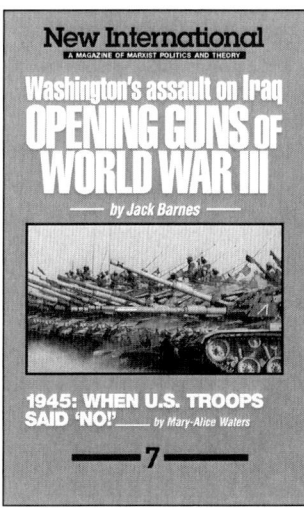

Opening Guns of World War III: Washington's Assault on Iraq

JACK BARNES

The murderous assault on Iraq in 1990–91 heralded increasingly sharp conflicts among imperialist powers, growing instability of capitalism, and more wars. Also includes:

1945: When US Troops Said 'No!'
by Mary-Alice Waters

Lessons from the Iran-Iraq War
by Samad Sharif

In *New International* no. 7. $14. Also in Spanish, French, Farsi.

The Clintons' Anti-Working-Class Record
Why Washington Fears Working People

JACK BARNES

What working people need to know about the profit-driven course of Democrats and Republicans alike over the last three decades. And the political awakening of workers seeking to understand and resist the capitalist rulers' assaults. $10. Also in Spanish, French, Farsi, Greek.

Socialism on Trial
Testimony at
Minneapolis Sedition Trial

JAMES P. CANNON

The revolutionary program of the working class presented in federal court in 1941 on the eve of US entry into World War II. The frame-up charges of "seditious conspiracy" targeted leaders of the Socialist Workers Party. $15. Also in Spanish, French, Farsi.

PATHFINDERPRESS.COM

EXPAND YOUR REVOLUTIONARY LIBRARY

New Expanded Edition!
Cosmetics, Fashion, and the Exploitation of Women
MARY-ALICE WATERS
JOSEPH HANSEN, EVELYN REED

"Norms of beauty and fashion are inseparable from the class struggle." That's the title of the opening chapter of this timely new edition of a lively 1950s debate in the *Militant*, a socialist newsweekly. How cosmetics and fashion monopolies rake in profits from social insecurities of women and adolescents. Why women's integration into the workforce and unions is a major advance in the fight for emancipation. A Marxist classic on the origins of women's oppression and the working-class road forward. $15. Also in Spanish, French, Farsi, Greek.

Thomas Sankara Speaks
The Burkina Faso Revolution, 1983–87

Under Sankara's guidance, Burkina Faso's revolutionary government led peasants, workers, women, and youth to expand literacy; to sink wells, plant trees, erect housing; to combat women's oppression; to carry out land reform; to join others worldwide to free themselves from the imperialist yoke. $20. Also in French.

Democracy and Revolution
GEORGE NOVACK

The limitations and advances of various forms of democracy in class society, from its roots in ancient Greece through its rise and decline under capitalism. Discusses the emergence of Bonapartism, military dictatorship, and fascism, and how democracy will be advanced under a workers and farmers regime. $17